The book of Acts is an acco[...]ead around the world, transfo[...]ple. Even people like Paul of Tarsus . . . and Frank Majewski of Detroit! This story is a continuation of Acts in our day, as the Good Shepherd is still rounding up his sheep, bringing in the strays.

PAT BOONE

singer, composer, actor, writer, and television personality

I am always moved by reading how the love and power of Jesus can transform a broken life, rescue that which was lost, and bring that soul to a place of restoration and healing. That is just what God did for Frank in this story!

The mercy of the Lord endures forever, and His love never fails! Frank was broken and forsaken. He fought, ran away, and fell deeper into despair and desperation. All the while the loving Lord of heaven was keeping His eye on this young man—all for a purpose!

Read this fine story—riveting and compelling, but true as can be. I am glad I met this brother, Frank Majewski. We are both sons given mercy—a mercy that is free to all because of the One who *is* Mercy!

PHIL KEAGGY

guitarist, vocalist, and Christian musician

Bring Him to Me: The Frank Majewski Story is a well-written account of how broken lives can collide with the living Christ through the work of the Holy Spirit. A must-read for followers of Christ, as well as those who do not yet know Him. I loved this book . . . couldn't put it down!

DOUG SCHMIDT

Senior Pastor, Woodside Bible Church, Troy, Michigan

In this compelling narrative Sally Zito shares the remarkable conversion story of Frank Majewski and how the Holy Spirit used his charismatic preaching to draw the hearts of hundreds of lonely and lost young people to Jesus, their hope and Way to the Father.

BISHOP DALE MELCZEK

Bishop Emeritus of the Diocese of Gary, Indiana

Sally Zito gives us a lively glimpse into a time that has faded too soon from our memories. The Lord used Frank, Alex, Joyce and Bruce, and many others to ignite our lives with the fire of heaven. We saw the hand of God as never before as we answered the Master's call to joyfully and recklessly abandon our lives to him. We became laborers in an awesome harvest. As I read these pages the Spirit seemed to say, "Keep your eyes open; there's more ahead, if you're willing to pay the price."

DICK BIEBER

Pastor Emeritus, Messiah Church, Detroit

A riveting story of redemption. If you need encouragement that no person is too bad, too messed up, too far gone for God to save them, this is a must read. You will discover that God does some of his best work in and through those of whom society would say "No way!"

JEFF BONZALAAR

Director, Life Challenge, Detroit

Sally Zito's telling of Frank Majewski's life and transformation is remarkably written and a fascinating read. This book shows the amazing, redemptive power of God and how God uses the most broken among us for His glory. *Bring Him to Me* is an excellent account of a true story that needed to be told.

BOB DUTKO

Christian Talk Radio Host, Detroit

Over 2,000 years ago Jesus said to a man named Nicodemus, "Unless one is born again he cannot see the kingdom of God." *Bring Him to Me* is an exhilarating and enthralling story of the transforming power of God. As you read you will discover how God, the giver of new life, can use some of the most improbable candidates for His glory.

TERRY ROBINSON

Director, Cru Inner City, Detroit

Bring Him to Me

Bring Him to Me

The Frank Majewski Story

WHEN GOD CHOOSES THE
LEAST LIKELY TO DO THE
MOST EXTRAORDINARY

SALLY ANN ZITO

credo
house publishers

To Tommy Z, with love.

"Now . . . what about us?"

"OH GOD, THOU HAST TAUGHT ME FROM MY YOUTH;

AND I STILL DECLARE THY WONDROUS DEEDS.

AND EVEN WHEN I AM OLD AND GRAY, O GOD,

   DO NOT FORSAKE ME

UNTIL I DECLARE THY STRENGTH TO THIS GENERATION,

THY POWER TO ALL WHO ARE TO COME."

PSALM 71:17–18

In loving memory of

SUE SILVA

and

BRUCE AND JOYCE TODD

Contents

Foreword

It came as a total surprise. No one had planned it. Suddenly, out of nowhere, the climate changed, and the name "Jesus" rose above all others, as the lives of many of us were transformed forever.

As Sally Zito reminds us in the following pages, the Lord used unlikely agents to wake us up. Flawed, broken lives were caught up in Heaven's Net and changed into servant-prophets in barbershops, bars, drug-dealing parks, . . . and even churches.

A maverick nun, a drug dealer, an itinerant preacher, a musician at loose ends, a biker-barber, and countless others—all had one thing in common: they were plucked out of the churning sea of this world and fit into a program dropped down from heaven.

So why is Sally Zito telling all this now, so many years later? Is this a history lesson? Or is it a reminder to those who have ears to hear that "those days" were but a foretaste of something awesome and ominous just ahead? Something that will require us to unclutter our lives, pick up our crosses, and follow our Lord to whatever Calvary he chooses for us.

May the Spirit of the Lord Jesus enable us to connect what we read in the following pages with the call he has placed on each of our lives.

This book is not a history lesson. It is a reminder that the Lord Jesus can even use unlikely servants like ourselves. It is an invitation to turn from our distractions and focus on the one thing needful: to follow the Master all the way to the end.

Dick Bieber
Pastor Emeritus, Messiah Church
Detroit, Michigan

Prologue

June 21, 1968
Warren, Michigan

Summer vacation had begun, and cars were peeling out of the school parking lot like jailbirds released from prison. Fresh-faced teens drove with one hand on the steering wheel and the other on the radio dial as they headed for Peppy's Burgers. Peppy's had been around since 1962 and was everyone's favorite hangout. The parking lot was littered with old jalopies: a '60s Comet on threadbare tires, a GTO with its rearview mirror on the dash. One car dragged a tailpipe, shooting sparks in the air as it jounced along the road. Greasy hamburgers and jukebox music drew teenagers from miles around. Girls wore black stirrup pants and squeezed into Naugahyde booths to sip on chocolate milkshakes. Boys stood in huddles near the front door to ogle the girls.

Everyone turned to watch as a Ford Falcon pulled into the parking lot. It was a sleek little number, candy-apple red with a white 12-inch stripe that stretched from front to back. Two blond, pony-tailed girls sat in the front seat. The windows were rolled down and the radio blasting. The girls waved at two boys inside the restaurant—a signal for them to come out.

Frank took a last sip of his Pepsi and elbowed his friend MoJo. "It's Carolyn and Cindy," he pointed out, nodding toward the Falcon. Frank was a tough-looking 17-year-old kid. His hair was greased back and dipped into a waterfall on his forehead. He wore tight black jeans and a sharkskin suit jacket he had stolen from JCPenney. His arms were muscular, and the near-perpetual scowl on his face caused everyone to give him a wide berth. No one wanted to mess with Frank. If they did, they were soon sorry. MoJo shoved a few fries into his mouth and followed Frank out the door.

"Good evening, ladies." Frank sidled up to the car and leaned into the window. "Ready for a joy-ride?"

"Hop in," Carolyn smiled.

Both boys clambered into the back seat, another friend, Johnny, close behind. Cindy turned up the radio, and the speakers pulsed: *Jumping Jack Flash, it's a gas-gas-gas . . .* The Falcon turned out of the parking lot and headed down Twelve Mile Road.

Frank drummed on his knees in beat to the music and then pointed to a party store. "Hey, Carolyn, pull over."

"What for?"

"Just do it."

Frank collected money from the boys in the backseat and then headed into the store. He came out with a case of beer, climbed back into the car, and began passing out bottles to his friends.

MoJo fished in his pocket for an opener, while Carolyn watched through the rearview mirror. At the sound of bottle caps popping she pulled over to the curb and turned down the music. "Listen, guys, if you're gonna drink, you have to get out of the car."

Frank glanced at Carolyn in the mirror, and then turned to MoJo. "I think she's serious, man."

"I mean it, Frank," Carolyn repeated. "My dad'd kill me if he found out."

"One beer ain't gonna hurt anything, Carolyn," Frank brushed her off. "And nobody's gonna tell your dad." He took another swallow and nudged MoJo to do the same. MoJo suppressed a smile and raised the bottle to his lips.

Carolyn swung around in her seat. "I'm serious, Frank. You can drink if you want, but not in the car. I'll swing by later to pick you guys up, okay?"

"Let's go, man," Johnny retorted, climbing out of the car. MoJo handed him the case of beer and stepped out as well, Frank on the other side.

"See you later!" Cindy waved her hand out the window as the car pulled away.

"So much for our joy ride." Frank took a swig of beer and started down a side street toward Hartsig Junior High. Construction had just begun on a new gymnasium, and a huge mound of dirt was piled up next to the building. Frank scaled the mound and waved down to his friends. "Good view from up here, bros. Bring the brew!"

MoJo left Johnny behind as he scuttled to the top and dropped down next to Frank. He leaned his head back and gazed up at the sky. MoJo's curly brown hair, rugged good looks, and easygoing nature made him a favorite with the girls. Frank had jet-black hair, a dark scowl, and a temper that could make your knees knock. Both had blue eyes. MoJo's were friendly, twinkling whenever he smiled. Frank's eyes only glinted when he was up to no good. Most of the time they were cold and hard. As different as the two boys were, MoJo and Frank were the best of friends.

Johnny reached the top of the mound and dropped the case with a thud. Two hours and several beers later the boys rolled down the hill, laughing and cursing when they hit the dirt. By now it was dark. They stumbled to their feet and wove their way through the empty school parking lot, drinking and shoving each other as they went.

Frank held up his hand to signal his friends to stop. Up ahead in the shadows a dark sedan was parked underneath a tree. Frank squinted to see whether anyone was in the driver's seat and was startled to catch a pair of eyes staring back. A police detective who had been watching the boys for several minutes stepped from his car and unfolded his six-foot-two frame to its full height. "Hold it right there," he ordered, flashing a badge at Frank.

"What for?" Frank took a few steps in a backward direction.

"Warren Police. I want to see some I.D."

Frank bolted toward his friends. "It's the cops! Let's get outta here!"

MoJo and Johnny ran, holding onto their beer, and hid behind a hedge. Frank joined them just as the detective began to scan the parking lot with a searchlight. Frank had had run-ins with the law in the past—shoplifting, fighting, and vandalism—and didn't want to add underage drinking to the list.

When the light passed the boys made a run for Twelve Mile and then cut down a side street. Frank paused to catch his breath, while MoJo leaned over, resting his hands on his knees, and Johnny stretched out on the grass. Another car was slowly making its way down the street, a dark blue Pontiac with a black vinyl top. It pulled up next to the curb and stopped. Frank took a few steps toward the car and motioned for his friends to follow.

"Hey," someone called from the passenger side, "what are you punks running away from?"

Frank moved in closer to see two men seated in the front. "What's it to you?" he challenged.

"What're you doing around my apartment," the passenger demanded, "pulling a B & E?"

Frank swaggered up to the window and leaned in, only to find himself staring down the barrel of a .25 caliber pistol. "*Whoa!*" Frank cried, instinctively recoiling with his hands in the air. "What'd ya hafta pull a gun on me for?"

"I don't know what you got hiding under that fancy coat of yours." The gunman waved his weapon at Frank's suit.

"I don't have no *gun*, man!" Frank gingerly opened up his jacket to prove it. "Now what's this about breaking and entering? Has your place been hit or something?"

"Can't say as I know . . ." The man's eyes narrowed. "I haven't been home yet."

He pointed the gun at Frank's face—and fired. A lightning bolt flashed in Frank's eyes, and a bomb exploded in his ears. He grabbed the side of his head, stumbled backward, and fell to the ground.

MoJo stood frozen as the man took aim and shot him in the stomach. Twirling in a slow-motion half circle, he dropped to the grass. Johnny started to run, but the gunman fired again, the bullet catching him in the groin. All three boys were down as the sedan squealed its tires and sped away.

Dogs began to bark, and several porch lights flicked on. Neighbors peered from behind living room curtains to see what had happened, but no one ventured out. Johnny rolled back and forth in the grass, while MoJo wrapped his arms around his torso and writhed in pain. Frank was barely breathing.

○━○━○

Several minutes passed before Frank could lift his head. He feared he was dying: his ears rang in a high-pitched whine, and blood streamed from his mouth. His nostrils were filled with a revolting, acrid smell, and a sharp pain stabbed at the side of his head. He couldn't move his legs. "What happened, man?" Frank cried as he tried to pull himself to his knees. "What just happened to us?"

MoJo was the first to respond. "You been shot, Frank! We all been shot!"

Frank groaned and dropped back down. The pain was excruciating now, and blood was everywhere, on his clothes and in the grass. It left a trail as he dragged his body toward the nearest house. His legs hung lifeless behind him as he pulled himself onto the porch. Frank pounded on the metal screen until a woman, wrapped in a robe, appeared at the door. She clutched her throat, slammed the door shut, and cut the porch light.

Undeterred, he crawled back down the steps and moved on to the next house. By now his head was severely swollen. MoJo and Johnny continued to writhe in pain on the grass while Frank made his way up the next set of steps. He banged on the door several times with his fist before collapsing.

This time a young woman responded. She knelt down and touched his shoulder. "Don't move," she insisted in efficient, clipped tones. "I'm calling the police." She glanced down the street in both directions before disappearing back into the house. Seconds later she returned; gently lifting Frank's head, she settled it onto a pillow. "You'll be all right. Just take it easy, okay?"

Frank groaned and closed his eyes.

The detective from Warren was the first to arrive. Two ambulances and several more cruisers followed. By now the street was lined with curious spectators who watched, mesmerized, as Frank was lifted onto a stretcher and placed in an ambulance. MoJo and Johnny were on stretchers too. Police lights flashed and sirens wailed as all three boys were rushed to the nearest hospital. Meanwhile, eager reporters collaborated with their camera crews to beat their competitors in airing the lead story for Detroit's nightly news.

As Frank stared out at what little was visible to him through the ambulance window, streetlights and buildings whizzed by in a blur. He hadn't thought about God in a long time, but tonight Frank wondered whether God knew what he was going through. He tried to remember a prayer he had once learned as an altar boy, but the words were jumbled in his head. *God,* he pleaded as they reached the entrance to South Macomb Hospital, *just get me out of this and I promise I'll be good.*

A team of orderlies met the boys in the emergency room and immediately set to work cutting away at Frank's clothes. They tossed his sharkskin jacket to the floor in a bloody heap.

Father Dale Melczek was making his rounds at South Macomb that night. As co-pastor at Saint Sylvester Catholic Church, he also served as the hospital chaplain. When the gurney carrying Frank to surgery passed him in the hallway, Father Melczek asked the orderlies to stop. Taking in the sight of Frank's swollen, bloody head, he grasped the boy's hand. "Would you like to tell me your sins right now, son, before they operate?"

Frank looked into the priest's eyes and blinked. His mouth felt glued shut.

"Just say you're sorry, son," the priest urged.

"Sorry . . ." Frank mumbled, his mouth feeling as though it were filled with marbles.

Father Melczek watched the gurney disappear down the hall. "Lord," he prayed, "please help that boy make it through the night."

Frank was lifted onto a surgical table and his arms and legs secured. An I.V. was started and a mask placed over his nose and mouth. As he breathed in ether, his stomach churned and his head began to spin. Glancing toward a nurse, Frank tried to recall a rote prayer from his childhood. "Oh my God," he muttered, uncertain whether he was speaking audibly, "I am heartily sorry for having offended you . . ." The lights went out and Frank forgot the rest.

The surgeon carved a thin line across Frank's cheek, grazing his skin with light sweeps of the scalpel. Carefully working his way around bone and tissue, he searched for the bullet lodged somewhere deep within his skull.

As Frank plunged into a troubled sleep, scenes from his childhood played in his head like an old movie. He was back at the orphanage again. It was winter on Cape Breton Island, and outside the wind howled and rattled the windows as the sky dropped a fresh blanket of snow onto the ground.

Crouching in the cellar beneath the basement steps, Frankie hugged his toy donkey to his chest. His bottom was bruised from yet another beating, and a tear dislodged itself and rolled slowly down his cheek. All he could think about tonight was running away.

Part One

"HOW LONG HAS THIS
BEEN HAPPENING?"

MARK 9:21

Part One

CHAPTER 1

"It Wasn't Me!"

December, 1956
Little Flower Institute
Cape Breton Island, Nova Scotia

"**B**end over, Frrankie."

"No."

"It'll be the wurrse furrr ya if ya don't." When Sister Ellen was angry, her temper was fierce and her Scottish *burr* prickly.

"I didn't do anything!"

"Aye, then who *wrrote* 'Frrankie is Zorro' on the wall outside?" she asked, wielding a radiator stick high in the air.

Frankie was the only boy at the orphanage with a Zorro costume. It had been donated by one of the villagers last Halloween. He also had a reputation for getting into trouble and was the prime suspect in any crime. Last fall, when Mother Superior's rosebushes had been trampled, all of the children had claimed innocence, including Frankie. But Sr. Ellen had forced a confession from him after finding his muddy brown loafers hidden in the basement. He had been beaten and sent to bed without supper. In fact, by the time he was five years old Frankie had the dubious honor of having received more floggings than any other child at the orphanage. Most of the time he deserved it, but today he was innocent and stubbornly held his ground.

The cold December air had turned the shower room into an icebox. It felt especially chilly after Frankie, under orders, had removed his clothes. *She can't make me bend over,* he thought fiercely to himself, shaking more from anger than from cold. "It wasn't me!" he protested once again, then squeezed his eyes shut to brace for the blow.

As the administrator of corporal punishment at Little Flower Institute, Sister Ellen took her job seriously. She flicked the radiator stick several times across Frankie's bare bottom, while he screamed loudly enough for everyone to hear. *That should do him some good,* the nun thought smugly. *He'll think twice before lying to me again.*

When the thrashing was over, Frankie grabbed his clothes, and his toy donkey, and scuttled down the basement steps. The cellar was a dark, dreary chamber with a monstrous looking furnace that moaned, clunked, and labored against the arctic air. Ductwork crawled across the ceiling like octopus arms reaching for Frankie as he entered the room. A large, circular eye opened and shut in time to the blower. The cellar was enough to frighten most of the children, but Frankie, finding solace out of sight near the rumbling furnace, nestled into a warm, dark hiding place behind a stack of boxes. Hugging his plush animal to his chest and twirling the small wheels on its feet with a finger, he buried his face in the matted fur and sobbed.

"Frankie," someone whispered huskily from the top of the stairs, "get up here." It was Charlie.

"Shut up, *Charles.*"

"*You* shut up," his brother snapped. "You wanna get us both killed? Get up here. I've got a plan." He closed the door with a click while Frankie wiped his nose on his sleeve. *Better not let him see I was crying,* he thought. His big brother Charlie was eight years old and had never cried a day in his life—at least not that Frankie had seen.

Charlie was tall and skinny, with blond hair like their mother's. (The boys had only one photo between them—of their mother cuddling a blond baby.) Charlie was tough too, probably the toughest kid in the orphanage. When he was six years old he had punched a kid in the nose for laughing at his glasses. No one had ever laughed at him again.

Frankie didn't look a thing like his brother. His jet-black hair and sapphire blue eyes were more like their father's. He was dark and brooding—a little French-looking; that was like his father too. Since he was also on the short side, it was easy for the nuns to grab him when he got into trouble. More often than not the nuns suspected Frankie was up to no good. In all fairness, most of the time they were right.

Frankie rubbed his bottom and crawled over the boxes before bounding up the three flights of stairs to the boys' dormitory to find Charlie. Four straight rows of metal cots filled the room, each topped with a thin wool blanket. Underneath each pillow was a gray flannel nightshirt (along with a stuffed animal or perhaps a wrinkled photo). The furnace could scarcely deliver enough heat for the building; only a tentative stream of warm air wafted its way up to the third floor. At bedtime the children rushed for their cots, dove underneath the blankets, and pulled the thin covers up over their heads.

As Frankie approached his bed, the frosty windows rattled and the floor creaked. A winter storm was blowing in from the bay tonight. Charlie sat on his own cot, jabbing the air with Frankie's toy sword. He glanced up before handing the sword to his brother.

"So, what's the plan?" Frankie asked expectantly.

"We're busting outta here. You know those bikes down in the basement?"

"Yeah."

"Well, when the weather warms up we'll sneak down, steal us a couple of bikes, and ride away."

Frankie's eyes grew wide. "Are you *serious*? Where would we go?"

"Who cares? As long as we get outta here."

"But what if they catch us?"

"Who's gonna catch us—the *nuns*? Nah. It'll be easy; you'll see. Just keep your mouth shut and don't tell nobody. We'll surprise 'em all. And by the time they notice we'll be long gone."

Frankie could hardly believe his ears. Running away from the orphanage was something they had dreamed about for a long time—up till this point it had been all talk. *If anyone can pull this off*, he thought triumphantly, *it's Charlie*. Charlie was smart and fast on his feet. And once he got an idea in his head there was no stopping him. Last Halloween when all the kids lined up to bob for apples, Charlie kept dunking his head into the barrel till he pulled up every last one. Sister Ellen smacked him on the head to make him stop, but he refused to quit. Everyone had been mad at him for hogging the apples, but Charlie didn't care. He'd just laughed, tossed one to Frankie, and ambled away.

Frankie gazed up at his brother in awe. He wanted to be just like him when he grew up. Charlie caught the look and punched him in the arm.

"Ow!" Frankie rubbed his shoulder. "What'd you do that for?"

5

"In case you decide to tell one of your friends about our plan." He jabbed a finger in the direction of Frankie's face. "And don't ever call me *Charles* again."

∞∞∞

Francois Josef Briand (Frankie) was born on January 7, 1951, the youngest child of Charles and Annie Briand. Francois bore a striking resemblance to his father with his black hair, deep blue eyes, and rascally disposition. When Charles left Brittany, France, in the early 1940s, he had crossed the Atlantic and settled on Cape Breton Island, where he'd started a taxicab business he called Frenchy's Cab. His wife, Annie, was a young, flaxen-haired girl of German descent who stayed home to care for the couple's three children, Margaret, Charles Jr., and Francois.

Frenchy's Cab had become a lucrative business for Charles, allowing him to invest money in two other industries for which Nova Scotia was becoming infamous: bootlegging and gambling. As Charles moved up in the world he started to dress the part. Strutting about town in tailored suits and fancy fedoras, he soon caught the attention of the local constables, who kept a close watch on the owner of Frenchy's Cab.

One officer in particular took an active disliking to Charles and vowed to put the man behind bars. Nothing would have pleased him more than to rid Sydney of one more shady businessman. In early 1952 the officer received a tip on Charles and prepared to arrest him on gambling charges. Charles knew himself to be backed into a corner; not only did his gambling debts threaten to destroy his cab business, but he now faced a jail term. If the police managed to squeeze any information out of him, it would put his family in danger. And if he were released he would be a marked man. Feeling that his luck had run out, Charles turned to the only solution that guaranteed an immediate escape: he checked out. One bitterly cold night he drove his cab into the woods, finished off a pint of Crown Royal, . . . and shot himself in the head. His body was found two days later. Charles left behind a grief-stricken wife, three small children, and a mountain of debt.

Annie had few friends in the world. One couple by the name of Mac-Dougal offered to care for the boys while she figured out what to do next. After the funeral she packed her bags and, with only Margaret in tow, headed for New York City, hoping to find a job and living quarters before sending for the boys. At first she sent money regularly to the Mac-

Dougals— usually once a week. But then the checks began to arrive less frequently—once a month and sometimes not at all. Finally they stopped coming altogether, and Annie was never heard from again.

The MacDougals, to their credit, tried to locate her, but their letters were returned unopened. As far as they could tell there were no living relatives in Sydney and no family to contact overseas. Charles Jr. and Francois were orphans in every sense of the word. The MacDougals had no interest in raising the Briand boys, so they took them to Little Flower Institute—the only orphanage on Cape Breton Island. Mother Superior listened as the MacDougals described how they had cared for the children for more than a year. They had trusted the boys' mother, they told her, to send for them. But now the two were to become wards of the province. The MacDougals patted Frankie and Charlie on their heads, directed them to be good for the nuns, turned tail, and left. Mother Superior took the boys by the hand and led them upstairs to their new home.

◯─◯─◯

Life on Cape Breton Island was never easy, but it was especially hard in the winter. The days were short, the nights long, and the wind bitter. Heavy snowfall slowed city traffic to a crawl, while ice floes from Labrador jammed the harbor and brought the coal and steel shipments to a halt. The older residents—an amalgamation of French, Scottish, and Irish immigrants—knew how to survive: basically, they huddled near their fireplaces and waited for spring. Younger men worked in the coalmines or at the steel yards in Sydney—backbreaking labor at any time of the year.

The women of Nova Scotia were strong and resilient. In spite of so many of their men having been lost at sea or crushed in the mines, they too knew the skills of survival. But occasionally a penniless widow would lay her starving baby at the door of Little Flower Institute. The Sisters of Saint Martha always took in the crying infant, knowing the mother would never be heard from again.

Father John Webb, Director of Catholic Charities on Cape Breton Island, oversaw the work at Little Flower. The nuns had cared for abandoned children ever since the home had opened back in 1927. But few of the children were truly orphaned; the majority came from broken homes. One night Father Webb stumbled upon two scantily clad boys, both under the age of three, wandering the streets of Sydney. Their intoxicated parents were located at a nearby pub. Father Webb took the boys by the hand and led them to the orphanage.

The Glace Bay police sometimes dropped off children as well. Two little girls, ages five and seven, were discovered in an abandoned building where their mother lay in a corner, passed out. In another instance a local doctor requested that six children be placed in the nuns' care after the mother was declared a threat to their well-being.

While the Sisters of St. Martha were the primary caregivers, additional hands were required to keep the orphanage running smoothly. Doctors, lawyers, school inspectors, and social workers helped the nuns, all reporting directly to Father Webb. His was a challenging role. Between Little Flower, his parish, and his other charitable work, the priest's schedule was beyond full. Everything else came to a screeching halt however, when the orphanage caught fire in 1953. Hundreds of townspeople rushed to the scene to help rescue the children and salvage as much of the building as possible.

Father Webb kept the news article in his top drawer:

> SYDNEY - Seventy-six children, including 24 infants, were evacuated in safety when a fire of unknown origin swept through the Little Flower Institute here early Wednesday afternoon. . . . [p]aths were blocked when billows of smoke poured from the boys' dormitory, which immediately adjoins the room where the fire had been discovered only minutes before. A call was at once put through to the Sydney Mines Fire Department and the major task of evacuating the children from the big wooden structure began.[1]

Three years later Father Webb stood at his rectory window gazing out at the falling snow. While the fire had nearly demolished the orphanage, sufficient funds had been raised to construct a red brick, more fire-retardant building. During construction several foster parents adopted the boys and girls who had been left in their care, greatly reducing the number of children sent back to Little Flower. Charlie and Frankie were among the 40 who returned. This was no surprise to Father Webb when he saw them. *It would take an extraordinary couple,* he thought ruefully, *to adopt those two boys.*

CHAPTER 2

The Great Escape

Charlie and Frankie adapted to life in the new orphanage. The people of Sydney provided food and festivities for the children to enjoy. There were birthday parties with cake and ice cream, summer picnics featuring lobster caught off the coast, and Halloween parties replete with candy and colorful costumes. The townspeople understood that life at an orphanage could be hard—the Sisters of Saint Martha were known for their discipline—so they were happy to offer the children an occasional treat.

Frankie's favorite event took place on weekends when the bagpipers came to play. Each Sunday afternoon the children were dressed in colorful kilts and lined up in the hallway to await the arrival of the pipers. Sydney was proud of its Scottish heritage, and the children loved it as well. Sunday became Frankie's favorite day of the week.

Prior to their arrival he could hear the pipers playing in the distance—a low wailing sound announced their approach. The other children giggled and jumped with excitement, but Frankie stood still and listened. Soon enough the pipers would round the corner and enter the hall. With silver swords glistening at their sides and cheeks puffed up like bellows, they would blow into their bags, producing a distinctive, droning melody. Next, dancers would draw their swords and place them in a crisscross pattern on the floor. They would leap and hop around the blades in time to the music while the pipers played *The Highland Fling*, a dizzying Scottish dance distinguished by its series of leaps and twirls.

On one memorable occasion Frankie could hardly contain his excitement when he was invited to join in. He jumped over the swords and twirled and spun until his legs grew weak and his sides hurt. Long after the event was over he lay awake in bed replaying the afternoon in his mind.

In spite of the good times, however, the boys grew tired of the nuns' heavy-handed discipline. In the spring of 1957 Charlie worked out every detail of their planned great escape. One night in late April, as the moon slipped behind a cloud Charlie shook Frankie awake and handed him a pair of trousers. Frankie sat up, rubbed his eyes, and slipped them on.

"Hurry up," Charlie hissed, tossing his little brother a pair of shoes as well.

Frankie gripped Charlie's hand as they descended the dark stairway to the cellar. Every creak of the steps sent a chill down Charlie's spine. He held his breath and hoped Sister Ellen wouldn't discover their treachery. "Over there," he whispered, pointing to a stack of bicycles. "Find the one you want, and I'll look over here."

Frankie grabbed a small red bike and rolled it toward the door. Charlie wheeled a bike across the room too, pausing near a rolltop desk on which he spied an orange bucket filled with candy. Waving Frankie over, he pointed to his find.

"Must be leftovers from Halloween," Charlie figured as he stuffed several Hershey bars into his pocket.

Frankie's eyes grew wide. "Do you think it's okay if we take it?"

"Here, idiot," Charlie scoffed, handing him three packs of m&m's. "Put these in your pocket—you'll need 'em for later." He pushed Frankie toward the door. "C'mon, let's get outta here." But Charlie paused once more: several bills lay temptingly on the desk. Pausing for only a moment he proceeded to stuff them into his pocket before turning to leave.

The moon was breaking through the clouds as the boys rolled their bicycles onto the sidewalk. Charlie hopped on board and started pedaling. Frankie, following, began pumping his little legs as hard as he could. A freighter bellowed in the distance as Charlie cut through the cemetery before continuing down the street. He pulled to a stop near a fire hydrant and waited for Frankie to catch up. "The harbor is that way," he announced, pointing down Alexandra Street. "So we'll go *this* way." He turned his bike and started up the hill without looking back.

Frankie sighed and began pedaling again. "How long are we gonna ride?" he asked sulkily. Charlie didn't answer. When they reached Churchill Drive Frankie called out again, "Hey Charlie, how 'bout we take a break?"

Charlie looked over his shoulder with a scowl. "You tired already? Geez, what a baby."

"I'm not tired. Just hungry."

Charlie couldn't argue with that. Leaning his bike against a tree, he pulled out a Hershey bar.

Frankie shoved a fistful of m&m's into his mouth. "Sure beats going to school today, don't it?" he reflected through a mouthful of chocolate.

Charlie squinted in the direction of a red glow at the horizon. "I'm thinking we can make the bus station before sunrise."

"*Bus* station?"

"Sure. I found us some fare in the basement." He patted the money in his pocket. "We'll ride the bus to . . . I don't know, maybe Halifax."

"Where's that?"

"Far away, dummy. We'll go to Halifax, and after that we'll just see what we feel like doing."

"We can do whatever we want now, right, Charlie?"

"Yeah, sure. We just gotta lay low for a while so the cops don't find us. When the coast is clear, we'll figure out what to do next."

As the boys planned their future a pair of headlights shined in their direction.

Charlie cupped his hand over his eyes as a car pulled up and came to a stop.

A police officer stepped out. "You boys are out a bit a*rr*ly this mor-*rn*in', a*rr*en't ya?" he asked, a touch of scorn in his tone.

Charlie nudged Frankie with his elbow before calling out in studied nonchalance. "Just getting some exercise, sir."

"Su*rr*e ya are," the constable replied knowingly. He stepped closer and patted Frankie on the head. "Why don't I give you boys a *rr*ide back to the o*rr*phanage before the sisters sta*rr*t to wo*rr*y? I'm su*rr*e Fr. Webb'll be wantin' a wo*rr*d with you as well."

Charlie, wondering how the officer knew where they lived, shoved the rest of the candy bar into his mouth, gave Frankie another nudge, and headed for the squad car.

Frankie shrugged his shoulders and followed his brother. He didn't much care about running away anymore. His legs were tired and his stomach growling. Walking wearily next to the police officer, he admired the shiny gun swinging at his side.

"Hey Charlie," Frankie called out hopefully, "d'ya think we'll make it back in time for breakfast?"

CHAPTER 3

"I'm Not Leaving"

News of the boys' escape spread quickly. Mother Superior was furious, but the other children were impressed. When Charlie and Frankie bragged about their ride in a police car, they became instant celebrities. Sister Ellen's flogging served only to elevate them to celebrity status in everyone else's eyes. Frankie enjoyed his new status immensely and walked down the hall with a swagger. Although he still slept with his toy donkey, he no longer felt the need to hide beneath the basement steps.

Now more than ever Mother Superior wanted to find a home for the Briand boys. It was obvious that Charlie could no longer be trusted. And Frankie was a loose cannon: she never knew what would set him off. On top of that, the boys were having a negative influence on the rest of the children.

Potential adoptive parents visited the orphanage every weekend. Each Saturday the children were dressed in their best hand-me-downs, hair combed and teeth brushed, and lined up in the big hall for visitors who would stroll by, smile, pat heads, and even pinch cheeks. Frankie always ran his hand through his hair to mess it up before joining the line. He hated these inspections.

"How would you like to come live with me?" a short, plump woman asked Frankie one morning as she patted his shoulder.

"No!" He shook off her hand. "I don't wanna live with you."

The woman glanced at Mother Superior, who waved her on to the next child.

Frankie leaned over to look down the row of kids. He winked at Charlie, who winked back. Already years earlier the boys, then very little, had made a pact that they would never be separated. If one of them were fostered out alone, he would make such a fuss that the frustrated parents would return him within a week. The plan had worked well on more than one occasion.

∞

One morning, in the spring of 1959, Mother Superior was seated at her desk sorting mail and planning the week's activities when a knock sounded at the door. "Who is it?" she asked.

"It's Sister Daniel, Mother. May I come in?"

"Come in, Sister."

A wisp of a woman entered the office and closed the door. Her face was framed in a white cotton cap tucked underneath a crisply starched coif, over which was draped a black veil that flowed over her shoulders and down her back. A stiff white collar held her chin high and kept her gaze perpetually forward. Her black robe hung in soft folds to the floor, and a leather cord cinched her waist. Sister Daniel wore a crucifix around her neck and carried a rosary in her pocket. After smoothing the front of her habit, she clasped her hands together and looked toward Mother Superior with a smile. "I have some good news for you, Mother," she announced.

"What is it?"

"I just received a letter from a friend of mine in America. She wants to adopt two boys— preferably brothers. I've known Jean Majewski for several years, Mother, and I think she's up to the task. Of course, the boys I'm thinking of are . . ."

Mother Superior, leaning back in her chair with a smile, finished the sentence: " . . . the Briand boys."

∞

Harold Majewski came from good Polish stock. Hardworking and devout, he had emigrated from Poland during the 1930s and settled in Michigan, one of thousands seeking employment in the burgeoning automotive industry. At the time Poles made up the largest group of immigrants in Detroit. Knowing he would need to work hard to get ahead, Harold earned a degree in engineering and later found a job at Stellar

Engineering Company. He married Jean, and the couple purchased a two-story wood-frame house on the southwest side of Detroit. Harold was a small man: short and wiry. But his hands were strong: he spent long hours tinkering on woodworking projects in the garage. When he wasn't sawing wood Harold was relaxing in front of the television. It was the Golden Age of Television, and Harold, like many others, never missed an episode of *What's My Line* or *The Ed Sullivan Show*.

Jean was a strong, fiery-tempered woman. She had lost four babies at birth, one right after another and the neighbors said she had never gotten over it. While Harold buried himself in his work, Jean trudged through her days mopping floors, cooking meals, and doing the laundry. The bitterness that she carried in her shoulders eventually caused her neck to grow stiff. So stiff, in fact, she could barely turn her head.

So it was a bit of a shock to the neighbors when a car pulled in to the Majewski driveway one day and two young boys stepped out. Hoping that adopting two children might bring some happiness into their home, Jean had written a letter to her friend at Little Flower Institute in Nova Scotia. Two weeks later Sister Daniel wrote back telling Jean that the orphanage did indeed have two brothers, Charlie and Frankie Briand, who needed a home. Pleased, Harold and Jean painted the upstairs bedroom a bright shade of blue.

⊂━⊃

Sister Daniel closed the office door behind Charlie and Frankie, and Mother Superior pointed to two chairs in front of her desk. "Have a seat, boys," she invited.

Charlie couldn't figure out why they had been called to the office. They hadn't done anything wrong—at least not lately. He glanced over at Frankie. *Unless the squirt ratted on me for beating him up last week.* He had pounded on Frankie's shoulder 60 times, making him count aloud each blow. But Frankie had taken it like a man, and it wasn't like him to go crying to the nuns.

"Boys," Mother Superior began, "I have good news for you. We've found a family who would like to adopt the two of you together." Charlie and Frankie exchanged a look. "So we won't need to separate you when you move to your new home . . . in America."

"America!" Charlie protested. "We don't want to go to America, Mother. This is our home."

Frankie, figuring Charlie could handle it, didn't say a word.

"Nevertheless, Charles," Mother Superior continued, "you're moving to Detroit, Michigan. If this couple is kind enough to take the two of you together, I should think you'd be grateful."

Frankie watched his brother in search of a cue for his own response. He knew Charlie would never agree to leave Nova Scotia. After all, this was where they'd been born—the only home they'd ever known. America was too far away. But Mother Superior was using her stern voice. She slipped a piece of paper in front of them.

"This is how you will spell your new name: M-a-j-e-w-s-k-i. It's pronounced *Ma-jes-kee*. It's longer than Briand, but you'll get used to it."

Why doesn't Charlie say something? Frankie wondered. *We're not changing our name!*

Charlie sat quietly, staring at his hands, while Frankie started to cry.

Sister Daniel led the boys from the room and took them upstairs to pack. There wasn't much to gather—most of their meager belongings would be passed along to the other children. "Besides," she informed them, "the Majewskis have enough money to buy you new clothes."

After crawling into bed that night, Frankie, tearing up anew, wiped his eyes and pulled the blanket under his chin. He looked over at Charlie and sighed. "New clothes . . ." Frankie whispered with a wry half-smile. "Maybe they'll throw in some toys, too."

"Who cares about new clothes or some dumb toys?" Charlie countered before turning his face away.

"Well, at least we'll be together, right?" Frankie waited hopefully, but when Charlie didn't answer he closed his eyes and tried to get some sleep.

The next morning there were no sad goodbyes on the front steps of the orphanage. The nuns, who seemed happy to see them go, waved from the porch with bright smiles. Several of the boys had slapped Frankie on the back, called him a lucky dog, and promised to write. Frankie knew they'd forget; he'd probably never see or hear from any of them again. At the airport he boarded the plane—an intimidating new experience—slipped into a seat, and pressed his nose against the window. As the plane lifted high into the air, Frankie squeezed his stuffed donkey tight and gazed down at the ground below. Soon Cape Breton Island looked no bigger than a dot on the Atlantic Ocean.

When they landed at Detroit Metro Airport Frankie knew he was on his own; one glance at his brother told him this was so. For the first time in Frankie's recollection Charlie looked small and weak—barely able to take care of himself, let alone his little brother.

"All right, boys," the stewardess announced in a cheery voice. "We've landed in Detroit. Time to meet your new parents."

"I'm not leaving," Frankie pronounced with an air of finality. He put on his angriest face and folded his arms across his chest. Charlie rolled his eyes, unfastened his seat belt, and stood up to leave.

"Oh, you don't mean that." The stewardess smiled reassuringly, patting the little boy on the shoulder.

Shaking off her hand, Frankie rose to follow Charlie toward the exit. He knew he couldn't stay inside the plane, but if he played this right no one would be able to get him down. He remembered the pact he and Charlie had made at the orphanage. *I'm keeping up my end even if Charlie doesn't keep his.*

Charlie made his way down the gangplank, while Frankie grabbed the railing and swung himself up and over the side of the plane. He landed on top of the wing and then scooted back from the edge. Wrapping his arms around his donkey, he shot down a fiercely challenging glance at a middle-aged couple who stood watching in horror.

"Hey!" the stewardess cried in alarm. "What do you think you're doing? Get down from there!"

"No."

"Listen, buddy." Her kindly demeanor was gone. "Come down right now or I'm calling security."

"I don't care. You can't make me."

The stewardess stepped into the cockpit.

"I've got an eight-year-old boy here sitting out on the wing," she spoke into a handset. "I don't know how it happened. He was getting off, and the next thing I know he's up on the wing. He refuses to come down. I'm going to need some help."

She hung up and seated herself on a step close to Frankie.

Security arrived in the form of a tall, thin man in a blue uniform. He strolled onto the airstrip with his hands in his pockets, looked up at Frankie, and smiled. "How ya doin' pal?" he asked. "How's it going up there?"

The man's friendly eyes caught Frankie off guard. Still, tightening his grip on the donkey, he yelled, "I'm not coming down!"

The man shrugged his shoulders. "Who said anything about coming down? I just wanted to ask you a question."

Frankie didn't trust him, though he did look like a nice guy.

"I was just wondering what your favorite ice cream flavor might be."

This could be a trap, Frankie realized, but decided to answer anyhow. "Chocolate."

"Chocolate? That's *my* favorite too." The man turned to point toward the terminal. "Did you know that inside our new airport there's a place that sells chocolate ice cream cones? It's the best ice cream in town. Did you know that?"

"No." Frankie glanced down at Charlie, who stood impassively next to the security guard.

Charlie tugged on the man's sleeve. "Do I get some too?" he asked.

"Sure," he replied. "You and your brother both get a cone . . . *if* he ever comes down from the plane, that is." He called out to Frankie. "Whenever you're ready, son."

"C'mon, *stupid,*" Charlie put in, his expression both resigned and impatient. "Let's get some ice cream."

"All right." Frankie scooted on his bottom toward the edge of the wing.

The man climbed up the steps and reached his arms toward the boy. "Nice and easy, son," he encouraged. "How about handing me the stuffed animal first, and then you can scoot a little closer?"

Frankie tossed his toy to the man before sliding into his arms.

"So you like chocolate, huh?" The guard took Frankie's hand and started to walk. He nodded toward the Majewskis and then continued on to the terminal. Frankie and Charlie ordered double-dip chocolate cones and licked their ice cream as they were introduced to their new parents.

CHAPTER 4

"You Can't Make Me"

"**H**urry up, boys," Jean called up the stairs. "You don't want to be late for school."

Frankie sat on the edge of the bed, clutching his new teddy bear in one hand and a toy gun in the other. It was Monday morning, the first day of school, and he was miserable. He hated school in the first place and dreaded having to meet new kids. He missed the orphanage— the crowded hallways, the breakfast oatmeal, and noisy boys thundering down the stairs. He missed the pushing, shoving, and teasing of his friends and the smell of the ocean when it blew in off the coast. He wanted to watch the seagulls and hear the freighters bellowing in the harbor. He wanted to go home.

Charlie stood, preening, in front of a full-length mirror admiring his school uniform and shiny new shoes. "Listen, Frankie," he announced matter-of-factly, turning toward his brother, "you better start calling me Chuck from now on. It sounds better."

Frankie frowned. "Then you better call me Frank," he conceded, not to be outdone. "I don't want people making fun of me either."

Chuck sat down on the bed and threw his arm around Frank's shoulder. "Listen," he declared, making a fist, "anybody laughs at you, they answer to *me*." Grateful to have Chuck at his side, Frank set down the teddy bear and headed downstairs.

Jean was in the kitchen, waiting to inspect the boys in their uniforms. She looked over Frank carefully and wet a finger to smooth back a stray lock of hair from his forehead. Wide-eyed and somber, he studied his new mother's face as she did so, noticing that she couldn't turn her head all the way. *Something's wrong with her neck,* he recognized. *Is she paralyzed or something?* He instinctively recoiled from her touch.

"Maybe she was born that way," Chuck suggested as they left the house. He knew better than to ask. He had already witnessed Jean's temper a few times and knew it was better to keep his mouth shut.

The boys had joined a traditional Polish family. Several times a week their house was filled with noisy relations dropping by for dinner. Jean worked long hours in the kitchen, cooking pierogies and kielbasa; it fell to Harold when they were entertaining to pass around the beer. Later he would mix highballs while everyone relaxed in the living room. As the evening wore on tempers tended to flare and old arguments resurface. This would be Chuck and Frank's cue to hurry upstairs to their room. They would huddle under a blanket in Chuck's bed, snickering at the coarse language drifting up from the living room. Loudest and foulest of all was their new mother.

From what the boys could tell, their dad was the smarter of the two. Harold had a college degree and was savvy enough to stay out of his wife's way. The boys took their cues from him, avoiding her at such times as well. This was the only way to maintain peace in the house.

On this first day of school Chuck and Frank grabbed their metal lunch boxes from the kitchen counter and headed out the door. School was less than a mile from the house, so the boys could easily be there in ten minutes. Neighborhood kids stopped along the way to stare. All had heard about the foreigners and knew they'd been orphans. They figured something terrible must have happened in their past. "Hi, *orphans,*" a few called out from a safe vantage point across the street before scampering away, sniggering.

Frank's jaw tightened as he cast a sidelong glance at his protector. "You gonna beat them up, Chuck?" he asked.

"Nah. Just let 'em cross over to *our side,* though."

Frank trudged along and watched the offenders run ahead to join another group. *This isn't gonna be easy!* he acknowledged to himself.

As they entered the school building Chuck made sure no one saw him walking with his little brother. Turning abruptly down the first hallway and lengthening his stride, he disappeared. Frank planted himself before a class roster posted on the wall and ran his finger down to the third grade list. When he found his name he took a deep breath and headed resignedly for Room 103.

The chalkboards and nuns reminded the boy of Little Flower Institute, but everything else seemed strange. His desk, for example. It was attached to his chair on one side and had a smooth wooden top with a horizontal well carved out for his pencil. When he raised the top it lifted on hinges and opened to a storage area big enough for books, papers, and crayons.

Everyone stored their lunchboxes on a wooden shelf above the radiator. Frank walked over and did the same. He was proud of his new lunchbox, with Matt Dillon's picture stamped on the front, and hated to part with it even temporarily. The tough, ornery television marshal was Frank's favorite. Nobody messed with Dillon. Jean had packed in the box a bologna sandwich in wax paper, squished alongside a thermos of chocolate milk next to an apple and a Hostess cupcake. Lunchtime was going to be Frank's favorite time of the day.

After lunch came recess. Frank slipped his hands into his pockets and strolled the playground in search of a friendly face.

"Hey kid," a boy called out. "Wher*re*'s the bahth-*rr*oom?"

"What?" Frank asked, caught off guard.

"I said, wher*re*'s the bahth-*rr*oom?"

"A*rr*e you making fun of me?"

"Did you hear that?" The boy elbowed his friend. "I told you he was weird."

Frank's hands curled into fists. His immediate impulse was to knock the kid out. But he had no desire to be sent to the principal's office on the first day of school. His tormentors laughed and ran away, leaving Frank in red-faced shame. He would have to get rid of the Scottish *burr* if he ever hoped to fit in. He decided to work on that. "Three more hours," Frank told himself with a sigh as he headed back into the building.

When the dismissal bell rang Frank burst through the doors in search of Chuck. Spying his brother standing outside with a group of sixth graders, Frank ran up and tugged on his sleeve. "Let's go, Chuck. Let's get outta here."

"*You* get outta here," Chuck countered, shaking off his hand. "*I'll* go when I'm ready. Beat it, squirt." He turned back to his new friends with a dismissive laugh.

Frank ran all the way home. It didn't feel like home, but there was nowhere else for him to go. *Chuck's a jerk,* he thought angrily. *He thinks he's tough just 'cuz he made a couple of friends.*

Jean was in the kitchen when Frank burst in. Leaving the outside door wide open, he brushed past her, bounded up the stairs to his room, slammed the door shut, and reached for the teddy bear lying on his bed.

Jean called up the stairs. "Frank, get back down here and close this door."

"No!"

"*What* did you say?"

"You can't make me."

"You come down here *right now!*"

Frank could hear the rising edge in her voice. Slowly opening the bedroom door, he started down the steps, still clutching the teddy bear in his arms.

When he reached the kitchen Jean squeezed the back of his neck and led him to the door. "*Now*, you close this the right way," she ordered.

"Make me!" Frank challenged, pulling away.

"*Make* you?" Jean reached for a dishrag on the counter and hurled it at his face. It snapped around his cheek before dropping to the floor. Frank lunged for the rag and stretched back his arm to whip it.

Just then Chuck reached him from behind, blocking his aim. "What're you doing, *idiot*?" He squeezed Frank's wrist hard, making him drop the rag.

"What do you care, Chuck?"

Frank darted out the door with his teddy bear. In a headlong hurtle he reached the end of the street and scuttled up a tall oak tree. *I hate them!* he thought furiously, ascending higher into the branches. He perched on a limb and dangled his feet in the air. *And I hate this stupid bear, too.* On an impulse Frank pulled a string from his pocket, wound it several times around the stuffed animal's neck, and secured it with a knot. Tying the other end of the string to the limb and then releasing the bear, he watched in satisfaction as it swung in the air. Frank scrambled back down to the ground and gazed up at his grisly work. Wiping a tear from his eye he started home, wishing he could trudge all the way back to Nova Scotia.

CHAPTER 5

"Make Him Apologize"

Summer, 1962

Jean folded the letter and placed it back in the envelope. She would show it to Harold when he got home from work. Sister Daniel had answered her request for more children by offering two little girls from the orphanage. One was an infant, abandoned last month on their doorstep. The other was a year older—her mother had also disappeared without a trace. Sister Daniel was surprised to receive Jean's request, however. She had thought the Briand boys would be quite enough to handle, and said so in her letter. But she agreed to draw up the necessary papers and arranged for the girls to arrive within a month.

Sister Daniel was right about one thing, Jean had to admit: the boys *were* a handful. At 14 years old Chuck was rude and disrespectful, and Frank at 11 was even more trouble than his brother. The boys were continuously fighting—with each other, with other kids on the block, . . . even with teachers. Phone calls from the principal's office brought Jean to the school office several times a month to pick up one or the other of her sons. At home Chuck and Frank were lectured, grounded, and beaten, but nothing could alter Chuck's defiance or calm Frank's volatile temper. Jean complained to the relatives, admitting she had made a mistake. She wished they'd never adopted the boys and didn't care who knew. Chuck and Frank could hear her from their bedroom.

"If they knew the truth about their parents," Jean told her sister-in-law one night, "they'd never believe it. I'm sorry we ever adopted those two. Especially Frank. The only hope I have is that these two little girls might bring some peace into this house."

Frank started to worry. Was his mother thinking of sending him back to Nova Scotia? It wouldn't surprise him if she did. But after living in the United States for three years he no longer wanted to return. He decided to work harder at getting along with everyone—even his little sisters to come.

"I'm gonna become an altar boy," he announced to Chuck on the way to school.

Chuck snorted. "*You?* You gotta be kidding, Frank. There's no way you'll ever be an altar boy."

"Oh *yeah?*" Frank had a twinkle in his eyes. "You just watch me. I'm not sitting through any more of them boring masses. I'm gonna do important stuff like ring bells and light candles and stuff."

"You get the craziest ideas, Frank," Chuck shrugged, thumping him on the head. "Besides, you're not holy enough to be an altar boy."

Within a month Frank was indeed dressed in a black and white cassock—the vestment worn by mass servers on Sunday mornings. Harold and Jean watched proudly from their pew as their son stood at the altar and assisted the priest. Chuck shook his head and rolled his eyes, knowing it was all a sham.

One Sunday Frank and another boy were hanging up their vestments when the priest walked in. It was typically his job to rinse and dry the chalice, but this time Father handed it to Frank. "Take care of this," he instructed before walking away.

Frank glanced inside the goblet. "What do you want me to do with the leftover wine, Father?"

"You can finish it," the priest called back as he left the room.

"Is he serious?" Frank shot a puzzled look at his friend, then shrugged and took a swallow. It burned his throat.

"This is nuts," the other boy commented, nonetheless taking a swig as well.

The following week Father stood by to watch the two empty the chalice again. This time the priest poured more wine into the cup. The boys drank until they felt giddy. Frank hadn't realized that being an altar boy could be so much fun.

There were other benefits as well. He no longer dreaded going to church. Each Sunday morning Frank was the first one up, hurrying off to mass to put on his vestment. The neighborhood kids respected him, and he had finally made some friends. Best of all, his parents were pleased, and there was relative peace in their home.

Soon afterward Frank decided to try out for the football team. He and Chuck tossed a ball around each night until it was too dark to see. He learned how to pass, block, and tackle. Frank made the team as fullback and looked forward to playing his first game. But week after week he found himself sitting on the bench. By mid-season he was ready to throw in the towel.

One afternoon, as the team celebrated a victory in the locker room, the door swung open and the Monseigneur strolled in, his black robe swishing along the floor as he walked. His somber gray eyes scanned the group as the boys stood at attention. The Monseigneur often made surprise visits at the school and occasionally liked to drop in on sporting events as well. Whenever he appeared unannounced, the team snapped to attention.

"Good morning, Monseigneur," the boys chanted in unison.

Frank alone didn't bother to look up. Leaning over a bench with one foot raised and continuing to unlace his shoes, he sneered, "Good *after-noon*, Monseigneur."

The team held its collective breath as the priest trained a fiery glare on Frank. He took several long steps, paused in front of the boy, and backhanded Frank's face, leaving an imprint from his ring on his cheek. Frank dropped to the bench, holding his cheek with one hand while covering his eyes with the other, not wanting his teammates to see the smarting tears.

Heading toward the door, the Monseigneur turned to address the coach. "That boy is finished playing football," he announced emphatically.

"*Frank!*" the coach roared after the priest had gone. "Grab your things and get out of here. You're off the team."

Frank ran home as fast as he could, slammed down his gear on the kitchen floor, and retreated to his room. Putting down his newspaper, Harold followed him up the stairs. "What happened, Frank?" he asked.

"They kicked me off the team."

"Who did?"

"The coach. And the Monseigneur, too. They both did it. They hate me."

"They got no right kickin' you off the team," Harold shouted over his shoulder as he tramped down the stairs. Grabbing his keys, he sped to the rectory and demanded to see the priest. No one answered the door. Harold shouted and cursed for a full 20 minutes, but the door remained closed. As he drove away the Monsignor stepped openly onto the porch, arms folded. Harold cursed him one last time before heading for home.

Frank was finished with sports. He quit being an altar boy, too. He wasn't sure why his father had defended him that night—they never talked about the incident—but Frank heard from a neighbor that his dad had pounded on the rectory door loudly enough to alert everyone within earshot. No one had ever stood up for him like that before. Despite his shame, Frank was proud.

He didn't care about trying to fit in anymore—he didn't want or need anyone else's approval, especially at school. By the time Frank turned 12, most of his classmates in the sixth grade steered clear of him. The nuns, too, tried to avoid a confrontation, turning a blind eye unless he caused egregious trouble. No matter how many times Frank was lectured, paddled, or suspended, his behavior only grew worse and his attitude more obstinate. There was only one place Frank hated more than school—and that was home.

The situation there had grown volatile. Frank's parents were as frustrated in dealing with him as the school was. They beat their son and confined him to his room, but nothing they tried managed to control his behavior. As time passed Harold and Jean began to fear for their own safety.

One day Jean received a call from the owner of the local Woolworth drugstore. He had watched Frank stuff a fistful of candy into his pants pocket that afternoon and walk off without paying. "If you don't want me calling the police, Mrs. Majewski, you'd better do something about your kid," he informed her.

Frank trudged home, wondering whether anyone had observed his shoplifting. If his mother found out, he knew, he'd be in big trouble. Taking a deep breath, he opened the back door. Jean, facing the stove, didn't say a word as Frank entered the kitchen. She preferred to wait for the sound of Harold's car in the driveway before launching into an argument with their son. Within ten minutes Harold pulled into the garage.

"So, Frank," Jean began, turning around and facing him before Harold had made his entrance. "I hear you stole some candy from Woolworths's today. What do we have to do now, call the police? Because that's what's going to happen if this doesn't stop."

Frank could feel his face growing red and his jaw tightening.

"Why are you looking at me like that?" she challenged. "Don't you care if you go to jail?"

"No," Frank replied, honestly for a change. "I don't care. Anything would be better than living here with you."

Harold, overhearing this last comment as he approached the house, unfastened his belt and pulled it from his waist before opening the back door. "What's going on in here?"

"She's yelling at me over nothing," Frank accused, pointing at his mother.

Without waiting for an explanation from Jean, Harold backhanded Frank across the face. "I've told you before: don't ever call your mother *she*."

"Make him apologize, Harold," Jean shouted.

"Are you going to apologize?"

"No! She's making a big deal out of nothing."

"What did I just say? You don't call your mother *she*. Now say you're sorry."

"I'm *not* sorry."

Jean, her fury escalating, lunged at Frank and pulled his hair. Her equally enraged son shoved her roughly aside as Harold snapped the belt across his arm.

"You gonna say you're sorry?"

"No!" Frank rubbed his arm, taking a step back.

"Make him get down on his knees and apologize, Harold." Jean was nearly hysterical.

"You gonna get on your knees, boy?"

"No, I'm *not* getting on my knees!"

Harold swung the belt again. This time it wrapped around Frank's chest, causing him to lose his balance and stumble to the ground. The next thing Frank knew he was pinned to the floor, his wiry father on top of him, holding down his arms with his knees. Frank struggled to break free as Jean leaned over him, deliberately scratching Frank's cheek with her diamond ring. Her chest was heaving and her eyes flashing as she proceeded to cut the other cheek too. A thin line of blood oozed from each wound. Frank screamed in pain while Harold, dumbfounded, stumbled to his feet and fell back into a chair.

CHAPTER 6

"Every Family Has Its Problems"

Frank crawled to the door before bolting from the house. There was only one place to run, only one friend to whom he could turn: Jerry Butcher. Jerry's parents were good people; they would take him in. And once they heard what had happened, they'd probably call the police. Frank pounded on the back door. "Jerry," he screamed. "It's me, Frank. Let me in!"

Mrs. Butcher opened the door. "Frank! Dear God, what happened? Come inside!" She took his arm and led him into the kitchen. Frank slumped into a chair, dropping his head on the table, while Mrs. Butcher grabbed a damp towel and began dabbing the blood on his face.

Jerry entered the room. "What happened, Frank? Did you get in a fight?"

"My parents," Frank moaned, cradling his head in his arms. "My mother did it to me." The taste of blood in his mouth, Frank swiped at it with his sleeve.

"Jerry," Mrs. Butcher instructed, "go get your father."

But Mr. Butcher had already appeared in the doorway. He was a soft-spoken man with kind eyes; Frank couldn't recall ever having seen him angry. He sat down next to Frank and studied his face. "Who did this to you, Frank?"

"His mother," Mrs. Butcher answered grimly. "What kind of woman would do that to her own son?"

"Jerry, go get some bandages." Mr. Butcher turned back to Frank. "We'll get you cleaned up, Frank. Just keep your head down and leave the towel on your face."

Jerry came back with bandages and sat in a chair next to his friend. Mrs. Butcher poured a glass of Vernor's ginger ale and set it in front of the boy. "Take some sips, Frank," she urged. "It'll settle your stomach."

"Can he sleep here tonight, dad?" Jerry asked. "He can't go home, right?"

"I'll call his parents and see what they say," Mr. Butcher replied as he taped gauze onto Frank's cheeks. "It's up to them, not us."

Harold responded that this was fine with him, and Frank followed Jerry upstairs to his bedroom.

The next day was Saturday, so the boys slept in. Frank lay on his back with his hands behind his head while Jerry sat cross-legged on the bed, tossing a ball into the air and catching it with his mitt. "So," Jerry invited slowly, "you gonna tell me what happened last night?"

"Not much to tell."

"What's with your mom?"

"She's crazy. She was waiting for my dad to get home so he'd hear us fighting and then beat me up. She does it all the time. Next thing I know he pinned me to the floor and she's cutting my face up with her ring. That's all I remember."

Jerry turned the ball in his hand and rubbed the stitching. He couldn't imagine something like that happening in his house. His parents had never hit him; in fact, his dad never even raised his voice. He wished his family could have adopted Frank instead of the Majewskis. "So, what are you going to do?" Jerry asked.

"I don't know. Think your dad will call the cops?"

"I doubt it."

"Why not?"

"I don't know. People don't do that with neighbors."

Frank grasped the ball and threw it at the wall.

"Don't be mad, Frank."

"Who's mad? Forget it. You got a mirror around here?"

Jerry pointed toward the dresser.

Frank crawled across the bed and picked up a hand mirror. Tugging gently at the bandages on his face, he spat out, "Man, that stings!" following up with a cuss word.

"Shut-up, Frank," Jerry hissed. "My folks'll hear you."

"You should hear *my* folks," Frank retorted, pulling the bandages off. "They're worse than a couple of sailors." He turned his face first to the left and then to the right, studying the scratches on his cheeks. "Man, she got me good. Look at that. All with her ring. I'll probably hafta grow a beard someday just to cover it up."

Changing the subject, Jerry hopped out of bed. "I'm starved. Let's get something to eat."

Mrs. Butcher was in the kitchen, cracking eggs into a bowl and heating up a frying pan. Her husband sat at the table reading the morning paper. "How'd you sleep, Frank?" he asked.

"Fine, sir," Frank replied. He reached for a glass of orange juice on the table and took a sip. "Thanks for helping me out last night."

"Have a seat, Frank," Mrs. Butcher directed. "I'll cook some eggs up for you boys."

Frank slipped into a chair and looked around the room. The sun peered through lace curtains over the kitchen sink while Mrs. Butcher worked at the stove. She wore a flowered housecoat with fuzzy pink slippers. Her hair was in rollers, and a pair of glasses hung from a chain around her neck. Jerry sat down next to Frank and opened a box of Sugar Smacks. Digging his hand deep into the box in quest of the prize at the bottom, he pulled out a tiny pirate ship on a string and hung it around Frank's neck. Mr. Butcher sipped his coffee and kept reading.

The scene struck Frank as almost too perfect. The Butchers didn't argue or throw things at each other. Jerry's world was totally opposite his own. It all seemed too good to be true. *Too good for me, at least*, Frank thought ruefully.

After breakfast Frank headed home to face his parents. It was bad enough to argue and fight, his father told him, but Frank had humiliated them all by running to the neighbors. Every family has its problems, but you keep them to yourself, he insisted. Frank was grounded for three months—one month each for stealing candy, fighting, and calling his mother "she." That meant no playing outside for the rest of the summer.

There's no way I'm staying cooped up in this house all summer long, Frank told himself, immediately beginning to plan his escape.

That night Frank climbed out his bedroom window and stepped out onto the ledge. Grabbing a nearby branch, he swung himself to the ground and headed for the alley behind their house. He walked quickly, his anger boiling and his cheeks still burning—from emotion and from his mother's ring. The scene replayed over and over again in his mind as he reached into his pocket for a book of matches. Following through on an impulse, he lit a match and flicked it into an open garage, where it landed on a stack of newspapers and burst into flame. Frank lit another and tossed it onto a pile of greasy rags, which ignited as well.

"*I hate you!*" Frank spat out before breaking into a run. He continued down the alley, tossing matches into all of the open garages. "*I hate all of you!*"

Some of the matches fizzled out, but others sparked into flame. It didn't take long before the sound of a fire engine wailed in the distance, and Frank hurried home to climb back into his room. Neighbors gathered on porches while firemen dragged heavy hoses toward the burning garages. Two burnt to the ground, and several others were damaged.

"Who would do something like this?" Harold stood with his hands in his pockets, looking up and down the street. Jean watched the firemen for a few moments and then stepped back into the house. "Frank," she yelled, "get down here!"

Frank took his time descending the steps. "What'd I do now?"

"You know exactly what you did," she shouted, leaving no room for benefit of the doubt. Grabbing a frying pan from the kitchen, she shook it menancingly at Frank. "What did you do to those garages? Don't bother denying it, either. I knew it was you the moment I heard those sirens." The pan flew through the air, striking Frank on the head. He slumped to the ground.

Harold, running into the house to see his son lying prone on the floor, gazed at his wife incredulously.

"He's no good, Harold," she sobbed, wringing her hands. "He's rotten through and through."

Harold watched Frank rolling on the rug, writhing in pain.

"Send him back where he came from," Jean pleaded, tugging on her husband's arm. "We can't keep him, Harold. He's no good. He'll never change."

"Get up, Frank," Harold instructed. "Go to your room and stay there till I call you."

Frank pulled himself with difficulty to a standing position and groped his way to the stairs. With one hand he held his head and with the other grabbed the railing. Upon reaching his room he fell across his bed and curled up into a ball. His ears were ringing, and his head throbbed in pain. He had never hated anyone as much as he hated his mother. He wanted to kill her—could picture himself wrapping his hands around her throat . . . *They'll have to lock me up to keep me away from her now*, he vowed through clenched teeth.

To Frank's surprise his parents never reported him to the police. The garage fires remained an "unsolved mystery" in the neighborhood; though no one broached the subject with his parents, everyone knew it was Frank. The cold stares said it all, and Harold wondered whether it was time to start looking for a new house.

Frank finally found some friends, public school kids who were daring and defiant—risk-takers just as he was. Some of them had police records and had spent time in reform school. They were criminals already in the seventh grade, but Frank didn't care. He was accepted and welcomed, and it felt great. The kids formed a gang, putting Frank in charge. He liked his new position and took the job seriously.

One of his closest friends in the gang was a boy known as Head—his head was larger than average, and his hair was crawling with lice. The other kids pointed and laughed whenever Head walked by, but Frank liked him. The two boys regularly stole candy from Woolworth's and chugged beer late into the night. Nearly every garage in the neighborhood housed a case of beer: an open invitation for boys on the prowl. One night Frank lifted a case and handed it to Head. They ran toward Cooley High School and climbed onto the roof of the building. There they popped open the bottles, leaning back to appreciate the view of Detroit. Frank and Head sat for hours, drinking and watching police cars as they cut through alleys with sirens blaring and lights flashing. Later that night, as Frank made his way home, an officer pulled him over and ordered him into the car. At the police station Frank placed a call to his father and then waited for him to arrive.

"Thank you, officer," Harold, still in his robe and slippers, responded in a resigned tone. "I'll take it from here."

When they got home the arguments and beatings resumed. Jean fired anything she could lay her hands on across the room at Frank—pots, pans, and doorbell chains all became missiles. In the morning Frank bolted from the house and headed back to the street.

One night after midnight the phone rang. Harold took the call. Frank was at the police station once again, this time charged with breaking and entering.

"Officer," Harold informed the police chief when he arrived, "I'm through bailing this kid out. Lock him up for the night. Maybe that will knock some sense into him."

The next day Frank stood before a judge while his parents sat impassively in the back of the courtroom. They refused to plead his case, so Frank was sentenced to six months of reform school.

When the judge rose to leave Frank turned around to locate his parents. As he watched them slip from the room, an officer approached him from behind and placed him in handcuffs.

CHAPTER 7

"Lead with Your Left"

Spring, 1963

Frank paced nervously in the hallway as a steady stream of boys filed past him into the classroom. Everyone took a seat, many making snide remarks about the new kid out in the hallway. Frank wanted to bolt from the building. He had no desire to face another new school, with new teachers and a class full of strangers.

"Think you're something special, Majewski?" The challenge came from Fonte, the most popular kid at Don Bosco Hall. Frank had heard his name mentioned several times since arriving at the reform school.

"No," Frank responded with a shrug. "I just don't wanna go in."

"What are you, a sissy?"

"No, man. It's bad enough going to jail, but being thrown into a new school is torture. At least for me it is. Everybody just stares at you like you're some kind of freak."

Fonte was a good-looking Italian boy with dark, wavy hair and a square jaw. At 14 years old he had earned the respect of everyone at Don Bosco. Even the guards liked him. Fonte had worked hard to get on good terms with the guards and was given free use of the gym as a reward. He worked out five days a week and sported the muscles to prove it.

Fonte looked Frank over and immediately liked him. Frank, though short, was well built. And with those piercing blue eyes he could probably beat anybody in a stare-down. Fonte had heard about Frank, too—about his red-hot temper—and liked him all the more for it. He decided to take him under his wing.

"Tell you what, Majewski," he invited. "Meet me in the gym after school today."

"What for?"

"Just do it."

Frank had no idea what Fonte could want, but one thing was certain: if the two became friends life would go more smoothly for him at Don Bosco. Frank took a deep breath and stepped into the classroom.

Father John Finnegan had founded Don Bosco Hall in 1954. For the next eight years he had taken in boys like Frank, turning many from a life of crime. The courts in Wayne County were more than happy to supply Father Finnegan with wayward adolescent boys—enough to keep his dormitory filled year round. While many of them were rehabilitated, some merely did their time and returned to the street. Frank was 12 years old when he arrived at the school. Angry and bitter, he was ready to pick a fight with anyone who might dare to cross him. The judge had sent Frank to Father Finnegan in the hope that he might be able to turn him around. But Frank wasn't interested in anyone's help. He had sat in too many principals' offices and endured too many beatings to believe that anyone really cared. He would never fit in anywhere—including home or school—and was resigned to the fact. He was just there to do his time.

After the short bus ride back to Don Bosco after school, Frank dropped his school bag in his dorm room and headed for the gym. Fonte was waiting for him in the workout area, dressed in black sweatpants and a sleeveless t-shirt. He straddled a weight bench, curling a set of dumbbells. Despite his youth, the muscles on his arms bulged with each repetition.

"So what's up?" Frank asked noncommittally.

Fonte handed him a dumbbell. "From now on," he announced, "I'm gonna be your personal trainer."

"What does that mean?" Frank lifted the weight up and down tentatively a few times, weighing the possible implications of this unexpected offer.

"It means you do as I say." Fonte laughed, giving Frank a shove with his shoulder. It was like a rock, hard as steel. "First thing tomorrow, I'm gonna teach you some things about fighting. And I'm talking about *real* fighting. You're interested in learning that, aren't ya?"

"Yeah, sure." Frank set down the weight before hurrying to catch up with Fonte as he walked away.

"I'll show you how to handle the guards too," Fonte added, picking up where he had left off. "It's easy once you know how. And if you're real good"—he turned with a wink—"I'll loan you some of my personal library."

Frank could hardly believe his luck. Fonte was the best fighter in the school, and everyone knew it. People were sure to respect him after he'd learned how to fight.

For the next several weeks the boys worked out each day after school in the gym. Fonte showed Frank how to lead with his left, jab with an uppercut, and deliver a sharp hook. He also taught him how to position himself with a punching bag. "Put your feet here," he instructed, "and keep your wrists straight." He grabbed Frank's fists and raised them to his face. "And remember, keep your dukes up, like this."

Frank was feeling stronger and more confident every day. His already stocky arms grew strong, and his fists felt like rocks. He was getting fast on his feet, too. He liked boxing, along with the feeling of power that surged through his body when he pounded the punching bag. Now, as he walked down the hall, kids stepped aside. Long hours spent in the gym were already starting to pay off.

Fonte introduced Frank to another of his favorite pastimes: smoking. He showed him how to take long, slow drags on a cigarette and how to dangle it from one side of his mouth as he talked. Frank tried it in front of a mirror, dropped the cigarette several times, and then stuck it back in his mouth. He liked the way he looked and started hiding packs of Marlboros underneath his mattress. Thanks to Fonte the guards never "noticed."

One afternoon Fonte lay stretched out across Frank's bed, his hands locked behind his head as he talked about his plans after reform school. "One thing's for sure," he emphasized, "I'm not going back to school when I get out of here."

"What are you gonna do?" Frank asked.

"I know someone that can put me up for a while," Fonte replied, sitting up. "I'm not goin' back to live with my old man, either. He hates my guts, and the feeling's mutual." Fonte reached under his pillow and pulled out a folded magazine, which he tossed with a smirk onto the bed in front of Frank. "Ever seen one of these?"

Frank stared at the cover and whistled. "Where'd you find this?"

"Wanna borrow it?"

"Are you kidding?" Frank took the magazine into his hands. "Where'd you get it?"

"My old man had a regular collection. Kept a stash under his bed. I grabbed a few before I left." Fonte flipped the magazine open for Frank. "I've pretty much looked at all of 'em. You can have this one."

Frank's face turned red. "Man, Fonte," he shook his head appreciatively, "you're somethin' else."

"Don't mention it."

"I mean it, man. You taught me everything you know about boxing, how to handle the guards, . . . and now this."

Fonte threw a jab that Frank blocked with his hand. They both laughed, and Frank stuffed the magazine under his mattress next to the cigarettes. Later that night he slipped the magazine out to take another look. His face grew hot and his hands shook as he slowly turned the pages. He pulled the bed sheet up over his head until the lights went out.

Once a month the boys from Don Bosco took a bus across town for a swim at the local pool. This was a highlight for all, incenting most of the boys to be on their best behavior. One hot afternoon Frank stood in line waiting to board the bus. A new kid—whom Frank had already sized up as big, tough, and ornery—stepped in behind him. As the line moved forward the boy pressed his knuckles hard into Frank's back and shoved him from behind. Frank spun around and raised both fists. "You better knock it off, man." The boys stood toe-to-toe for a moment as Frank stared up at his face.

"Who's gonna stop me, *man*?"

Frank turned back around as the line inched forward again. He felt another shove from behind, followed by an elbow in the mouth as the boy pushed past him. Infuriated, Frank lunged. Grabbing the boy by the throat with his left hand, he started punching with his right. Rivulets of blood dripped from his nose as Frank continued to pummel the boy's face.

Everyone began to cheer. "Get 'em, Frank!" they shouted. "Smash his face in!"

The approval of his peers goaded Frank on as he threw punches again and again. Finally a security guard blew a whistle, and the boys fell silent. The guard squeezed through the crowd and separated the two boys. "Everyone turn around," he ordered, to a collective groan. "This trip is cancelled. Everybody into the gym—*now!*"

The boys slowly did an about face and headed back. This wasn't the first time swimming had been canceled.

"Let's *go!*" the rest of the guards barked in unison.

Whenever a fight broke out at Don Bosco the fighters, along with their audience, were shuffled into the gymnasium and forced to finish what they'd started with boxing gloves. Fellow inmates formed a ring around the pair to watch and cheer. The guards made sure things didn't get out of hand; when one of the challengers collapsed, the match was declared over.

Frank studied his opponent as Fonte laced up his boxing gloves. "He's gotta be six feet tall," Frank protested.

Fonte glanced over at the challenger and nodded. "Just remember what I taught you," he directed. "Keep your feet moving and your dukes up. Lead with your left." Patting Frank, he took his place in the crowd.

Frank shuffled his feet and beat the air a few times with his fists. He knew he was in for the trouncing of his life but wanted to put on a good show. The referee blew his whistle, and round one began. The gym echoed with shouts and catcalls as Frank stepped into the ring.

His opponent descended upon him with fists swinging wildly. He was a beast whose prey was already cornered. Frank took several hard punches to the head, lost his balance, and stumbled into the crowd. The kids as one pushed him back into the ring, laughing and cheering him on. He threw a hard left hook, his opponent barely flinching. Frank felt as though he had hit a wall. A sharp punch to his ear sent throbbing pain through his head, and a blow to his nose released a wash of blood, which Frank tasted in his mouth.

When he raised his glove to wipe his nose, the bully moved in for the kill, pounding Frank in the stomach, the ribs, and again in the head. Finally Frank collapsed on the ground. The crowd screamed for him to get up, but Frank couldn't move. Dark rings circled his eyes, and blood gushed from his nose and mouth. Raising himself on one elbow, he stared across the ring, only to drop once again to the floor, spent. The referee raised his opponent's arm, and the crowd booed.

Fonte hurried into the ring. Along with a group of other boys he lifted Frank in his arms and carried him to his bed. Fonte sat down on edge of the bed and began pulling off the boxing gloves, Frank wincing with each tug.

"You did all right, Frank," Fonte encouraged. "You almost had 'em."

Frank raised a limp fist and took a mock swipe at Fonte's jaw. "You're nuts," he murmured, "but thanks." With that he closed his eyes and dropped off to sleep.

CHAPTER 8

"When Will It End?"

Nine months later . . .

The porch light flicked on, and the door opened a crack as Harold peered out into the dark. "Who is it?" he asked.

"This kid belong to you?" A police officer stood on the porch, gripping Frank by one arm.

Harold paused for what seemed a moment too long before sighing. "Yes, he's ours." He held the door open. "Get in here, Frank."

"I'll need to make out a report," the officer continued, catching the door with his foot.

Harold waved him into the house.

"Our records show that your son just spent some time at Don Bosco Hall."

"And a lot of good it did him, too."

The policeman jotted a few notes in his report as Frank headed up to his room. "Mr. Majewski, you realize that your son broke parole again. If he keeps this up he's going to wind up back in jail . . ."

Frank lay in bed with a pillow over his head to muffle the sound of their voices. *I hate them!* he thought again—an all too familiar refrain. *I hate this house, this family, and this neighborhood, too. The first chance I get I'm busting out of here.* The prospect of jail no longer intimidated Frank. *Anything is better than living here*, he thought fiercely.

Chuck wanted out too. He was sick of fighting with his mother and tired of his father's stringent rules. He figured he and Frank could make it on their own, so the next night the boys, in a renewed alliance, climbed out the window and slid to the ground. They hurried across Six Mile Road before ducking into an alley. It was after midnight, and the streets were empty. Chuck tried the door on a parked car, and it opened. He shoved Frank into the back seat. "Lay down here," he ordered, "and I'll go in front."

"You gonna hotwire it, Chuck?"

"Not now, stupid. I'm gonna get some sleep. We got a big day tomorrow."

This is great! Frank thought excitedly. *On the road with Chuck—it can't get any better than this.* He slept for an hour before awakening to the thunk of a nightstick against the window.

"Come on out of there," an officer yelled.

Someone must have seen us getting into the car, Frank thought. *Now he's gonna march us back home.* Frank climbed out of the back seat and looked around for Chuck, who was already in the squad car.

On the ride home Chuck and Frank were already planning their next escape. When they arrived at the house Jean held the front door open for Chuck but pulled it shut in Frank's face. "Lock him up, officer," she called through the screen. "We don't want him back."

Frank couldn't believe his ears. His own mother had told the police to throw him in jail.

"Well, kid," the officer addressed him as they walked back to the car, "looks like you're coming with me to the station."

The next day a judge sentenced Frank to 60 days in the Wayne County Youth Home. For the first time in his life Frank was scared. He had never been there before but had heard it was bad—like real jail. Last week he had been in school, doing math problems and hanging out with friends. Now he was heading to one of the toughest juvenile homes in the state, housing some of the worst underage offenders. These were the kids Father Finnegan couldn't help.

But when Frank arrived he looked and acted as tough as the rest of the boys, so no one bothered him. The moves Fonte had taught him at Don Bosco came in handy. Frank spent the rest of the school year in and out of the youth home. Each time he was released from jail he returned to the streets. Harold and Jean wished their son could just stay in jail. Each time he ran away they hoped it was for good.

There's only one person in the world who cares about me, Frank reasoned, *and that's Chuck.* But Chuck had problems of his own. His last drinking binge had forced Harold to place a restraining order on him. Chuck wasn't allowed within 100 feet of their house.

One winter night, however, he appeared at the back door. It was January 7, 1965, Frank's 14th birthday. Chuck was a full-blown greaser now. His hair was slicked back with Brylcreem, and he sported skin-tight pants. He had a pack of Marlboro's rolled up in his T-shirt sleeve, and a cigarette dangled from his mouth. His blond hair was combed in a waterfall, giving him the "James Dean" look every teenaged boy coveted. Chuck was tall and muscular and packed a hard punch, . . . and he had come to take his little brother out for a night of carousing. Harold had no desire to fight with Chuck, so when he appeared at the back door he let him in. Frank grabbed his coat, and the boys headed out.

"Be back by curfew!" Jean shouted unnecessarily as the door slammed. She smiled to herself: if Frank violated his curfew she would have him thrown in jail.

The backdoor creaked as Chuck and Frank tiptoed into the house. The smell of whiskey followed them as they bumped into the kitchen table and snickered. Jean flicked on the light and stood with her arms folded across her chest. Seeing her scowl, Frank started to laugh.

"Harold!" Jean yelled, her face turning crimson. "Call the cops! Tell them to arrest Chuck *and* Frank!"

Chuck pushed Frank out of the way and strode over to his mother. "Why don't you just shut up?" he challenged, giving her a shove.

"Yeah," Frank shouted. "For once in your life, shut-up!"

Jean grabbed a dishrag and fired it at Frank's face. It wrapped around his cheek and snapped at his eye to deliver a stinging blow. Crying out in rage and pain, he lunged for his mother, knocking her to the ground. Jean could feel his weight on her chest as he wrapped his hands around her throat and started to squeeze. This was the moment Frank had been waiting for—the one he had imagined all these years. He squeezed harder, murderously. He had envisioned doing this countless times before, and the more Jean struggled the more unrelenting became the vice-grip on her throat. "*I hate you!*" he screamed. "*I hate you! I hate you! I hate you!*"

A sharp blow to his back knocked Frank to the floor. Chuck had come up from behind and hit him with his knee. Frank gazed up at his brother, bewildered, while Jean crawled away, gasping for air. Harold stood stock still in the doorway, frozen in disbelief.

Chuck pulled Frank to his feet. "Let's get outta here," he scoffed. "She ain't worth killin'."

The brothers hurried out the door as Harold dropped into a chair. Jean, sick to her stomach, dragged herself to the kitchen sink, leaned over the edge and began to retch.

Harold hung his head and sighed. "When will it end?" A defeated man, he addressed his incredulous words to no one in particular. "When will this nightmare ever end?"

CHAPTER 9

Nowhere to Run

Spring, 1965

"Welcome to Gibault School for Boys."

Big Willy's voice was as deep as a well. At 6 feet 4 inches tall, he towered over the boys now gathered in the hall. He was in every way a giant of a man, with flashing black eyes and powerful arms that he kept folded across his chest. He looked over the group with a frown. The top of Big Willy's head was smooth and shiny, and his brown skin glistened with tiny beads of perspiration. "I'm Brother William, the prefect of discipline." Big Willy paced a few steps and then paused in front of Frank. "I have only one piece of advice for you boys: don't mess with me, and I won't mess with you."

Big Willy wore the coarse brown robe of the Brothers of the Holy Cross. A braided leather belt tied at his waist doubled as a switch if he happened to need it. Frank knew it was no coincidence that he had been assigned to this colossus.

Big Willy led the group down a narrow corridor, assigning each boy to a room as they went. They were instructed to unpack their bags and reconvene at the swimming pool in five minutes. Frank stepped into his room. *Not much better than a jail cell,* he observed, and tossed his bag onto the floor. Besides the bunk beds there were a dresser, a wooden desk, and a chair. A small grated window was propped open with a stick; through it wafted the excited voices of boys playing ball in the yard. He plopped momentarily onto the lower bunk, stretched his legs, and clasped his hands behind his head. *Could be worse, though,* he assessed. *At least I'm not living in that house anymore.*

Frank recalled his father's last words as he was being arrested. "Lock him up," Harold had said, "and throw away the key. Any kid that tries to kill his mother deserves to stay in jail."

He had to admit that he'd lost control. But Jean had pushed him too far. While most kids don't try to kill their mother, Frank reasoned that Jean had never been much of a mother to him. All they had ever done was argue and fight. Frank stared at the ceiling and tried to remember his real mother's face. *I wonder what happened to her. She never did come back. Does she even care about me?*

Frank headed for the swimming pool, where Big Willy was about to bark his instructions. The Brothers of the Holy Cross believed in hard work, he told them, and the jobs they assigned would keep the place running. When the boys weren't studying in class, they'd be working in the field: plowing, planting, and harvesting. There were farm animals to care for as well. And hay to gather. There wouldn't be a whole lot of free time.

Gibault School for Boys, named after Fr. Pierre Gibault, "the patriot priest of the American Revolution," was a 360-acre farm in Terra Haute, Indiana. This reform school was unique in that the brothers combined hard labor and discipline with religious instruction. Their goal was to instill submission and obedience into wayward boys.

Frank had been sentenced to a year at Gibault—the court's final attempt to rehabilitate him. The judge hoped the monks might succeed where the youth home had failed. Gibault was a last-ditch effort to save young men about to be swept up into the penal system. It was usually reserved for the toughest cases—the notorious killer Charles Manson had been there in 1947. Frank was another tough case. The court had concluded that if Frank's life couldn't be turned around at Gibault it was just a matter of time before he would become a ward of the state.

"This'll be your first job here." Brother Willy pointed to the empty pool. Deep cracks spread along the walls like spiders' webs. The bottom of the pool was littered with mud, leaves, wrappers, and broken bottles. It hadn't been used in years and functioned now as little more than an oversized garbage dump.

"We want this pool to sparkle again, boys," Big Willy informed them—flashing his teeth in the first smile they had seen. "So it's all up to you." He handed each boy a bucket and pointed to the ladder leading down into the filth. "You can start by hauling up all the garbage and dumping it into these bins."

No one dared question Big Willy, but Frank was fuming as he lowered himself into the pool. The stench made his stomach turn. He scooped a handful of thick slime with his hands and tossed it into the bucket. After tossing in another he stood up. "Hey!" he challenged, "I ain't doing any more of this BS, man."

Big Willy stepped over to the edge of the pool. "C'mere," he beckoned to Frank. Frank climbed up the ladder and strolled over to the monk. Big Willy once again folded his arms across his chest. "Did I just hear you say a foul word?"

"Yeah," Frank replied. He glanced back at the other boys and grinned. "What of it?"

"Follow me."

He seems calm enough, Frank thought as he trailed Big Willy across the yard. They entered a small maintenance building filled with mops, buckets, and other cleaning supplies. Big Willy closed the door, reached to the top of a shelf, and pulled down a bar of Philip Lye soap. Frank swallowed as he watched the monk unwrap the bar and drop the wrapper to the floor.

Big Willy grabbed Frank by the head and locked him firmly underneath his arm. Next he shoved the bar deep into his mouth. Frank coughed, gagged, and struggled, but Big Willy persisted. "You're gonna eat this whole thing, Majewski," he announced. "You might as well start chewing right now. You're not getting out of here till it's all gone."

Frank squirmed and kicked as hard as he could, but nothing could release him from Big Willy's grasp. He chewed the soap in his mouth, his stomach heaving with each thrust of the bar. When he was finished Frank stumbled out the door and vomited. Big Willy dragged him by his shirt collar to the pool and ordered him to kneel in the sludge for the rest of the day. The other boys climbed out and headed for lunch with empathetic glances back at Frank. It was dark by the time he was allowed to drop into his bed. Punching his pillow several times, he turned his face to the wall. His back ached, his knees burned, and the bitter taste of Lye soap hung in his mouth. It was Frank's first day at Gibault, and already he wanted to bolt.

"I think you just broke the record for the most whacks at Gibault," Gorgo acknowledged with a chuckle. Frank's new friend, John Gordon—Gorgo—was also from Detroit.

He was right about Frank's breaking the record. In three short months he had received more wallops than anyone else in the history of the school. And Big Willy aimed his thwacks carefully, striking the upper thigh in order to inflict maximum pain. Frank always held his breath, refusing to give Big Willy the satisfaction of hearing him cry out.

"I don't know anybody who's been whupped by Big Willy more than you, Frank," Gorgo repeated, a touch of admiration in his tone.

"Yeah, well, that s.o.b. has whacked me for the last time. And he's gonna have some explaining to do after you and me bust out of here," Frank declared.

Gorgo was as tough as Frank. In Detroit he had run with a street gang known as the Toledo and Junction Boys in an area Frank knew well. When he first heard that a fellow Detroiter had found his way to Gibault, Frank looked him up. As soon as they met the boys began to plan their escape.

"Tomorrow's the day," Gorgo announced. "My mom said she'll pick us up near the cornfield. If everything goes according to plan we should be home by Thursday night."

Frank scoffed. "We can't just get up and walk out the door, man. What we gonna say: 'See ya, Big Willy . . . it's been real, but we're takin' off!'?"

Gorgo laughed before lowering his voice. "Look, nobody's gonna pay any attention to us if we leave right after dinner. Just meet me behind the chicken coop, and we'll run to the cornfield. Once we get in there we'll cut over to the main road where my mom'll be waiting for us."

Frank ran his hand through his thick hair. "I wonder what the punishment is for breaking outta jail," he reflected aloud.

"You turnin' yellow, Majewski?"

"No man, I'm in." Frank gave Gorgo the secret handshake. "You're sure your mom will come through, though, right? I mean, she could get in a lot of trouble for this."

"She don't care. My mom wants me outta here. She'll do whatever it takes. Just meet me by the coop."

Frank couldn't pass this up. Gorgo's plan sounded foolproof as long as his mom did her part. He hoped Gorgo could get them through the maze, because Frank had no sense of direction. He rehearsed the plan in his mind as he drifted off to sleep that night. *If this works*, he thought, *I should be back home in two days.* He felt sure the police would give up their search after a week or so. Then he would figure out what to do next. If he couldn't stay with Gorgo he'd try to find Chuck and move in with him.

The next evening, right after dinner, the boys met behind the chicken coop as planned. It was dusk—dark enough to hide their movements but not too dark to find their way. Frank could hardly keep up as Gorgo made a dash for the cornfield. The two jumped over logs and ducked under low tree branches before plunging into the maze. The full moon lit the trail, but still Frank struggled to keep up. If he lost sight of his friend he might never find his way out. He knocked over cornstalks and listened for Gorgo's movements. Finally both boys emerged from the field on the other side. Frank held on to his side and heaved short, shallow breaths, while Gorgo stood at the edge of the highway and gazed down the road in both directions. There was no sign of his mother.

"Maybe she got lost," Frank suggested.

"She'll be here," Gorgo reassured him, squatting along the side of the road.

Frank was getting nervous. Surrounded by hundreds of acres of farmland, he couldn't find his way back to Gibault even if he wanted to. If their plan failed there would be hell to pay at the hands of Big Willy. Frank continued to watch the highway, straining for any sound in the distance. Gorgo at last stood up and pushed him back into the field.

"What's going on?" Frank whispered.

"She's coming," Gorgo hissed. "But it might be the cops. We need to be sure." Frank held his breath and listened as a car slowed down and then flashed its headlights twice—off/on, off/on. Gorgo waved his hand in the air and pulled Frank up by his arm. "It's her. C'mon. Get ready to jump in."

The sedan idled as the boys hopped into the back seat and dropped onto the floor. Gorgo's mother pulled a blanket up over their heads and sped away. "Sit tight boys," she instructed. "We'll be past the Indiana border in a few hours."

Frank laughed hoarsely as he and Gorgo huddled beneath the blanket. Their plan had worked beautifully. By the time anyone discovered them missing they would be well on their way to Detroit.

It was 2:00 a.m. when they finally arrived at Gorgo's home. Mrs.

Gordon directed Frank to crash on the couch, while she headed upstairs to her bedroom. Gorgo made for his own room in the basement, only to slip out the backdoor first thing in the morning. Frank, figuring Gorgo must have wanted to lie low somewhere with the gang, wondered why he hadn't been invited to do the same. The Gordon house would be the first place the cops would look.

Two days later a loud knock at the door propelled Frank into the kitchen, where he hid inside the pantry. He could hear Mrs. Gordon letting two officers into the house. Their muffled voices made his heart pound. Suddenly the pantry door flew open, and a policeman grabbed Frank by the neck. Within seconds he was in handcuffs and being escorted out the door. Mrs. Gordon was nowhere to be found.

Frank could hardly believe what had happened. *She must have finked on me,* he fumed. *Probably didn't like me eating all her food.* He was mad at Gorgo for taking off and disgusted with himself for trusting him. Frank stared glumly out the window; heading for the police station, he vowed never to trust anyone again.

⊂⊖⊃

Mr. Papajohn strummed his fingers on the table several times and then made some notations in Frank's file. "So, tell me what happened, Frank." He leaned back in his chair and studied the boy's face.

Frank didn't know what to say. Mr. Papajohn was a good probation officer, and he hated to disappoint him. "I don't know, Mr. Papajohn. I just screwed up."

"I'll be driving you back to Gibault tomorrow," he conceded as he closed Frank's file. "You just added five months to your jail sentence. I wouldn't expect anyone to be too happy to see you."

The next day Big Willy met Frank at the door. After shaving Frank's head he thwacked him with a 2 x 4. According to Big Willy a paddle wasn't good enough for a jailbird. This time Frank didn't care if the whole place heard him screaming. He was sentenced to 30 days hard labor and locked in his room each night.

Frank felt cornered. Like a rabid dog he attacked anyone who got in his way; the more he fought the wilder he became. He punched, kicked, and threw buckets at people. In fights he attempted to gouge out his opponents' eyes. Even Big Willy had difficulty restraining him. He doubled

Frank's workload, confining him to his room on the rare occasions he wasn't working.

One afternoon Big Willy led Frank out to a hill near the edge of Gibault's property. There stood dozens of tree stumps needing to be pulled. He handed Frank a shovel. "Maybe after you're done clearing these stumps, Majewski, you'll be fit to live among human beings again."

Frank watched Big Willy as he turned and walked away, continuing to gaze across acres of rolling hills and then eying the narrow path leading back to Gibault. *No point in running away,* he told himself. *There's nowhere to go.* He plunged the shovel into the ground near the first stump and gave it a shove with his heel. After burying the blade deep in the dirt, he paused to unbutton his shirt. A full hour later the stump finally yielded and fell on its side. Frank wiped his brow and climbed down into the large hole left when it fell. The moist earth cooled his hot skin, and he squatted and folded his arms across his knees. The position reminded him of his hideaway under the basement steps at Little Flower. Frank stretched his legs up over the top of the hole and leaned back to enjoy the solitude.

For the next month Frank continued to pull out stumps . . . to his surprise finding the labor more rewarding than he would ever dream of admitting. Each time a thick root surrendered to his shovel he felt like a mighty warrior engaged in battle. Afterward he'd slip into the cool refuge of the hole and lean back his head to study the clouds. One day as he rested he began to contemplate the future. He didn't want to spend the rest of his life in prison. Frank climbed out of the hole and perched on a stump, wiping his brow and gazing, deep in thought, across the field. *Maybe I should try to be good for a while,* he mused. *Then maybe they'll shorten my sentence and let me go home.* Shielding his eyes from the relentless sun, he glanced toward Gibault. It was almost lunchtime. Kicking the shovel aside he began his trek down the path toward the mess hall.

Within a few short months of that defining moment Frank had not only earned the highest grade-point average in the school but had become the starting fullback on the football team. Everyone watched in amazement, wondering whether the turnaround would last. Big Willy in particular had his doubts. It's only a matter of time, he warned his superiors, before something ticks Frank off and he's back to his old ways. "Now that the hill is cleared," he informed Frank one afternoon, "I'm going to start you on the farm."

Gibault's farm supplied the school with all the vegetables it needed. In addition, the cows, chickens, and pigs raised there made the establishment to a large degree self-sufficient. The kitchen depended on daily deliveries of fresh eggs and poultry, so Frank filled an important role when he was assigned to the chicken coop.

But the dirty, cackling poultry got on his nerves. He hated every one of them. The only pleasure Frank found was in kicking the birds as he forged his way across the yard. Whenever an order arrived from the kitchen for fresh poultry, Frank would handpick the specimens that had irritated him the most. Holding a mock trial for each of the condemned, he would sentence them to death.

"You!" he would call out to his first victim, a brown speckled chicken with a shrill cackle. The bird would flap its wings and, seemingly aware of its fate, scurry across the coop as though to escape. Frank would grab it by the throat and hold it high, like a trophy. "You squawk too much," he would pronounce. "I sentence you to *die!*" Thwack! The blade would fall sharply across the poor bird's neck.

The mock trials went on for weeks, until the chickens would scatter in raucous terror whenever Frank approached. In time the trembling hens began to lay fewer and fewer eggs. When complaints arrived from the kitchen, Big Willy headed down to the coop to investigate. "We usually get hundreds of eggs from these chickens," he observed, looking around. "Now we can't get ten. I want to know why."

"I dunno," Frank shrugged.

Big Willy stepped inside the pen, and the skittish birds squawked, flapping their wings and scattering. "What did you do to these birds, Majewski? You've been abusing them, haven't you? Chickens don't scatter like that, not if you treat them the right way."

Frank didn't answer. He had endured enough beatings from Big Willy to know what would come next. Several hard whacks from the paddle, and he was back to pulling stumps. Frank didn't care; he much preferred the field work anyway.

For the next few months he tried to stay out of Big Willy's way, continuing to play football and keep up his grades. By the summer of '66 Frank was finally released from Gibault to take the first bus home.

CHAPTER 10

A Real Thug

Summer, 1966

"I don't like the way this neighborhood's changing." Harold set down his coffee cup and pushed his chair back from the table.

Frank glanced up from his bowl of Cheerios, his spoon suspended in the air, and Jean wiped her hands on a dishtowel.

Harold continued, "We're going to find a house in the suburbs."

"I'm not going," Frank announced with finality, wiping his mouth on his sleeve. "All my friends are here."

"You don't have anything to say about it, Frank." Harold could be as stubborn as his son. "Your friends are no good anyhow. We're selling the house and moving to a better neighborhood."

"What about Chuck?"

"Who cares about Chuck?" his mother put in. "He's worse than your friends. We're sorry we ever adopted either of you, aren't we, Harold?"

"Don't start, Jean," Harold cautioned.

"He should know the truth."

Frank got up to leave. He wasn't in the mood for a fight, not first thing in the morning. And he had just gotten home from Gibault.

Despite his protests Frank wasn't totally averse to leaving Detroit. Several of his friends had already moved to the suburbs, and Frank figured he wouldn't be living with his parents much longer anyway. Once he got his driver's license he could come and go as he pleased.

Frank's parents found a house in the city of Warren—a small brick ranch with a two-car garage and fenced-in yard. Every house on the street looked exactly the same: cookie cutter homes with fake shutters and small porches, . . . right down to the nearly identical six-foot maple saplings planted in each front yard next to freshly poured sidewalks.

After they had moved in Frank would slip out at night to walk the streets. He missed the grittiness of Detroit and was disappointed to find no back alleys, no downtown, and only a handful of party stores. He strolled along 12 Mile Road, where there seemed to be no end to the rows of houses looking tediously like his own. Occasionally he would walk past a lonely strip mall, sterile and uninviting.

Harold and Jean were happy in their new home, however, and proud of the parish they had joined. Saint Sylvester Catholic Church was a few short blocks from home, and walking to mass each Sunday morning would be a treat. A public school was within walking distance as well, and they immediately enrolled Frank at Hartsig Junior High, hoping he would adjust to his new surroundings and maybe even make a few new friends.

But when the neighbors learned about Frank's past—his arrests and jail time—they kept their distance. No one wanted anything to do with a juvenile delinquent. Frank found himself wandering the neighborhood alone, eager for companionship. By the time school began he already felt like an outcast.

Nor was Hartsig Junior High prepared for Frank's arrival on the first day of school. Heads turned as the new kid swaggered into the building alongside his probation officer, Mr. Papajohn. Frank's hair was slicked back, and he wore peg-leg jeans and pointy leather boots that clicked on the tile as he strutted down the hall, shooting fiery glances at curious onlookers. Mr. Papajohn held open the door to the principal's office to let Frank inside. Students in the hallway glanced at each other with knowing looks.

Mike Cassady, a slim, brown-haired eighth-grader, watched from his locker as Frank passed by. No one needed to warn him to keep his distance; one glance marked Frank as a thug. Grabbing his history book and slamming his locker door, Mike turned to his buddy, Chuck Cardamone, commenting, "Man, *that* is one mean-looking dude."

Chuck turned around to watch Frank as he entered the principal's office. "Looks like an angry bear," he agreed, "growling at the world."

After that first day of school Frank walked home, pausing to look at a motorcycle for sale. It was a 1958 Harley Davidson, orange, with a metal flake finish and a 15-degree extension on the front. Frank walked a circle around the bike and whistled. "Man," he said to himself, "that is one bad-looking chopper."

Frank wanted that Harley, and all he had to do was raise $100. He lacked a driver's license, but Frank had already owned two cars by his 15th birthday. One, a '57 Chevy, was a sharp-looking number that had never even started. He'd finally had it towed away. The second was a '56 Ford, a stick shift he'd kept parked in front of a friend's house. While Frank was doing time at Gibault the Ford had disappeared.

Now he had his eye on a chopper.

Frank picked up odd jobs around the neighborhood, cutting grass and raking leaves. In a few weeks' time he'd saved enough money to buy the bike, a leather jacket, and a pair of sunglasses. He climbed onto the Harley, revved the engine, and opened up the throttle. Frank nodded to other bikers as he whizzed past them on his way to Detroit.

School had never been a priority for Frank. And now that he owned a bike he skipped class nearly every day. His parents didn't check up on him, and the teachers never asked questions. At home or at school Frank came and went as he pleased. One day, however, Mr. Papajohn received a note from the principal: Frank had violated parole. The next day he stood before a judge. Despite Mr. Papajohn's request for leniency, Frank was sentenced to 30 days at the Macomb County Youth Home.

Frank had heard about this youth home from some of his friends. It was a cramped, outdated building with a cafeteria that served lousy food. There was one bathroom for every 13 inmates, and the staff was under-trained and overworked. There were rumors of physical abuse as well.

The home was tucked away directly behind the county sheriff's office and surrounded by a heavy steel fence with barbed wire rolled along the top to discourage thoughts of escape. Frank had heard that the kids at Macomb weren't nearly as tough as the Wayne County crowd, but the guards were another matter. Two in particular, Mr. Thatcher and Mr. Bott, seemed to enjoy harassing the kids—especially hotheads like Frank. Beatings by Thatcher and Bott ensured that none of the inmates ever wanted to return.

Daytimes were spent in a large multi-purpose room, allowing the guards to keep a close eye on the boys' activities. No one could leave the

room without permission. On his first day Frank glanced around the cafeteria to size up his surroundings. Thatcher, a tall, black, muscular man
with penetrating eyes and a smooth round head, had planted himself
before the only exit with his arms folded across his chest. Reminiscent
of Big Willy, Thatcher looked like someone Frank would want to avoid.
Bott appeared a little friendlier. From time to time he would even crack
a smile, showing off a row of straight white teeth. But Frank knew better
than to think the man was good-natured. A smile from a guard usually
meant trouble.

After several days life at the youth home settled into a routine, and
Frank began to wonder how he could get his hands on a cigarette. Smoking was banned, making tobacco a prized commodity. Through the black
market inmates were able to buy and sell cigarettes with ease; the tricky
part was not getting caught. And since there were never enough matches
to go around, the boys had devised a plan. Every match could be broken in half lengthwise, making one into two. Almost everyone walked
around with half a matchstick in his pocket.

One day Bott observed Frank slipping something into his pants
pocket. "Majewski," he barked, "come over here."

Frank followed Bott out the door, down the hall, and into a small
room.

"Let me see the match," the man ordered, holding out his hand.

Frank reached into his pocket.

"Where'd you get it?"

Frank kept his mouth shut. Nobody snitches in jail.

"Okay," Bott conceded, as though reluctantly. "Fifty push-ups right
here."

Frank lowered himself to the ground, did thirty, and then rested. But
Bott grabbed him by the back of the pants and raised him up. "Who told
you to stop, Majewski? You got twenty more to go."

Frank did another ten and paused. This time Bott reached underneath him, grabbed the front of his pants and lifted him high into the air.
Hurling Frank against the wall, the man watched in silent glee as Frank
fell to the ground. The boy curled into a ball, his crotch on fire and his
head pounding from the blow.

Thatcher heard the commotion and opened the door a crack. "Everything okay in here?" he asked.

"Toss him in the hole," Bott muttered as he stepped out of the room.

Frank didn't like the sound of that. Thatcher pulled him to his feet and led him across the hall to another room. It was empty—no bed, pillow, or blanket. One small window high above Frank's head admitted the only sunlight he would see for days. A light bulb dangled from a wire in the middle of the ceiling. Brick walls and a cement floor made the room colder than a freezer.

Thatcher ordered Frank to strip down to his underwear and then walked out with his clothes. Frank was in solitary confinement. A key turned in the lock as he wrapped his arms around his bare chest and shivered. A thin stream of air blew into the room from a register so Frank huddled close to warm his hands. He hated being cold, but even worse was being alone. The bare bulb glared for 24-hours, its garish light, visible even through his eyelids, keeping Frank awake for most of the night.

For three days he hunched near the register. The guards delivered trays of food and escorted him twice a day to the bathroom. Some afternoons Frank could hear the shouts and laughter of boys outside the window. He covered his ears to block the sound and wondered whether anyone cared that he was in the hole. Frank had lost the ability to cry a long time ago; all he could do now was stare up at the blinding light and wait.

Following the incident the guards effectively shut down the black market for tobacco. By the time Frank emerged from isolation it was impossible to find a cigarette. He had heard that smoking was allowed at the county jail; it was said, in fact, that a kid could get as many cigarettes as he wanted if he was lucky enough to be transferred. But "arranging" a transfer wouldn't be easy. This recourse was reserved for the worst offenders. Frank figured out how to qualify.

Thatcher, expecting another slipup from Frank at any moment, watched him closely in the mess hall. One afternoon Frank stood up and headed for the door. Arms folded, Thatcher stepped in front of him. "Hold it right there, Majewski," he ordered.

"Get outta my way you big, fat n-----!" Frank challenged.

Thatcher grabbed Frank's wrist, twisted his arm up behind his back, and shoved him through the door.

"Need any help, Thatch?" Bott called out, sounding hopeful.

"Nope, I got this one."

Thatcher tossed Frank into his room and left, locking the door behind him. This wasn't what Frank had expected. He was looking for a transfer, not confinement to his cell. He screamed and hurled himself against the window, after which he scratched and clawed at the screen with his bare hands. For two hours Frank shouted at the top of his lungs while continuing to tear at the screen. By the time his cries had been reduced to whimpers and his hands were covered in blood, Thatcher re-appeared outside the door. He waited for Frank to quiet down, and then cracked open the door far enough to glance inside. Frank was on the floor, slumped into a corner with his eyes closed and his shirt splattered with blood. Before arranging a transfer to the county jail, Thatcher brought in a roll of gauze to bandage Frank's hands.

Upon arrival at the jail, however, Frank was placed in isolation for 30 days . . . on the women's floor: no cigarettes and no special privileges. The guard who delivered his food was his only contact. By the time Frank returned to the youth home his hands had healed, but his heart had been torn in two.

CHAPTER 11

The Devil Inside

After Frank was released from the youth home he met a tall, wiry 20-year-old who had escaped from the state penitentiary. Doyle was serving time for safe cracking when he managed to break out of prison and hitchhike to Detroit. He and Frank were a good match. Doyle was classy, confident in his ability to dress, dance, and handle the ladies, while Frank was a risk-taker, tough and daring—precisely the qualities Doyle looked for in a sidekick. Doyle also knew how to fight and come into money the easy way. Frank, never one for school and homework, was game for an adventure, and Doyle had some big ideas.

One night the pair drove to Detroit to stay at Doyle's apartment on 2nd Avenue. Adjacent to the building was a smoke-filled pool hall, Doyle's favorite hangout and an ideal place for picking up drugs, booze, and female companionship. Doyle pulled out a marijuana joint and lit it with a match. Frank, who had never before smoked pot, decided to give it a try. He leaned back in his chair, relaxed, as Doyle stepped across the room, returning with a woman on either arm. He introduced the two to Frank and offered him first pick. Frank laughed nervously, a strange warmth beginning to travel up his neck and into his face. He had thought he was ready for anything Doyle could dish out, but this caught him off guard. Frank cleared his throat, however, stood up, and followed one of the women to a back room. The door closed behind them as she smiled alluringly, edged up to Frank, and slipped her arms around his neck.

The next morning Frank and Doyle drove down to Cincinnati, Ohio. Doyle wanted to visit some old friends—a Mexican family by the name of Gonzalez. Frank smiled when a beautiful, dark-haired girl named Gladys answered the door. The Gonzalezes offered to put up Doyle and Frank for a couple of weeks, and Gladys even found them a job at Big Sixties, a hamburger joint down the street. Frank, who had never before held a job, relied on Doyle to show him the ropes. By the second day he was flipping hamburgers on the grill like a pro.

One evening several members of a gang—greasers dressed in black leather jackets and tight blue jeans—wandered into the restaurant. Their hair was slicked back, and they smelled like pot. Doyle was working behind the counter while Frank wiped down the tables with a rag.

"Hey dude," one of the greasers directed his taunt at Doyle, "where'd you get that funny little hat? I want one too." His buddies, obviously high, guffawed with him, and Frank glanced over at Doyle. He knew Doyle could handle the situation and watched as his buddy tore off his hat and leaped over the counter. With lightning speed Doyle began to shadow box with a phone booth. The greasers, mesmerized by his moves, stepped backward as one. Doyle was fast on his feet, and his jabs radiated a message that was loud and clear: don't mess with me! The greasers took slow steps toward the door. "We'll be right back, man, okay?" the leader called out as they retreated.

Doyle ran his fingers through his hair before putting his hat back on, after which he jumped back over the counter and returned to work. Frank broke the tension with an appreciative laugh. "Did you see their faces, Doyle? You freaked them out with them crazy moves!"

Doyle didn't say a word—just continued methodically cleaning the counter. Moments later, though, the gang returned with two cases of beer and half a dozen girls. "Let's party, man!" they shouted as they set the beer on the counter.

Doyle tore off his apron, strode over to lock the front door, and turned the "Closed" sign to face the window. Frank, caught off guard, recovered immediately; taking Doyle's cue he turned up the jukebox, and everyone started to eat, drink, and dance. For the next few hours Doyle dominated the dance floor, dazzling the girls with his fancy moves. One of the greasers threw a beer bottle across the room, shattering the mirror, and everyone paused to take in Doyle's reaction. Reaching for a jar of mustard, he proceeded to fling it at the mirror as well. Suddenly ketchup, relish, and French fries were sailing through the air as the party dissolved into a food fight. Frank tossed hotdogs and hamburger buns, while Doyle squirted mustard across the floor and then slid purposely in the slimy mess. Hoots of laughter filled the room as Big Sixties was transformed into a war zone. By midnight everyone had had enough, and the greasers took their leave. Doyle and Frank emptied out the cash register, turned off the lights, and locked the door behind them.

"We'd better get out of town now, man," Frank announced as they trudged back toward the house.

"We gotta hit the school first," Doyle reminded him. "It's now or never."

Doyle had planned a break-in at Oakley Elementary, a small public school just down the street. It was a quick way to fill their pockets with cash. Now that Doyle and Frank had to leave town, they decided to move forward with their plans.

An hour later the trio, which included Gladys, had posted themselves outside the darkened school building. Frank climbed in through a window, landing feet first in a classroom, while Gladys hid in the trees holding a walkie-talkie. Doyle waited nearby, listening and waiting for a signal from Frank. The plan was for Frank to locate the safe and notify Gladys. Once Gladys received the go-ahead Doyle was to enter the school.

Frank paused inside the blackened classroom to get his bearings. Probing with his fingers he came upon what felt like a statue. Surrendering to an insane impulse, Frank lifted the bust and threw it to the ground.

"Frank," Gladys hissed through the walkie-talkie. "What just happened?"

Frank didn't answer. Instead he kicked over a desk and flung a shelf-full of books to the floor. His frantic thoughts latched on to everything he'd always hated about school: teachers, principals, homework. He threw a chair at a window and shattered it. When his groping hands discovered a sledgehammer in a maintenance closet, he began to smash display cases and overhead lights. Leveling the hammer at a teacher's desk, he cracked it in half. Moving like an automaton, he smashed desks, broke more windows, and tore books in half. After the first room Frank moved on to the next. A strange thrill coursed through his body. He couldn't have stopped if he'd wanted to.

"Frank," Gladys called again. "What's going on in there? Where are you?"

"D--- you!" Frank shouted into the walkie-talkie. "D--- all of you!"

Frank threw down the walkie-talkie and smashed it with his foot. He headed for the second floor, systematically ripping doors off lockers and lifting desks in the air to hurl them against walls. He ran through the building, unleashing years of pent-up fury.

"I'm going in!" Doyle announced grimly, easing himself through the window. "Frank! Where *are* you?" The sound of crashing furniture reverberated from the third floor. Doyle took the stairs two at a time. Frank stood, transfixed, in the hallway, sledgehammer in hand. His eyes were glazed over, and his chest heaved.

"What're you *doing*, man?" Doyle gasped. "Are you *crazy*?"

Frank looked possessed, and Doyle took a step backward. "Take it easy, man," he intoned, backing toward the exit. "What's going on, Frank?"

Frank lowered the sledgehammer and let out a ragged breath. "I went on a nut, man," he uttered, shock registering on his own face.

Doyle looked around and shook his head. "We gotta get outta here. This place'll be crawling with cops." He turned on his heels and ran. Once he had made his way back the way he had come, Frank climbed out the first-floor window and started to run. There was no sign of Gladys or Doyle, so he took cover in a wooded area till morning. At daybreak he headed in the direction of downtown Cincinnati.

Frank walked the streets looking for a way to raise the bus fare for Detroit. Passing a blood bank, he stopped in to inquire about donating plasma for cash. But when he rolled up his sleeve and revealed his tattooed arm the nurse shook her head. Heading down an alley, Frank came upon a drunk passed out on the ground. He reached into the man's pocket to lift his wallet: no money, just a piece of I.D. Frank figured it might come in handy and slipped it into his pants pocket.

His aimless steps took him past a Catholic church. *Nuns are a pushover for homeless kids,* he thought, based on years of experience, and knocked at the convent door. "Sister," he pleaded when a nun appeared, "I'm here by myself and need to get back to my family in Detroit. Can you help me out with a bus ticket?"

Soon Frank was reclining in the rear seat of a Greyhound bus, heading home. He dozed for an hour, then sat bolt upright when the bus ground to a stop. The sign outside the window announced Dayton; they were still miles from Detroit. It was only then that Frank registered with a start what he hadn't realized at first: it was the cops. Flashing lights bounced off the ceiling of the bus, and he glanced out the window to see two police cars flanking the bus, one parked horizontally at the front and the other in back. *This can't be a good sign,* he realized with a sinking heart.

The door swung open, and two officers boarded the bus. Strolling down the aisle, they stopped to check each passenger's identification. Frank stared in studied nonchalance out the window.

"Roll up your shirt sleeve, kid." An officer hovered over him, watching, as Frank rolled up his sleeve. He pointed to one of the tattoos. "This one here says Frank. Is that your name?"

Frank reached into his pocket and pulled out the wallet. The officer studied his fake I.D. "Robert Miller. So that's your name?"

"Yeah."

"Then why do I see Frank tattooed all over your arm? Is that your boyfriend?"

Frank rolled his sleeve back down.

"Let's go, Majewski." The officer, abandoning the pretense, took him by the arm. "You're coming with us."

Frank wondered how they had found him and whether they knew about the school. When he arrived back at the Cincinnati police station he got his answer. Gladys was seated at a desk, dabbing her eyes with a handkerchief. She glanced over at Frank and then looked miserably away. Doyle was nowhere in sight.

For the most part Mr. Papajohn liked his job as a probation officer. But getting through to some of the kids was tough, a little like peeling an onion. Layers of pain and abuse could make it virtually impossible to reach their heart. Frank was like that. He had grown so bitter he shut everyone out, refusing overtures of help. As Mr. Papajohn made the drive to Cincinnati, he wondered how long it would take before Frank wound up in prison or dead on the street. When they met at the police station Frank looked beaten. The pair walked out to the car side by side.

Mr. Papajohn broke the silence while lighting a cigarette: "Sorry about the handcuffs. I'll take them off at the first stop. We'll try to get you off with some time at the youth home, Frank. But you gotta promise me nothing like this will happen again."

Frank promised, determined for the moment to turn over a new leaf. *Mr. Papajohn's a good guy,* he conceded. *I can't keep doing this to him.*

February, 1967

The school secretary glanced over the top of her glasses as the superintendent flipped through Frank's file, which was more than an inch thick. Frank had spent 90 days at the Macomb County Youth Home and was back home living with his parents. Harold and Jean wanted him enrolled in school, and the task of finding a placement had fallen to the superintendent, who was flipping through the pages of the file without looking up. "So, what's the last grade he completed?" he asked.

"Eighth. He spent most of ninth in the youth home. So technically he's a sophomore."

"Eighth grade." He closed the file and pulled off his glasses to emphasize the point he was about to make. "So he was at Hartsig for a few months, then wound up in jail again. And now they want him back in school." He rubbed his eyes and leaned back in his chair. "We can't place a juvenile delinquent with middle school kids now, can we?" Tossing the file on the desk he made his pronouncement: "Looks like Frank Majewski just got promoted to the tenth grade."

"That would be Cousino High," the secretary replied, reaching for the file. "I'll notify the school that he'll be starting Monday."

She walked to the door as the superintendent reached for a cigar. "Better let his parents know too," he called after her.

Everyone stared as Frank entered Cousino High School. Mike Cassady, a little taller now and more filled out, was surprised—and hardly pleased—to see him again. The last time their paths had crossed Frank was being handcuffed and escorted out of Hartsig Junior High. Now here he was again, walking into another school with a probation officer at his side. *Some things never change!*

"You can see it in his eyes," Mike told his friend Chuck the first time he ran into him in the hallway. "It's like he's got the devil inside."

Chuck too knew enough to stay out of Frank's way. But attending the same school once again meant that some contact would be unavoidable. One day, as he sat in the cafeteria eating lunch, Chuck leaned back his head to guzzle milk from his carton. A kid pushed by, bumping Chuck's elbow and sending chocolate milk streaming down the front of his shirt. Chuck was furious. His pants were soaking wet and his shirt ruined. The culprit, sniggering, joined his friends at another table.

Frank had watched the thing unfold. Rising from his seat, he walked over to the kid, and stood above him. The boy looked up with a nervous grin, and Mike nudged Chuck to observe what would happen. Frank lifted a carton of milk and pried it open with the fingers of one hand, after which he slowly and deliberately poured the contents over the boy's head. The room fell silent as a stream of chocolate milk rolled down the front of his shirt. Frank opened a second carton and emptied it over his head as well. No one challenged him when he reached for the third. The boy, horrified, sat frozen in his seat. Mike stared in disbelief.

Much as he hated school, Frank enjoyed his status at Cousino. When he walked into the building everyone stepped aside. No one dared to cross him, evidently not even the principal. He even acquired a few friends to back him up—Pete, Dino, and Mooch Bob.

One afternoon Mike was standing at his locker as a red-faced student came running down the hallway in a panic, with Frank in hot pursuit. Mike knew something must have set him off and felt sorry for his victim. Within seconds Frank was on the kid, grabbing him by his shirt and hurling him against a locker. Next he began punching him in the stomach. The boy dropped to the ground in a heap, and Frank proceeded to kick him. Several teachers rushed to the scene, followed shortly thereafter by the police. Frank was handcuffed and led from the building, leaving his victim to limp with assistance to the school office.

Chuck made his way over to Mike. "That guy is totally out of control," he stated. "They oughta lock him up and throw away the key."

Thirty days later Frank was released from the youth home and back once again at Cousino. The following year saw a series of suspensions, arrests, and jail time. The principal, knowing Frank would never graduate, believed it would be only a matter of time before he wound up in prison for the rest of his life.

CHAPTER 12

Nothing but Scum

Frank was headed, slightly late, for his first hour speech class. Mrs. Harlow had just asked everyone to find their seats and take out last night's homework assignment. Stepping momentarily from the room, she passed Frank in the hall. Frank nodded and proceeded into the classroom, kicking the leg of a boy in his accustomed seat. "You're in my chair, man," he complained.

"It's mine now." The boy didn't move, and the class fell silent, every eye on Frank.

He reached down, lifted the boy by his shirt, and threw him to the floor. "No, it ain't your chair. It's *mine*." Kicking his classmate out of the way, he sat down.

Mrs. Harlow, who had appeared again in the doorway, made her way down the aisle and stood over Frank with her hands on her hips. Frank glanced down at her shapely legs and looked up again with an appreciative smile. "How ya doin', Mrs. Harlow?"

"Frank," she began, trying to conceal a slight tremor in her voice. Then she paused. "No, on second thought, I'm not sending you to the principal's office. This time you're going to sit up in front right next to me." She pulled an empty desk next to her own and pointed to the chair.

"Whoa . . . !" The other kids laughed and whistled.

Frank, playing the game, strutted to the front of the room and sat down. "I think she likes me," he announced with a wink. Glancing pointedly at Mrs. Harlow's soft blond hair, he nodded his approval. Everyone tittered again. Mrs. Harlow rapped on the desk with a ruler to bring the class to order.

The next day Mrs. Harlow asked Frank to remain after class. "Look, Frank," she informed him. "I'm moving your seat back where it belongs tomorrow, but from now on you'll do as I say."

Frank smiled. "Whatever you say, Mrs. Harlow."

"Everyone is giving a speech next week," she continued, "and that goes for you too."

"I can't do that, Teach. I got nothing to say."

Mrs. Harlow thought for a moment. "Why don't you talk about life as a juvenile delinquent? That should be easy enough—you've got plenty of material."

Frank, laughing, said he would give it a try.

The following week Frank stood before the class with a prepared speech. He talked about the orphanage, the youth home, and life on the street, stressing that all of these were better than living at home with his parents. He also talked about his Harley, going to jail, and pulling out tree stumps at Gibault's. The class was mesmerized. Everyone clapped when Frank was finished, and Mrs. Harlow smiled.

March, 1967

Every morning before school Mooch Bob pulled his GTO in front of Frank's house and honked the horn. When the weekend arrived the boys cruised down Van Dyke Avenue, drinking beer and on the prowl for girls.

One Friday night Frank, Mooch, and another friend named Pete headed over to Cousino for a Battle of the Bands concert. Frank's brother, Chuck, had agreed to meet them there. Frank hadn't seen his brother for a while. Chuck had his own apartment now and worked for a construction company. But he still liked to party and missed hanging out with his little brother. The concert was underway as the three boys strolled into the school. Frank, Chuck, and Mooch Bob hung up their leather jackets before heading into the dance hall.

Mooch elbowed Frank and pointed across the room. "Hey," he pointed out, "there's that dorky kid from music class—the one that ratted on me. What a chump." Mooch spit on the floor and began walking toward the boy.

Frank followed, randomly shoving people aside as he crossed the room. He didn't want to miss this. Within seconds the unfortunate boy was on the floor with Mooch on top of him. As he punched the boy's face, a general fight broke out, and fists began to fly. Girls screamed and ran from the room, while teachers tried to break up the skirmishes. Frank indiscriminately punched everyone he saw, then climbed onstage and rushed at the bass player. The boy swung his guitar in the air, hitting Frank in the head. Frank stumbled across the stage and leaned against a set of drums. When his head cleared, he grabbed the drumsticks and began to beat the drummer on the head. Smashing the bass drum with his foot, he kicked it across the stage. The drummer fled.

Mr. Ellis, the swimming coach, grabbed Frank from behind and wrestled him to the ground, only to have a flailing Frank punch him in the stomach and break away. Chuck raced to the stage and grabbed a microphone by the cord. Swinging it high above his head like a lasso to increase its momentum, he let it fly. As the twirling projectile made its way across the room, anyone who didn't duck was whacked in the head. Meanwhile, Frank continued to beat people on the head with the drumsticks. First he'd thump one side and then the other, treating each head like a snare drum.

Someone jumped on top of Frank and knocked him to the ground, while someone else punched him in the nose. For a moment Frank saw stars, and his nose began to bleed. Mooch-Bob and Pete pulled off the attackers and helped Frank to his feet. "You *okay*, man?" Mooch asked.

"Who just did that?" Frank's head was still spinning as he glanced around the room.

Pete pointed. "It was Mr. Lichter, right over there. He hit you while you were down!"

Frank lunged at Mr. Lichter, knocking the man to the ground. The crowd gasped in horror as their teacher took multiple blows to the face. Mr. Ellis grabbed Frank by the shoulders and peeled him off. "You're the scum of the earth, Majewski!" he snarled, shaking his finger in Frank's face. "You're nothing but scum!"

Frank opened and closed his fists several times. Mr. Ellis, recognizing his own peril, turned and ran from the gym, rushing through the hall slamming doors behind him as he ran. Frank was at his heels, forcing his way through every door. Soon he was upon the teacher, punching him in the face. A policeman finally arrived with a nightstick in his hand. Placing it across Frank's throat, he dragged him backward down the hall. Outside, Frank was handcuffed and shoved gruffly into a patrol car while Mr. Ellis, bruised and ashen faced, stood watching. Several teachers gathered around him as the patrol car pulled away.

There were no more suspensions left for Frank. The principal, who'd had more than enough of his violent outbursts, expelled him and pressed criminal charges. Frank found himself back at the youth home again, sentenced to another 90 days. He never returned to school.

April, 1967

"You got company, Majewski."

"Who is it?" Frank asked sullenly. He had never had any visitors before and hoped it wasn't his parents.

The guard leaned against Frank's cell with a smirk. "It's your folks."

"Tell 'em I'm not here."

"You don't have a choice, Majewski. I'm here to take you down to the visitor's hall."

Frank had been in and out of the youth home so many times he felt more at home here than at his house. When he wasn't drinking, shoplifting, or fighting, he was behind bars. Harold and Jean had never before visited their son and were doing so now based on a judicial summons. They drove the 15 miles in silence before pulling into the parking lot of the Macomb County Jail.

Harold glanced at the barbed wire fence as he stepped from the car, wondering whether Frank was watching from the third floor as they entered the building. Harold wished he could make things right with his son but realized it was probably too late. The guard escorted them to the visitors' center and directed Harold and Jean to a set of chairs. After several moments a loud buzz was followed by the slam of a heavy door. Harold glanced up as Frank shambled into the room. He knew instantly that his son had changed for the worse. His face looked hard, and his eyes were cold. Harold reached out to shake his hand, but Frank ignored the gesture and heaved himself with an audible sigh into a chair.

"So, how are you doing, Frank?" Harold leaned forward in his seat.

"How do you think?"

"We brought something here to show you." Jean reached into a bag. "It's an award from Father Gibault's."

"*An award?*" Frank sat up, genuinely interested. "For what?"

"They had a big dinner down in Terra Haute," Jean explained. "They wanted to give you this." She held out a polished wooden plaque. "It's for football." She read the inscription aloud. "The Amateur Athletic Union Award – 1965."

"*Well, I'll be —,*" Frank murmured, taking the plaque in his hands.

"It's too bad you're still in jail," Jean continued, a taunting undertone in her voice, "and couldn't make the dinner. You could've gone down there and accepted this award. Everyone would've clapped, but instead you're stuck here in jail."

Frank had heard enough. Handing back the award, he signaled to the guard. Harold tugged on Jean's arm and stood up. "Let's go," he stated in an uncompromising tone.

"I wasn't done."

"I said *let's go!*"

Harold led Jean out the door, while the guard escorted Frank back to his cell. He dropped onto his bed and clasped his hands behind his head. "Athletic Union Award," he repeated aloud, talking to himself. "What do ya know about that?" He thought back to the days at Gibault, recalling Big Willy, the chickens, and pulling up the tree stumps. He was proud of the way he'd made it to captain of the football team. Seemed like many years ago now.

Frank reached under his mattress for a piece of coil that he had hidden there the night before. Every mattress was made of coil springs, and Frank's buddy Lynn had shown him how to twist and turn a spring until it broke in his hand. Lynn was a good friend—Frank knew him from junior high and had occasionally spent the night at Lynn's house in Warren. Now his friend had a plan: the two of them would break out of the youth home as soon as Frank could produce a key. A nice, straight piece of coil could open any cell window. For several nights in a row Frank had twisted the coil until it had finally snapped in his hand.

That afternoon at lunch Frank slipped into a seat next to Lynn. "Got it," he whispered.

"Where is it?"

"Under my mattress. When do you want it?"

"Tonight. Slip it to me after dinner. Then sneak down to my room just before lockdown."

"Okay. This should go smooth, right?" Lynn nodded, and Frank positioned himself in line for lunch.

That evening he handed off the key to Lynn as they passed in the hallway. Before lockdown Frank made his way to Lynn's room. The boys had already stripped down to their underwear for bed, and Frank shivered when a cold breeze blew in from Lynn's window. The window was wide open, but Lynn was nowhere to be seen. He had already opened the grate, broken through the glass, and climbed out.

Frank had to think fast. Running into the hallway, he called for the guard. "Mr. Thatcher," he shouted, "c'mere, c'mere, c'mere!" Thatcher hurried down the hall. "Lynn broke out, Mr. Thatcher—you better get some help."

Mr. Thatcher stepped inside, glanced around Lynn's cell, and hurried down the hall to call security. After he left Frank too climbed out the window, scraping his knee against a shard of glass. Blood ran down his leg, but that didn't slow him down. Dropping feet first to the ground, he made a beeline for the steel-wire fence. Jumping as high as he could, he grabbed hold of the wire and started to climb.

"Hey!" Thatcher's voice sounded from the window. "Get back here, Majewski! You're not going anywhere."

The fence cut into Frank's bare feet as he climbed, but he kept going. Lights flashed across the complex, and guards shouted as they rushed from the building, but still Frank continued to climb. His hands scraped against metal and his feet were starting to bleed, but when he reached the top he managed to flip up and over the barbed wire, snagging his boxers in the process on a barb. *"Aw, man!"* he groaned, tugging his pants free. Frank lost his grip, tumbled to the ground, rolled a somersault in the grass, and scrambled to his feet. Ignoring the pain, he made for a building in the distance. The place looked deserted, so Frank grabbed hold of a downspout and pulled himself up onto the roof. It was low and flat—an ideal spot for a lookout. Dropping onto his belly, he held his breath.

Weather can change suddenly in Michigan, and April is notorious for throwing in one final blast of serious ice before spring. So when a mixture of snow and rain began to fall on Frank, he groaned. An icy blanket formed over his back, and he shivered uncontrollably while he scanned the area. Frank knew it was crazy to run without clothes, but it was too late to change his mind now. The sleet cut across his skin like a knife. Resting his chin in his hands, he gritted his teeth against the chattering and waited.

It was then that he heard them—excited voices shouting in his direction. There were a dozen guards, maybe more, all wielding flashlights and running straight toward the building. Frank lowered his head, willing himself to lie flat against the shingles. He wondered whether it would occur to anyone to check the roof. The guards swarmed the building like flies, their voices muffled by the blowing wind. Frank held his hand over his mouth and closed his eyes. Thatcher's voice was the loudest. "Over here, men." he shouted. "I found some tracks!" The group turned to follow as he led them away from the building.

Frank waited a few moments before slowly raising his head. It seemed too much to hope for, but his pursuers were gone. Giddy with relief, he slapped his side and laughed as he watched the guards scurry across the field in the wrong direction. He waited some more, the freezing rain continuing to pelt his back. Frank's arms ached, and his joints felt stiff, but still he waited. Finally he sat up, rubbed his arms and legs, and lowered himself to the ground. Sneezing a few times, he headed in the direction of the city lights.

Across Groesbeck Highway was a mobile home park—a small, dimly lit collection of old trailers with rusty hitches. The park, situated in the shadows behind a convenience store, looked to Frank like a promising hideaway until things settled down. Glancing once over his shoulder before sprinting across Groesbeck, he dodged several cars and hurried into the park. His bare feet scraped along the gravel as he searched for a pair of pants or a shirt hung out to dry. But no one hung laundry on a wet April night.

Frank paused in front of a small trailer and tried the doorknob, which turned in his hand. "That's more like it!" he whispered audibly before stepping inside.

The smell of stale cigar smoke hung in the air as Frank groped in the darkness in search of a light. He bumped into a table and cursed, then felt along the wall with his hand while calling out "Anybody here?" He didn't expect an answer and reached inside a dresser drawer for some clothes.

Footsteps crunched along the gravel path. Frank slipped into a seat and held his breath. The door swung open, followed by a blinding flash of light. Frank covered his eyes with one hand and waved the other in the air. "Wait a minute," he called out. "Hold on. I know what you're thinking."

No one answered, so he opened his eyes. A man stood in the doorway, one hand poised on the switch. With his other he rubbed a stubbly beard before brushing back a mop of hair from his eyes. He lowered himself into another chair and let out a deep breath, filling the room with the smell of whiskey.

CHAPTER 13

The Boy in the Sharkskin Suit

"**L**ook, I'm gonna explain what just happened, all right?" Frank knew he had to talk fast to stall for time. "It's Good Friday, man. Easter weekend, right?"

The man glanced at the door. "Did you just bust into my trailer?"

"No, man," Frank countered. "I didn't bust into anything. The door wasn't locked. I just walked in, okay? I'm tellin' the truth. Now I'm gonna explain everything to ya. I just busted out of the youth home tonight, all right? All I'm trying to do is get home for Easter. They wouldn't let me go home for Easter, man! I wanna see my family." Frank rubbed his hands together and shivered. It felt colder inside the trailer than out.

"Okay, kid, take it easy. Ain't nobody gonna hurt ya."

"Just don't turn me in. You're not gonna turn me in, are ya?"

The man rubbed his stubble again.

"Could you just find me some clothes?" Frank went on. "It's freezing, man. I just need something to wear and then . . . maybe you could give me a ride over to Twelve and Van Dyke. That's where my folks live. I just wanna see my parents, okay? Could you do that for me?"

The man studied Frank's face. He didn't like punks, especially from the youth home. But he didn't want to involve the police either. "I s'pose I could find something for you to put on," he agreed finally, walking over to a closet. He tossed Frank an oversized pair of workpants and a brown flannel shirt.

Frank scrambled from his seat and pulled on the pants. "Whoa, these must be size 50 or something," he commented, tying the waistband into a knot. The shirt was extra large too, but the flannel felt warm against his skin. "Now, about that ride—you think you can do that for me?"

The man, anxious to be rid of the intruder, climbed into his truck, a 50s model that shook when it hit 45 mph, and headed with his passenger for Twelve Mile and Van Dyke. After Frank had climbed down from the cab, he spun away without looking back. Frank walked over to a bin labeled as the property of a local thrift store and peered inside. Shirts, pants, and jackets were piled several feet deep. He flipped himself over the side, curled his body into a tight ball, and dropped into soft layers of clothing. Pulling down the metal cover and rolling a sweater into a pillow, he fell almost immediately into an exhausted slumber.

An hour had passed when Frank awoke to the crackling of a radio dispatch immediately outside the dumpster. *Somebody must have tipped off the police,* he thought fiercely, *and I think I know who.* He could hear his own breathing—short, fast pants that seemed to echo inside the closed bin. He could only hope the officer couldn't hear it too. Frank burrowed deeper beneath the clothes, all the way to the bottom of the bin. The lid was pried open with a nightstick, and an arm reached down into the mass of clothing, lifting shirts and pants from the top of the pile. "Frank," someone called out into the darkness, "come on out and nobody'll get hurt."

Frank held his breath, hoping the call was a bluff. Finally the lid dropped with a thunk, the muffled voices started to fade, and car doors slammed. When Frank heard the crunch of tires he knew he was safe. Still, he remained buried beneath the thick warmth for several more hours, not emerging until morning.

The lid on the bin opened only a crack as Frank peered out to feel the sun on his face. He lifted himself gingerly over the edge of the dumpster before dropping to the ground. The pavement was cold on his feet. *Gotta find me some shoes,* he thought, cinching the knot at his waist. Making his way to the west end of the shopping center, he strolled with a carefree air into Kmart. Spying a tube of Brylcreem and a comb, he slipped them into his pocket. On his way to the shoe department he snatched a pair of socks from a rack and pulled them onto his feet, feeling better already. Next he grabbed a pair of tennis shoes and laced them up. No one appeared to notice the boy in the baggy pants as he waddled out the door and headed for JCPenney.

In the men's department Frank fingered through several racks of expensive suits. An iridescent sharkskin number caught his eye—his size, too. Rolling the suit into a ball, he stuffed it underneath the baggy shirt before making his way outside and behind the store to change his clothes. *Like a butterfly sheds his cocoon,* he thought with a smirk while peeling off the flannel shirt.

Frank startled in response to a noise behind him. Someone was climbing over the cement wall. A boy scrambled over the top, then dropped to the ground. He rubbed his hands together, staring at the clothes at Frank's feet. "What're you doing, man?" he asked.

"What's it to you?"

"Just wondering what you're doing."

"Look, I broke out of the youth home last night." Frank reached down to pick up the clothes and toss them into a garbage can. "I needed something to wear, okay? So don't tell nobody."

The boy smiled broadly. "Wait a minute," he sang out in recognition. "I know you. You're Frank Majewski. Don't you remember me? We went to Hartsig together."

"No, sorry, I don't."

"Larry Wolf."

"That's cool, Larry. Say, you got any food at your house? I'm starvin'. I haven't eaten since yesterday."

"Yeah, c'mon home with me. I'll feed you."

Larry led Frank back over the wall and on to his home. His parents were still asleep as the boys tiptoed into the kitchen. Larry poured two bowls of cereal, and they sat down to eat. Next he led Frank into the basement, telling him he could lie low there for the rest of the day.

The next morning Frank shook Larry's hand, thanked him, and slipped out the backdoor. He still wanted to catch up with Lynn; even though the boy had punked out on him, Frank figured they were both on the lam and might as well travel together.

It was a bright—and warm—Easter morning. Frank's iridescent suit glistened as he strolled along Van Dyke Avenue. Folks heading to church turned to stare at the boy in the fancy clothes. Frank enjoyed the attention but diverted his eyes when he recognized an off-duty guard from the youth home.

The guard turned to stare as Frank walked by. "Say . . ." Mr. Hughes hadn't heard anything about Frank Majewski being released, and something didn't seem right. "What's going on, Majewski?" he challenged.

"G'morning Mr. Hughes," Frank called back airily.

The guard continued to watch as Frank ambled down the street, then hurried to find a pay phone. Frank, willing himself not to look back, turned down a side street and sat down on a porch. A squad car pulled in front of the house, and an officer stepped out. He squinted at Frank, shielding his eyes with his hand. "You happen to see a kid wandering around here? His name's Frank Majewski—broke out of the youth home."

"No sir, never heard of him," Frank replied in an even tone.

"We got a call he was seen in this area."

"If I see anybody, I'll let ya know."

The officer waved, climbed back into his cruiser, and pulled away. Frank chuckled. That was the third time he'd been cornered by the cops and allowed to go free. He stood up, stretched, and continued down Van Dyke. Turning onto Lynn's street, he climbed the steps to his front porch and knocked on the door. No one answered. Frank, feeling cocky and invincible after his recent near misses with the law, sat down on the porch to wait for his friend.

The officer returned, this time with several more squad cars, all of which screeched to a stop in front of Lynn's house. Strobes flashed as officers stepped from the cruisers and pointed their guns at Frank, ordering him to the ground.

"Where's the gun, Majewski?" an officer barked while snapping handcuffs on Frank's wrists.

"What gun?"

"Check the garage," he nodded to his partner. "He probably hid it in there."

"I don't have a gun," Frank protested.

"Shut-up and get in the car." The officer pushed Frank into the back seat and slammed the door. "The only reason I didn't arrest you before was those fancy clothes. Threw me off for a minute."

Frank stared out the window en route to the station. He wondered briefly whether Lynn had gotten away before turning his thoughts to Thatcher and Bott—how they'd react when he arrived back at the youth home and how much time they'd give him for busting out. Glancing down, Frank fingered the silky fabric of his suitcoat. "Hey," he called out, "do I get to keep the clothes?"

The officer glanced at his partner and laughed. "You won't be needing that sharkskin suit for a while, Majewski—not where you're going."

CHAPTER 14

Things Are Looking Up

Three months later Frank was back on the streets. For the Majewskis, living together as a family had long since proved impossible. Harold and Jean felt beyond exhausted, and knew that a permanent break with their son was inevitable. After kicking Frank out of the house one final time, there was peace in their home at last. Frank didn't much care. He shrugged it off and moved in with his new friend, Larry "MoJo" Wolf.

On this particular Friday evening Frank and his brother Chuck hopped into MoJo's car and headed for the Chicago Key Club in Warren. The windows were rolled down against the stifling air, and tensions were running just as hot between the brothers. As MoJo neared the already overflowing parking lot Frank noted to his satisfaction that the club was swarming with teenagers. Everyone's radio was tuned to CKLW, and girls were dancing in the street.

Inside the club band members warmed up their instruments, and girls in tight pants flirted with appreciative boys leaning against the walls. Jim Johnston, the 28-year-old proprietor—a hard-working "go-getter" who also owned a barbershop in the neighborhood,—stood just outside the door, cigarette in hand, leaning against the outer wall. He had opened his place back in September and was enjoying sell-out crowds nearly every weekend.

⊖⊕⊖

From where Jim stood he could inconspicuously screen every person who might attempt to enter . . . and turn away the undesirables. He had just received word that two punks—brothers—were fighting out in the street. Jim took a drag from his cigarette. As long as they stayed off his property he wasn't concerned. But if they wanted to enter the club they would have to abide by his rules. Jim had never met the Majewski brothers, but he knew the name. He also knew that trouble followed in their wake. When Frank and Chuck had resolved their scuffle the three boys headed into the club. Sending a puff of smoke skyward, Jim sized up Frank as the kid crossed the dance floor.

Soon after the band had started to play a burst of angry voices rose in crescendo above the thrust of the music. Frank and another boy were standing their ground, toe-to-toe, fists clenched. Before Jim could step in Frank had delivered a blow to the kid's stomach. A girl screamed, and the crowd stepped back as one. The boy landed a return punch to Frank's mouth, and he staggered and raised a hand to his lip. Blood trickled down his chin as Frank lunged at his opponent, knocking him to the ground.

When police sirens sounded in the distance, Jim pulled Frank to his feet and led him upstairs to his office. Concealing the boy behind his desk and ordering silence, Jim locked the door and slipped the key into his pocket. The last thing he needed was trouble with the cops. Smoothing back his hair with his hands, the youthful proprietor headed downstairs.

"You're a pretty good fighter," he observed to Frank later on, after the police had gone.

"I wanted to finish him off," Frank muttered.

"Not in *my* place."

"Sorry, man. I couldn't let that punk slide, though, after he hit me in the mouth."

Jim sat down at his desk and lit a cigarette, offering one to Frank, who winced at the pain in his jaw.

"Look," Jim invited, studying the young man in front of him, "why don't you come over to my house and we'll get you cleaned up? You should lay low for tonight anyhow—the cops'll be looking for you. I'll give my wife a call and tell her we're coming."

Frank agreed and, after closing time, rode with Jim to his home in Detroit. Judith met them at the door, set a cold plate of chicken on the kitchen table and cast a sidelong glance at Frank. Reaching for a drumstick, Frank took note of her silky tresses and blue eyes.

Judith wondered what Jim was getting involved in now. *Haven't we got enough troubles of our own? she thought.*

Jim sat back, scrutinizing their guest from behind partially closed lids. The kid looked tough; he was strong and obviously knew his way around. But most remarkable were his eyes—off-putting, really—the most penetrating Jim could recall having seen. The kid's scowl reminded him of a storm cloud ready to burst.

"Where'd you learn to fight like that?" Jim asked.

"I been around." Frank took a decisive bite of his drumstick.

"How old are you, Frank? Still in school?"

"Nah. Got kicked out of school, man. I'm done with all that."

"How about your parents? You got family?"

Frank chuckled. "No, man. I don't have any family." His face grew serious. "Look, I got nobody, okay? No place to live—nowhere to go."

Jim glanced at Judith. "Listen," he offered, "why don't you crash here for a couple of days? Let everything cool down with the cops, and then you can figure out what to do next."

⊖⊖⊖

"That kid needs something to do with his life," Jim commented. "I'm gonna see if I can get him into barber school. At least it's worth a try."

Judith was tight-lipped as she poured him a cup of coffee. It was 10:00 a.m. on Monday, Jim's day off, and Frank was asleep on the Johnstons' living room couch for the third morning in a row.

When Frank stumbled into the kitchen, Jim presented his idea. "What do you think about becoming a barber? I mean, you got kicked out of high school and got nowhere else to go. What if I got you into barber college?"

"Nah, man." Frank rejected the idea with a dismissive wave. "I don't wanna be no barber—that's sissy stuff."

"You calling me a sissy? I've been cutting hair for years. Besides, you got nothing else going on. I can take you down to the college today and get you enrolled."

Frank considered for a moment. Jim was right about one thing—there weren't many options open. If Jim was willing to help, maybe he should give it a try. "All right," Frank consented. "What do I hafta do?"

"Just fill out the form," Jim replied. "Leave the rest to me."

"How old are you, kid?" Dan Sade used his one good eye to study Frank as he handed him an application. Dan, the owner of Lamar Barber

College, did a little racketeering on the side. He could tell a lot about a person within their first few moments of meeting, . . . and he didn't feel good about Frank.

"Sixteen."

"You can't get into barber school till you're seventeen," he replied. "How much education have you got?"

"Got kicked out of tenth grade."

"You need at least a tenth grade education." Dan waved his hand indifferently toward the door in a gesture of dismissal. Shrugging, Frank stepped from the room. He had expected as much.

Jim, unwilling to give up so soon, headed without invitation into Dan's office, closing the door behind him. "*C'mon man!*" he pleaded, "give the kid a chance."

Frank could barely hear their muffled voices. Finally the door swung open. Jim stuck his head out the door and, in his "can do" manner, waved Frank back in.

"Alright!" Dan conceded, leaning back in his chair. "This is what I want you to do: go to your high school and get into the office. You probably know somebody on the inside, right?"

"Yeeaah . . ." Frank glanced tentatively at Jim, not sure where this was going.

"Find some blank letterhead from the school and bring it back to me."

"That shouldn't be too hard," Frank agreed with a nod. He thought of his friend Carol, a student volunteer in the front office at Cousino.

A week later he handed Dan the letterhead and watched as the man typed a memo stating that Frank had completed the tenth grade. Dan placed the memo in a file and handed the boy a registration form. Within an hour Frank was enrolled at Lamar Barber College, his tuition deferred until after graduation.

Jim found him a small apartment at Six Mile Road and John R, within walking distance of the school, telling the manager of the complex that Frank was his little brother and implying that the place was for the two of them. He paid the security deposit and first month's rent and, once they had stepped outside the office, handed the key to Frank. Frank couldn't believe his luck—a career opportunity and his own place! Things were definitely looking up.

CHAPTER 15

A Little Help from Heaven

Summer, 1967

In 1959 Jim and Judith were a couple of jittery kids, flushed with idealism, standing before a Justice of the Peace. Judith had just turned 18 and Jim was 19 when they'd exchanged wedding vows and set up housekeeping in a small, lower flat in Detroit. For the next five years Judith had raised the couple's three children, who had arrived like clockwork, one after another, and kept house while Jim finished barber school. The enterprising Jim went to work in 1964, soon becoming owner and proprietor of Plaza Barber, a shop at the corner of Twelve Mile and Van Dyke in Warren.

The business took off quickly. The shop, conveniently located across the street from General Motors, allowed auto executives to swing by on their lunch hour for a haircut. Jim was an outgoing man everyone liked, and the extra time he took with each customer paid off in the form of tips. All would likely have been well had he not begun frequenting local bars after closing the shop. All too soon this practice turned into a nightly affair, with him visiting multiple bars before heading home. Long after Judith and the kids had fallen asleep he would stumble into the house, drunk and reeking of women's cologne.

Judith suspected that her husband was cheating on her but lacked proof—until one morning when in the process of leafing through his wallet she came upon a scrap of paper on which a woman's name and phone number had been scribbled. Suspecting trouble and confirming it can be very different experiences; Judith's hands shook as she stared, grief-stricken, at the note. An open bottle of Jack Daniels sat on the counter—Jim never bothered using a glass. Like salt rubbed into a newly opened wound, his behavior repulsed her and hurt more than usual this morning. Judith rubbed her forehead and sighed. Both she and Jim had been raised in alcoholic homes, and she knew all too well the effect of alcohol upon the well-being of a family. Together she and Jim had vowed never to repeat the sins of their parents. This morning, though, Jim had proven that he was not only addicted to alcohol but unfaithful as well.

Her hands still trembling, Judith dialed the phone number. An older woman answered— probably the girl's mother. No, her daughter wasn't home. Did she want to leave a message? Judith's voice quavered. "Please tell her that the man she's seeing is married, with three children." Hanging up the phone without waiting for a reaction, she buried her face in her hands. That night she confronted Jim, who denied everything. All three kids, their security shaken by the angry words and tones, burst into tears.

The next morning Judith couldn't drag herself out of bed. An hour after waking she still huddled under the covers, crying into her pillow and contemplating the suicide that seemed in her devastation to be the only solution. She doubted Jim would care; any love between them was gone. But Judith couldn't bear the thought of destroying the children's lives as well; distraught though she was, that kind of collateral damage was unthinkable. Nor was there was anyone she could trust to care for them when she was gone.

Preoccupied with that thought, she slipped out of bed and tip-toed into the children's shared bedroom. The older two lay tangled together, their faces pressed close on a pillow as though for mutual support. The baby, oblivious to the tragedy uprooting her mother's world, lay fast asleep in her crib. Judith listened to their even breathing for a moment before gently closing the door and heading to the bathroom to splash cold water on her tear-swollen face. There was really only one option, she decided then: throw Jim out of the house, file for divorce, and end the vicious cycle. Drying her hands, she studied her face in the mirror. Angry smudges—dark as bruises—beneath her tortured eyes accentuated her look of desperation.

That evening Judith pulled Jim's carefully folded clothes from the dresser and removed his pants from the closet. Tossing everything into a pile on the driveway slab, she sat down on the couch to await his homecoming. When Jim stumbled into the house at 2:00 a.m. he reeked, as usual, of alcohol. Judith rose from the couch, a butcher knife in her hand, which she pointed at Jim. "I want you out of here *tonight!*" she pronounced through gritted teeth. Her hand shook, and her tone was shrill. "Take your stuff and get out of here. I never want to see you again."

Jim took a step toward her. "Hold on, Judith. Let's talk about this."

At precisely that moment Judith hurled the knife—a wild throw that struck the wall. Jim stared for a long moment in disbelief before gathering his wits sufficiently to flee. Alone in the living room Judith collapsed onto the couch and sobbed. Her once happy family life lay in a pile of ashes.

First thing in the morning she met with an attorney, and later that afternoon a courier served Jim the divorce papers at work. Jim lit a cigarette, collapsed into his barber chair, and shook his head. *I'm not giving up that easily, Judith,* he vowed. *If you're looking for a fight, that's what you'll get.* That evening he instructed his own attorney to contest the divorce.

Judith had joined the Catholic Church when she'd married Jim. Neither of them had been devout; far from it, the couple rarely attended Mass. And over the ensuing years Judith had given up on God. She had never looked to Him for help before, and it seemed pointless to do so now.

After signing the divorce papers, however, she cried herself into a fitful sleep night after night. In the mornings she would drag herself out of bed to stumble through her day in a daze. There was no one to turn to and no end to her wretchedness in sight. One evening, feeling utterly desolate, Judith dropped to her knees on the living room floor and folded her hands. "Oh God," she cried in anguish. "Please help me. I've made such a mess of my life." She bowed her head as tears formed rivulets down her cheeks. "I need your help, God," she sobbed. "Please forgive me. Come into my life and take over."

Judith's tiny, overwrought frame began to tremble. Wracking sobs rose from her gut as she clenched and unclenched her fists and then wrapped her arms tightly around her waist. She continued to pray for several more minutes before an unaccustomed peace began to wash over her and her tears subsided. She began to experience an uncanny sensation that she was no longer alone. Rising from her knees, she wiped her eyes and gazed intently around the room. No one else was present. Still, she felt herself being enveloped by an unshakable and profoundly comforting presence. Dropping to the couch she closed her eyes, savoring the peace that flooded her heart. Overcome by sudden weariness, she managed to stumble into the bedroom and ease herself between the sheets. Judith hadn't slept well in months, but when she lay her head on the pillow she dropped off into the deepest, most restorative sleep she'd experienced in years.

The next morning Judith awoke refreshed, and filled with a new and unaccustomed hope. God had heard her prayer—she was sure of it—and would somehow see her through the days ahead. After the children were up and readied for their day, she found her way to a Christian bookstore, purchased a Bible and hurried home to begin reading. To her great surprise Judith discovered the book to be filled with stories of people very much like herself—men and women who had run from God, only to discover how to find rest and assurance in Him. She could hardly put the book down and began reading her Bible every night after tucking the children into bed. Sometimes a verse would seem to leap off the page. She would grab a pen to underline—and thereby claim—the words as her own.

Once in a while, though, a passage would strike her as harsh and difficult to accept. Teachings on forgiveness proved particularly challenging. "If you don't forgive others, neither will your Father in heaven forgive your sins," Jesus himself declared in Mark 11:26. Judith recoiled at the implications. She had never to this point seriously considered forgiving Jim. To dismiss his unfaithfulness, to pretend it had never happened, sounded crazy. She needed the help of a minister.

"Well, you certainly have biblical grounds for divorce," the pastor conceded near the end of their visit. He leaned back in his chair, numbering off his points on the upturned fingers of his left hand. "Alcoholism, adultery, neglect . . . My advice to you is to move forward. Start a new life for yourself and the children."

Based upon what she'd read in the Bible, this wasn't at all what Judith had expected to hear. She determined to check out what the Bible itself had to say about divorce. Every verse she could find on the subject served to reinforce God's good plan for marriage, to reveal how vehemently He hates divorce. "But God," she cried out in protest, "Don't I have rights too? This is all Jim's fault. *He* has the problem. How can we go on like this?"

A gentle answer infiltrated her thoughts, whispering, unbidden, to her heart: "Don't worry about Jim; I can take care of him. We're going to work on *you* right now." Judith knew then that God, in His own way, in His own time, would handle everything. She could trust Him. God was asking her to surrender her marriage, broken as it was, to His care. She wrestled with the thought: *stay in this marriage? Really?* She and Jim had already been separated for 18 months, and the divorce would be final in one short week. That afternoon she phoned her attorney, asking him to cancel the proceedings. Next she phoned Jim to invite him home, stipulating one condition: marital counseling. Jim agreed.

"Marriage is like a wheel," the counselor explained. "If God is at the hub everything turns smoothly. But without Christ at the center there's nothing to hold your marriage together; everything starts to fall apart." The counselor explained to Judith that she needed to love Jim unconditionally. Change wouldn't come overnight, he cautioned. And Jim needed to pledge himself to Judith and the children—and then to follow through by coming straight home from work every night. They decided to give it a try, and for several weeks the Johnston family ate dinner together and even attended church.

The night came, however, when Jim invited a client out for a drink and didn't return till after midnight. Recognizing his drunken state, Judith struggled with an agonizing doubt that he would ever change.

For his part, Jim was sick and tired of his wife's self-righteous attitude; she was starting to wear him thin with all the God talk. "Listen," he insisted. "If we're gonna make this thing work we need a compromise: you keep your religion, and I'll keep my freedom."

Judith had a response ready, but she held her tongue. What was the point of arguing? She agreed to his terms, and Jim watched in amazement as his wife left the room, softly closing the bedroom door behind her. Judith, knowing that God could accomplish more in response to her prayers than she could imagine, dropped to her knees in submission.

⊂⊃⊂⊃

Frank was stretched out on the couch in his apartment. Beer bottles littered the coffee table, and his buddy Greg was passed out on the floor. The Rolling Stones blasted from a record player as Frank stood up and punched his fist into the wall.

Greg raised his head. "What'd you do that for, man?" he whined, unhappy at being disturbed.

"Just seeing if you're awake," Frank replied. His hand didn't hurt yet, so he swung again to make another hole.

Greg, rising too, threw a punch at the wall as well. Frank laughed, popped open two more bottles of beer, and handed one to his buddy. The two drank, hooted, and punched the thin apartment wall until both passed out on the floor.

The next morning Frank's petite, feisty apartment manager, Marie, pounded on his door. "I want you out of here *today!*" she demanded. "Where's that so-called brother of yours? You guys were lying to me, weren't you? You don't think I know? You're the only one living here, aren't you? Go on, get out!"

Frank's head hurt, and Marie's high-pitched voice grated on his nerves. Too hung-over to argue, he gathered what he could of his belongings, vacated the building, and proceeded to make a bed for himself in the alley behind the apartment. It was cold and wet outside, but he had nowhere else to go.

Marie watched from her window as Frank huddled next to a garbage can. She sighed, threw on a sweater, and went outside. "This is it?" she asked, looking resignedly up and down the alley. "This is where you're going to stay?"

"You kicked me out, Marie," Frank reminded her. "Where am I supposed to go?"

"C'mon," she beckoned. "You can't stay out here." She led Frank down the stairwell into a storage room underneath the apartments. "You're underage, so I can't rent to you, but I'll bring you a cot and you can sleep down here." She pointed to a pile of coal next to the furnace. "You can pay me by doing a little work, all right? Just keep the furnace going with coal. A load in the morning and one at night. That'll pay for your keep."

"All right, Marie," Frank consented. "Thanks."

Marie headed up the stairs, then paused. "I'll make you some dinner too. You just keep that furnace going."

Frank walked over to the pile of coal. *Room and board for a little bit of work,* he thought. *I can handle that.* He tossed several shovelfuls of the black stuff into the furnace before heading up the stairs to check out what was cooking on Marie's stove.

The summer of 1967 was a scorcher in Detroit. In addition to the temperature, tensions were heating up between black and white residents. Racial unrest was widespread, and not only in Detroit. All around the country cities were becoming powder kegs on the verge of exploding. On July 23 Frank and MoJo sat glued to the television set as reporters broadcast news of Detroit's darkest hour. A police raid at an illegal liquor store at 12th and Clairmont had led to 82 arrests. While the prisoners were being escorted to police vans, someone had thrown a rock. Pushing, shoving, and shouting had ensued, until the crowd transformed itself into an angry mob. Several men set fire to a shoe store, while others smashed local shop windows and began to steal merchandise. Teenagers ran down the sidewalk cradling television sets as mobs dragged shop owners into the streets and began to beat them with tire irons. As violence, looting, and arson fire spread across the city, police tried in vain to stem the relentless tide.

Detroit was following a trend set off by similar eruptions in Los Angeles, Chicago, and other major cities. Every store, theater, and sporting event was shut down. Residents holed up in their homes behind pulled shades, and baseball fans at Tiger Stadium watched in horror as acrid smoke darkened the sky over right field. When news of the rioting reached Tiger left fielder Willie Horton, he abruptly left the game and drove to his home near 12th Street. Climbing onto the hood of his car, he begged the rioters to disband. They paused long enough to hear him out before resuming their looting.

By Monday afternoon the city had declared a state of emergency. Entire neighborhoods were engulfed in flames as the carnage continued. On Tuesday 8000 National Guard troops were called in, and President Johnson dispatched two Airborne Divisions to the city. As green army tanks rolled down Woodward Avenue, armed guards were posted at every major intersection.

Lamar Barber College was situated near the center of the uprising, and Frank wondered how Dan Sade was holding up. Just down the street cars were being overturned by gangs, while enraged rioters marched by the college, shaking sticks and shouting threats. The enterprising Dan watched several tanks make their way down the street before stepping to the curb to offer free haircuts to any soldier parked in front of the school. By noon Dan was enjoying the full protection of the Armed Forces of the United States.

In a way Frank could relate to the rioters. He understood their fury, knowing firsthand how easily rage can flare out of control. Still, Frank breathed a sigh of relief along with everyone else when the rampaging finally subsided. In five short days 43 people had been killed, hundreds injured, and thousands more arrested. Detroit looked more like a war zone than a community, but the streets were quiet once again.

When the curfew was lifted Frank hopped into MoJo's car, and the two of them headed down Woodward to survey the damage. Everywhere they looked garbage and broken glass littered vacant, burned-out buildings. Detroit's commercial district looked like a ghost town, while in the residential areas despondent homeowners methodically picked up trash and shook their heads.

But strange demons were afoot in the 1960s. While Detroit crawled out of its darkest hour, Frank and MoJo plunged headlong into their own. The duo headed to Peppy's Burgers for a night of partying, never suspecting that within a year their revelry would end in tragedy.

CHAPTER 16

Aftermath of a Shooting

June 22, 1968
South Macomb Hospital

Frank opened his eyes and blinked several times. The hospital room was spinning. He tried to turn his head but found it wouldn't cooperate. Panic set in as he rotated his eyes from side to side, trying desperately to see where he was. The right side of his face felt numb, and his temples throbbed with pain.

Frank tried to remember what had happened the night before. There had been a gunshot and a sharp sting as the bullet had entered his head. He remembered that MoJo and Johnny were hit too. All three had been rushed to the hospital and taken to surgery. Frank recalled a priest who had held his hand and helped him pray.

He shifted his eyes to the right. An I.V. bag and a heart monitor stood next to the bed. Someone in a white coat walked in, studied his chart, and then stepped a little closer. The man patted Frank's arm. "I'm Dr. DeCampo," he told him. "How are you feeling, Frank?"

"I can't move."

"Don't try. Just lie still. I couldn't get the bullet out; it was buried too deep." Dr. DeCampo took his finger and traced a path in the air, just above the contours of Frank's face. "It traveled up your nose, curved underneath your eye and then lodged right here, next to your temple. You were lucky, Frank. If that bullet hadn't curved it would have gone into your brain. But your head is very swollen right now, and it'll be a while before I can go back in. You'll need to stay in the hospital for a few weeks."

He patted Frank's arm again before turning to leave. "Just get some rest, and we'll try again in a couple weeks."

Frank followed Dr. DeCampo with his eyes as he left the room. He wondered how MoJo and Johnny were doing, having forgotten to ask whether they had made it. He glanced up at the ceiling and swallowed hard. The first chance he got he would find out about his friends.

The doctor prescribed morphine for Frank's pain, so every few hours he buzzed the nurse's station to request a shot. "Hey!" he would call into the monitor, "the pain's back. Somebody come shoot me up!"

A nurse would appear at his side and inject morphine into his arm. Frank felt the effect almost immediately. A stream of warmth would travel down his shoulder all the way to his feet and then back up to his throbbing head. A deep calm would wash over his body, gently lulling him to sleep. As the pain disappeared this time he temporarily forgot about MoJo and Johnny.

Since Frank's assailant was still on the loose, an armed guard was stationed outside his room. The police weren't taking any chances. No visitors were allowed other than immediate family. And everyone who did come had to be searched before entering. For the first time in his life Frank was grateful for the police.

MoJo and Johnny were recovering in a shared semiprivate room down the hall, and Frank learned from the nurse that both were doing well. As soon as Frank was able to sit up he rolled his wheelchair down to their room. MoJo burst into raucous laughter when Frank appeared at the doorway—the sight of his friend's oversized head was more than he could take. MoJo laughed so hard, in fact, that he held his sides and begged Frank to leave. "It hurts too much to laugh," he complained, still chuckling. "Don't come around again; I can't take it. They stitched up my stomach, man, but you're killing me."

Frank scowled and turned to leave. Still hearing MoJo's sniggers as he wheeled back to his room, he climbed into bed and turned on the television.

Later that week a police officer entered Frank's room with a prisoner in handcuffs. He asked Frank whether this was the man who had shot him.

"Well," Frank replied, studying the man's crooked sideburns, "for one thing, he's got a bad haircut."

"But is this the guy who shot you?" the officer repeated.

"That's gotta be him," Frank agreed slowly rubbing his chin. "I mean, I'm pretty sure it's him, but it's hard to say for sure. It was dark out, and we'd had a few beers. Still . . . ," he mused, "how could I forget that face?"

The officer wasn't convinced. He took the prisoner and left.

"It was him all right," Frank told MoJo later. "I heard the guy's girlfriend turned him in after hearing him brag about gunning down three people. He had a .25 automatic berretta on him too—the same gun he shot us with. But I couldn't identify him for sure, so he'll probably walk."

MoJo and Johnny were released from the hospital within a week. When they said goodbye to Frank, neither realized how much pain he was in or how much suffering he had yet to endure. A second surgery was scheduled, after which Frank's real recovery could begin. Day after day he sat, dejected, in the hospital, feeling restless and alone. He had learned from his parents that Chuck had been drafted. His brother was stationed somewhere in Vietnam, but no one knew where. Listening to the war report on the news that night, Frank couldn't help but wonder whether he would ever again see his brother.

His days settled into a dull routine revolving around little more than mushy food and morphine shots. When he wasn't asleep Frank passed the time watching reruns or sitting in the patient lounge. As he gazed out the window to the street below, he saw cars racing along Twelve Mile Road, their occupants never glancing up. No one cared that a young man on the third floor was lonely and in need of a friend.

"Well, look at you, you s.o.b."

The familiar voice gave Frank a start. Turning his wheelchair, he gazed into the eyes of his brother. "Chuck!" he shouted in astonished elation, and threw open his arms.

Chuck hesitated for an awkward moment before wrapping his arms around Frank's neck. Never having hugged his brother before, he stepped back self-consciously after withdrawing from the embrace. Slipping his hands into his pockets, Chuck studied Frank's bandages. His brother's head was swollen, and black and blue rings encircled his eyes. Chuck figured that at this point Frank couldn't weigh more than a hundred pounds. Still, it was Frank—and he was alive.

Chuck grinned, pulled up a chair, and sat down. "How you doing, Franko?"

"Man, I thought you were in Vietnam," was Frank's reply.

Chuck looked around before lowering his voice. "I am. I went AWOL. I had to. My commanding officer wouldn't let me come see you. I had to know you were okay."

"You went *AWOL?* Man, are you nuts?"

"That's why I can't stay. If I go right back, maybe they'll take it easy on me—toss me in the brig for a few days."

"So you can't stay, Chuck?"

"Gotta get back, Franko. I just wanted to see you. I'd do it all over again if I had to, but I can't stay." Chuck reached into his pocket and pulled out a gold ring. "I bought this over there, and now I'm giving it to you. Keep it safe, all right?"

Frank took the ring and slipped it onto his finger. "Thanks, Chuck," he managed to respond in a choked voice, fighting back tears.

"This means a lot, coming from you."

Slipping on his cap, Chuck reached out to shake Frank's hand and squeezed it hard. "You take it easy, all right, Frank?" he directed. "I'll be back in about a year." He started down the hall but threw his brother a backward glance before stepping into the elevator. Pointing at him, he smiled. "See you in a year, okay?" Frank raised his fist in the air, lowering it slowly after watching his brother disappear.

During a second surgery Dr. DeCampo managed to remove the bullet from Frank's head, after which he wired together his jaw and placed him on a soft diet of milkshakes and eggs. Frank was miserable. He could hardly chew and was barely able to speak, not to mention that the pain in his jaw was excruciating.

After his release from the hospital he returned to Marie's basement and resumed his job of feeding the furnace. But shoveling coal had become a painful task. Each toss of the shovel made Frank's head throb and his sinuses ache. And now he had a new problem: Frank had grown accustomed to morphine in the hospital; long after he'd stopped needing them he had continued to ask for shots. Now he was hooked. Alcohol could never provide what morphine did for him. Frank needed another hit but didn't know where to find it.

It was 1968, and the hippie movement was in full swing. Guys sported wire-rimmed glasses and grew long hair and scraggly beards. Marijuana and LSD had become popular, and Frank had no difficulty finding a dealer from whom to obtain these street drugs. Every weekend he dropped a hit of acid before lying on his back on the floor in MoJo's basement. Frank Zappa music blared on the stereo, while strobe lights flashed across the ceiling. A little while after a hit every sensory stimulus in the room would intensify. Smells, colors, and textures all sprang to life. Frank would sit up, glance over at MoJo, and begin to laugh uproariously. His face, he would notice, looked elongated, stretching nearly to the floor. MoJo's eyes were huge, too, and his friend's breathing roared like the wind.

"What are you staring at?" MoJo would ask. "What's so funny?"

Frank guffawed even harder when he heard MoJo speak; his friend sounded like a record playing at slow speed. Frank held his sides and continued to chortle while MoJo turned away.

Although his weekends now revolved around LSD, Frank had re-enrolled in barber college. During the week he focused on schoolwork, still hoping to graduate. One Saturday night he and MoJo headed for a party. Frank recognized a girl from high school he had once dated. Debbie, he noted with satisfaction, was still beautiful.

He waited for her boyfriend to step away before approaching her with a come on: "You're looking good tonight, Debbie."

Debbie laughed. "You look good yourself, Frank." She sipped her beer as Frank moved in closer to slip his arm around her waist.

When her boyfriend returned, though, he pulled out a gun, aimed it at Frank, and ricocheted a shot off the wall. The partiers scattered, with Frank and MoJo pushing their way out the back door and rushing across the yard.

"Here come the guns again, MoJ!" Frank exclaimed as they hopped over a fence and dashed down a side street. He paused to catch his breath before draping his arm around MoJo's neck. "Moj," he announced, "I'm finished with this greaser scene. Peace and love is where it's at, man. Time for us to become hippies."

MoJo found this hilarious but had to admit that Frank was right; things were getting too dangerous in the greaser world. Times were changing; maybe they needed to do the same. He ran a hand through his short brown hair and announced that he'd been thinking about growing it out anyhow. Frank observed that he'd like to try a beard. He was ready to trade in leather boots for sandals, and tie-dyed shirts and peace necklaces were starting to sound pretty good.

Dan scowled as he took in Frank's new look: the shabby clothes, long hair, and scruffy beard. Now more than ever before he wanted this kid out of his school. He couldn't imagine Frank ever becoming a barber; he just didn't look—or act—the part. After the shooting episode Dan had hoped Frank might not return. It was disappointing to see him sitting in class.

One afternoon Dan flipped through Frank's file, perusing his test scores. It was obvious the kid would never pass his finals. The only way Dan could be rid of him for good was to rig the test, hand him a diploma, and send him on his way.

He called Frank into his office and asked him to sit down. "Look, Frank," he began, getting right to the point, "I don't want to see you flunk the exam." He shoved a pen and paper toward him. "Write down everything I tell you. Are you ready? Number 1 is "a." Number 2, "c." Are you getting this?"

Frank was incredulous. "Are you giving me the answers, man?"

"Just write 'em down," Dan cut in.

Frank started to write, shaking his head and chuckling.

On the day of the exam he filled in the answers before exiting the building with a grin. It had taken him two years to complete the one-year course, but with a diploma in hand Frank was certified to cut hair.

Jim "JJ" Johnston agreed to set up Frank in the back of his store at Tech Plaza with a barber chair and some haircutting equipment. It occurred to the ever resourceful Jim that Frank's appearance—his beard and tattoos—might attract a new clientele to his shop. Frank would service the hippies while Jim handled the GM execs and other businessmen from Warren.

Frank strung colorful beads at the entrance to his booth and burned patchouli incense in a burner. Jimi Hendrix music blared on his phonograph, and a lava lamp swirled colors on the ceiling. Within a week Frank's schedule was full. His chair became known as "the head booth"— a place where dope heads could obtain a decent haircut in a psychedelic setting. It was a rough-looking crowd that wended its way to the rear of the barbershop, but Jim didn't mind. As long as Frank's clients were paying customers, having him around was good for business.

Frank enjoyed receiving a weekly paycheck. He was living once again in an apartment, paying rent, and paying for food and gas. But there wasn't much left over for fun, and his student loan had come due.

Watching Frank struggle to make ends meet, Jim offered some advice. "Barbering is never gonna make you rich, man," he acknowledged. "Let me show you how to pay off your debt in one lump sum." Interested, Frank pulled up a chair as Jim explained. "Say someone in a car hits you from behind—you get what I'm saying?" Frank nodded. "So they hit you and—*bam!*—you fake a whiplash. You catch my drift? After that, you sue." Jim sat back in his chair, hands clasped behind his head, before once again picking up his train of thought. "My attorney will take it from there. He makes a little and you make a little." Jim smiled. "*That's* how you pay off a student loan."

Frank had always figured JJ for a scammer, but he hadn't realized the man was a pro. The plan sounded foolproof, so the next day he drove down Woodward Avenue and braced himself for a collision. At the first light Frank slammed on his brakes just after it turned green, inviting the accelerating car to his rear to smash into him. Barely feeling the impact, he grabbed his neck and moaned as the apologetic driver hurried to his side.

The next day Jim introduced Frank to his attorney, who immediately filed a lawsuit. Just as Jim had promised, Frank was awarded $4000—enough to pay off his entire debt.

Jim also introduced Frank to his nightclub of choice, Club 39 in Ferndale, a smoky pub in a seedy part of town, on the outskirts of Detroit. The club was frequented by hard-drinking rednecks who dropped nickels into a jukebox and listened to country music till closing time. Frank and MoJo dubbed it "the hillbilly bar."

One night Frank got into an argument with one of the patrons. It wasn't unusual for Frank to pick a fight, but this time the bartender stepped in. "Take it outside, Frank," he ordered. "I don't want any trouble in here tonight."

MoJo tugged on Frank's sleeve, pulling him toward the exit, but as they started to leave the patron drew a gun from his pocket and fired. Frank and MoJo rushed out the door and jumped into Frank's old car, the gunman following in his own. Frank careened down John R Road with the man in hot pursuit, cutting through back alleys and speeding along side streets on threadbare rubber. As he bounced over punishing curbs and crashed through garbage cans his tires began, one by one, to collapse, sparks flying as the rims scraped concrete. To Frank's intense relief the gunman gave up the chase, the image of his vehicle disappearing from the rearview mirror. Turning to MoJo, Frank shook his head—yet another potentially lethal encounter with gunfire. He turned the car around and eased it back, riding the rims, to their flat in Highland Park.

Upon arrival Frank collapsed into a chair, exhausted from the chase, while MoJo turned on a black light and lit a joint. He took a drag before handing it to Frank. A cockroach scurried across the room; Frank crushed it beneath his shoe before stretching out on the couch. Sinking into the weathered cushions, he gazed around the room, taking in the black-painted ceiling with its glow-in-the-dark stars and the deep purple walls covered with posters. *It's not much*, he admitted as the flashing strobe illuminated the walls, *but it's home.*

●━●━●

Every Saturday night Frank and MoJo headed for the Grande Ballroom. The two-story dance hall, built back in the '20s, had in its heyday, which lasted decades, hosted jazz, blues, and Big Band performers. But by 1960 the hall was run down and in dire need of repair. Early in the decade a local DJ by the name of Russ Gibb, determined to restore the iconic establishment to its former glory, had reopened it as a rock and roll concert hall. Frank and MoJo had already seen some of the biggest names in music perform for standing-room-only crowds on the Grande stage: MC5, The Who, and Cream.

On this particular Saturday evening Frank stood in the long line that wrapped around the building, waiting to hand the attendant his three dollars. Inside strobe lights, psychedelic colors, and thrumming rock and roll would, as always, bring the ballroom to life. Drug dealers lined the colonnade, holding up signs openly advertising their wares: marijuana, LSD, and speed, for the most part.

Frank, brushing through a string of beads at an entry point, studied the crowd as it surged into the room. The heavy scent of patchouli incense mingled with the pungent aroma of marijuana. Teens gathered in clusters along the colonnade, sharing drugs and getting high. MoJo slipped in next to Frank and handed him a joint.

"Thanks, bro," he acknowledged, lighting up. "This place is hopping tonight, man."

MoJo nodded, looking around. The warm-up band appeared on stage as Frank continued to scan the room. Leaning against the wall with a cigarette was Mike Cassady, his former classmate from Cousino. Frank thought the kid looked different from the last time he'd seen him. Mike's hair fell below his shoulders, and he sported a full beard. Frank made his way across the room and shook the hand of his former classmate. "Cassady, how you doin', man?"

Mike tried not to appear nervous. Who could forget Frank Majewski's hair-trigger temper? Shaking Frank's hand, he observed that the guy looked even crazier than before—demon-possessed! Mike glanced toward the exit, mumbled something about a phone call, and slipped away.

The crowd erupted into raucous applause as Janis Joplin crossed the stage, a bottle of Southern Comfort in her hand. She took a swig before grabbing the mike. Calling out in her signature raspy voice, she worked the crowd: "I'm giving you everything I got tonight, Detroit . . ." The fans cheered as Joplin took another swallow, and the band flung itself into "Piece of My Heart."

Everyone was high, and the atmosphere was intense, heavy with smoke, sweat, and exhilaration. As the music played and the giant strobe swirled circles on the ceiling, Frank took another hit from his joint, handing it back to MoJo with a sigh. *It didn't get any better than this!*

Part Two

"BRING HIM TO ME."

MARK 9:19

CHAPTER 17

East Meets West

The days of *Ozzie and Harriet* had run their course. In 1967 it seemed as though a whole generation turned as one from its traditional moorings to embrace a world of drugs and free sex. Young men burned their draft cards and skipped classes at school. Liberated young women set their bras on fire in front of television cameras before leaving home to join California communes. All across America anti-war protests broke out on college campuses. Professors joined in as well, with Timothy Leary encouraging students to "turn on, tune in, and drop out"— all with the help of a little LSD. Martin Luther King Jr. marched for racial equality in the South, while race riots erupted in the North. It looked as though America was coming apart at the seams, and newspaper headlines daily sounded the alarm.

In the midst of all this unrest 30 students from Duquesne University gathered at the Ark and Dove Retreat Center in Pittsburgh for a weekend of prayer. This seemed like a good idea to the devout Catholic students. Several of their professors agreed and joined them on the retreat. Participants were asked to read two books before the weekend began: *The Cross and the Switchblade* by David Wilkerson and *They Speak with Other Tongues* by John and Elizabeth Sherrill.

A junior at Duquesne named Patti prepared for the retreat by praying. Patti believed in God and trusted in Jesus but knew very little about the Holy Spirit. "Lord," she prayed one night, "if it's possible for your Spirit to be more at work in my life than He has been till now, I want it."

The format for the weekend was simple: a few worship songs, a couple of guest speakers, and a time of prayer. The professors had also suggested that everyone read the first four chapters of the biblical book of Acts. When the retreat convened on Friday night, a feeling of expectation pervaded the room.

One of the speakers began to describe the Holy Spirit. He's a Person, she explained, someone who empowers us for daily living. She encouraged all those present to give their hearts fully to the Lord before the night was over, inviting the Holy Spirit to come in. Patti listened as the woman spoke, feeling certain the message was aimed specifically at her. Afterward she strolled through the building, deep in thought, before wandering upstairs to the chapel. No one was inside, so she knelt to pray. Instantly Patti felt herself to be on holy ground. Slipping off her shoes, as Moses had done at the burning bush, she continued to pray. After several minutes she prostrated herself and lay face down, again as Moses had done. An overwhelming sense of God's presence permeated the room, and His love and peace began to saturate her heart. An hour went by before Patti hurried downstairs to tell the others what she had experienced.

The group followed her back up to the chapel, and everyone began to pray. Some found themselves speaking in an unknown, heavenly language, while others experienced a rush of warmth that washed over their heads, hands, and feet. The professors joined the students on their knees. Although no one had expected the evening to take such a turn, there was no doubt the Holy Spirit was at work.

A month later several of the same students visited Notre Dame University in Indiana. Two men, Ralph Martin and Stephen Clark, were present when the students described what had taken place at Duquesne. Afterward the men drove to Pittsburgh, anxious to see whether the Holy Spirit would manifest Himself to them as well. When they gathered in the chapel they too were touched by the presence of God and began to pray in tongues. Martin and Clark returned to Notre Dame bursting with excitement. They gathered more than 100 students and faculty members to pray together for God's Spirit to touch them as well. Thunderous praise echoed in the halls of Notre Dame that night. The Catholic Charismatic movement had been launched.

News of the event spread rapidly, and prayer meetings sprang up on campuses throughout the Midwest. Newly baptized students returned home for summer break and formed prayer groups in their hometowns. Martin and Clark settled near the University of Michigan in Ann Arbor and instituted a Christian community that would later become known as The Word of God.

As the Charismatic Movement continued to grow, it traveled west, joining forces with another revival moving east from California. In Los Angeles hundreds of young people were wading into the chilly waters of the Pacific Ocean to be baptized as a symbol of their new life— a sign to the world that a spiritual awakening had taken place. "The Jesus Movement," as it would come to be called, would bring a tidal wave of change into the lives of thousands of young people across the United States. On Sunday mornings churches were filled with frayed, ragged new members, most badly in need of a haircut. They wore blue jeans and granny dresses and walked around with guitars strapped onto their backs. Their influence changed the format of many traditional church services virtually overnight. Preachers began sharing the gospel in city parks, coffeehouses, and wherever young people were gathered. Drug use in California began to decline as thousands of new converts turned on to Jesus instead of pot.

By late 1969 Christian communes and coffeehouses were popping up all over the U.S. and Canada. Years later *Time* Magazine would feature a full-length article describing the phenomenon. An excerpt:

> Jesus is alive and well and living in the radical spiritual fervor of a growing number of young Americans who have proclaimed an extraordinary religious revolution in his name. Their message: the Bible is true, miracles happen, God really did so love the world that he gave it his only begotten son. In 1966 Beatle John Lennon casually remarked that the Beatles were more popular than Jesus Christ; now the Beatles are shattered, and George Harrison is singing My Sweet Lord.[2]

The Jesus People went to concerts and music festivals in order to hand out tracts and pray with new converts. As their numbers grew, campus violence and drug abuse were greatly reduced. *Time* Magazine continued,

> In Chicago's Grant Park band shell, Street Evangelist Arthur Blessitt last month warmed up a crowd

of nearly 1,000 with a lusty Jesus cheer, then led them off on a parade through the Loop, gathering people as they went. "Chicago police, we love you!" they shouted to cops along the route. "Jesus loves you!" Blessitt also passed a box through the crowd, asking for a special contribution: drugs. The box came back filled with marijuana, pills and LSD; it was turned over to the flabbergasted cops.[3]

CHAPTER 18

A Greater Power

Judith shuffled into the kitchen and plugged in the coffee pot. She took a mug down from the shelf, sat down in a chair, and dropped her head in her hands. It was Sunday morning, and the kids were still in bed. Jim was sprawled out on the couch, passed out from the night before. He had one leg draped over the arm of the sofa, and his face was buried in a pillow. Judith sighed. Jim was not only abusing alcohol, he was using drugs. She was sure of it. And Frank was his dealer: she was sure of that too. For several weeks now Frank had been selling drugs in the back of the shop while Jim looked the other way.

But something alarming had happened last night. Jim had come home late as usual, but this time he wasn't drunk—*he was high.* His eyes were bright, and his hands shook as he pried the lid off a bottle of beer. He jumped when Judith entered the room, then stumbled into the living room and collapsed on the couch. Within seconds he was fast asleep. None of the loud, angry fights at two in the morning to which Judith had grown accustomed.

As she poured herself a cup of coffee she tried to sort through her feelings. *If Jim is determined to destroy his life*, she reasoned, *I can't stop him. But I can't let him destroy me and the kids along with him.* She took a sip and stared out the window, wondering how much more she could take. Laughter from upstairs interrupted her train of thought. It was Sunday morning, and the kids were waking up. Judith wiped her tears and started upstairs to get everyone ready for church. Afterward, she closed herself in the bedroom and fell to her knees. "Lord," she entreated, "if you really want me to stay in this marriage, I'm going to need more of you. I need help, God. I can't do this by myself."

After loading the kids into the car, Judith drove down Van Dyke for several miles before pulling into the parking lot of Bethesda Christian Church. This was her new church—a Pentecostal, Holy Spirit-filled congregation. That day, profoundly aware that she needed God's help to live the Christian life, Judith prayed for and received the baptism of the Holy Spirit. This was a turning point for her, and she began to see how, with the Holy Spirit's love flowing through her, she could love Jim unconditionally. Jim hadn't changed; he was still an alcoholic desperately in need of God. Judith didn't know how the Lord would save their marriage, but for the first time she actually believed He would.

Back at the house Jim was waking up to a hangover. His eyes had been thin slits as he'd strained to hear his children's voices. But the house was quiet. Judith and the kids were at church. Jim raised himself on one elbow and ran his hand through his hair. *Things are getting out of control,* he admitted to himself. *I never should have listened to Frank last night.*

"Take it, man," Frank had invited, holding out a tiny pink pill. It had looked pretty harmless.

"What is it?"

"Just take it, JJ. It'll make you feel good."

Jim had swallowed the pill, only to find himself shortly afterward on his hands and knees crawling in the grass. He clawed at the lawn, picking one blade at a time and holding it up in the air for inspection. Next he tore out clumps of turf and tossed them high.

"What are you doing, man?" Frank asked, amused. "Are you nuts?"

Jim looked up. His thoughts were a blur and his eyes refused to focus. Bright colors swirled in his head as he stared back at Frank. "You . . . ," he accused, wagging a finger at his friend, "you did this to me. You took my mind . . . mind . . . mind."

Frank helped Jim to his feet. "You're just having a bad trip, JJ," he soothed. "Sorry 'bout that, man. It happens once in a while."

Now, back at home late Sunday morning, Jim headed for the kitchen to pour a cup of coffee. *Selling a little dope on the side is one thing,* he conceded, *but Frank is taking this too far.* His friend was peddling every drug on the street now: pot, LSD, PCP, mescaline—and something new on the market, STP. Last week two young girls had introduced Frank to STP in the backseat of a car.

Frank sold most of his dope at Peppy's, the hamburger joint from his high school days. It was still a favorite hangout for kids from Cousino, so Frank made his way over there almost every night of the week.

"What'll it be tonight, man?" he would ask, lugging his briefcase from car to car. "Downers, uppers, speed, acid . . . you name it." Dealing was becoming a lucrative business for Frank.

Jim had realized that Frank was in pretty deep when a Detroit man by the name of Dino dropped by the shop. *If Frank wants to cut hair and peddle dope, that's his business*, Jim had told himself. *But I don't want any of "the big boys from Detroit" showing up here*. Dino was the kind of guy who could get Frank hooked for life.

Rubbing the stubble on his chin, Jim turned his thoughts to the burning issue that had occupied him yesterday before the unwelcome episode of last night's bad trip. He'd just been offered free round-trip airfare to California by a cosmetics company. He was thinking of taking them up on the offer, maybe even looking up his old friend Jay. Jay Sebring had become a successful stylist among the elite movie stars of Hollywood.

When Judith arrived home from church he greeted her with his news. He would go to California alone, he told her, and see whether he could break into the Hollywood scene. Judith ignored the pounding in her heart, forcing herself to remain calm. She understood that God had Jim on a line—that He was reeling him in, letting him out a little, and then reeling him in some more. If God was at work—despite appearances to the contrary—she wouldn't allow herself to get in the way. "Well," she informed him matter-of-factly, working hard to quell the bubble of emotion rising within her, "I'll be waiting here when you get back."

Jim headed, then and there, to the bedroom to pack his things. The next day he arrived in California, only to fly immediately from there to Las Vegas to check out the nightlife. But his trip was shortlived. After squandering all his money within a week, he hopped on a plane and flew straight back to Detroit.

Shortly after his return, Jim was stunned to learn that his friend Jay Sebring had been murdered at a beach house on the California coast. It was all over the news. The cult leader, Charles Manson, had sent his followers to the home of Sharon Tate, where Jay had been staying. A bloody execution had ensued. Jim was badly shaken by the news, knowing that if he had remained in California he might have been murdered along with Jay. He began to think seriously about turning his life around. And as Judith continued to pray she felt certain it was just a matter of time before God would reel in her husband the rest of the way.

Frank continued to work at Plaza Barber, and life settled into a routine of cutting hair, selling drugs, and partying on the weekends. Frank was living the high life. He was also living dangerously close to the edge. He knew that—and wouldn't have it any other way. He had forgotten all about his prayer while lying on a hospital gurney with a bullet in his head. Hundreds of LSD trips later he wasn't thinking much about God anymore.

An undercover narcotics agent had set up a sting operation with the intent to arrest Frank and MoJo. The woman had bought some LSD but, in Frank's opinion, had asked far too many questions.

Drug dealing was a dangerous business, but Frank could usually size up a customer in seconds. "There's something about that chick, MoJo," he'd reflected as they drove to a party. "I don't like her, and I don't trust her. You can hang out with her if you want, but something just doesn't feel right to me."

MoJo wanted to change the subject. "You're too paranoid," he commented as he pulled into a gas station to use the restroom. Frank followed, glancing around him nervously as he walked. "I'm telling ya, Moj, I smell a rat," he went on as he washed his hands. "And I think it's that chick." MoJo just laughed, shook his head, and headed back to the car while Frank—responding to a strong premonition—stayed behind in the bathroom.

A little while later he cracked open the door and peered outside. He wasn't surprised to see that two police officers had approached MoJo and that now his friend was being handcuffed. Frank climbed on top of the sink, popped open the screen, and squeezed himself through the window. Dropping several feet to the ground, he ran as fast as he could, cut into a subdivision, and hid behind a garage. When he felt the coast was clear he zipped up his leather jacket and began to walk with backward glances and an uneasy stride. *Too bad about MoJo,* he thought, *but he shoulda listened to me. It was that chick all right—she was setting us up.*

"You and Frank should come to church sometime," Judith commented offhandedly to Jim one Sunday morning. Not waiting for his response, she picked up her purse and loaded the kids in the car.

Jim sat at the kitchen table in his pajamas, chuckling at the thought. *Me and Frank going to church . . . now that would be hilarious.* On an impulse, though, he decided to give Frank a call.

"Sure, why not?" Frank snickered in response to the unexpected invitation. "I'll meet ya there, and we'll surprise Judith."

The two men slipped into a back pew at Bethesda Christian Church. Drawing several surprised glances from the carefully dressed churchgoers, Frank nodded and smiled as he settled into his seat. Jim opened a hymnal as the organ music began and everyone rose to sing. When the first song ended the congregation broke into impromptu exclamations of "hallelujah" and "praise the Lord."

Frank nudged Jim with his elbow. "These people are nuts, man," he smirked.

All over the room people were lifting their hands in the air as they sang. One chorus led into another, and the "hallelujahs" crescendoed in volume.

After the final hymn Frank and Jim sat down to enjoy the show as an elderly woman stepped across the stage. Myrtle "Mom" Beall, the 75-year-old founder and pastor of Bethesda, approached the podium with sure steps, a Bible in her hands. She smiled at the congregation, and a hush fell over the room. Frank turned around to pinpoint the nearest exit.

"I won't be needing this." Myrtle Beall pushed aside the microphone, shooting a glance in Frank's direction; her steady gaze caused him to squirm in his seat. She opened her Bible and cleared her throat. "I want to read a passage from Psalm 7, verses 15 and 16," she began, going on, "'He has dug a pit and hollowed it out, and has fallen into the hole which he made. His mischief will return upon his own head and his violence will descend upon his own pate.'" Myrtle lifted her eyes and paused for emphasis. "Some of you have dug a hole," she declared. "You've dug a hole, and now you're trying to get out."

Frank glanced at the exit.

"I said, *some* of you have dug a hole!" Her voice thundered as she pointed directly at Frank, who grabbed his keys and made a frantic dash for the door.

After turning around to watch, Jim made his way over to Judith to sit with the family.

Out in the parking lot Frank collapsed into his car and, feeling unhinged, savagely thrust the key into the ignition. "Those people are nuts," he muttered again as he turned it. Revving the engine, he shifted into reverse, only to smash into the car behind him. Next he collided with the car in front. Flooring it, he sideswiped yet another vehicle. Finally, with a screech of the tires, Frank peeled out of the parking lot, leaving in his wake a cloud of black smoke as he headed for home.

◌●◌

A shaft of sunlight thrust its way through white lace curtains over the sink as Sister Angela Hibbard made her way into the convent's kitchen. The aroma of fresh-brewed coffee greeted her and, when the chugging of the percolator ceased, she lifted the heavy pot and poured herself a cup. Grabbing a magazine from the counter, Sister Angela seated herself at the table and dropped a sugar cube into her steaming mug. Savoring the hot brew, she perused *Ave Maria*, the Catholic periodical from Notre Dame University. One article described a series of prayer meetings being held at the college. Her curiosity piqued, Sister Angela leaned forward in genuine interest. She had heard about those meetings. The phenomenon the article described had happened first in Pittsburgh but had since spread to other cities. Now such Charismatic prayer meetings were popping up all over the country.

Five days each week Sister Angela taught third graders at Gesu Elementary School in Detroit. She was committed to her work and loved instructing children, but the spirited nun in her twenties retained an interest in college news. There had been a great deal of talk about renewal taking place, although no one was quite sure what the term signified. Sister Angela continued to read. Catholics young and old, the article purported, were experiencing the baptism of the Holy Spirit—a new and exciting expression that was creating a buzz everywhere.

"Are you reading about the Charismatics?" Gloria, a newly enrolled novice who had walked into the room, sat down at the table and pointed to the article. "Something similar happened in Monroe last month."

"What do you mean?"

"We had a guest speaker while I was visiting the convent down there," Gloria explained. "He offered to pray with us for the filling of the Holy Spirit."

"And what happened?"

Gloria's eyes lit up. "It's just like the article says. I could feel God's presence in the room. And while we were worshiping some sisters started speaking in tongues. I didn't, but others did. It was amazing. Beautiful, actually. They say it's happening all over. There's going to be a Renewal Day in Lansing next week—would you like to go? I didn't think to ask you before, but I don't really want to go by myself."

Sister Angela walked over to the sink and dumped the rest of her coffee. "I'll think about it," she replied.

"It's not a long drive . . ."

"I'll let you know."

The following Sunday Gloria and Sister Angela made the two-hour drive to Lansing, Michigan, where a group of clergy and some lay people were gathered at a small church. The leader of the group, a priest, explained that God was sending renewal to the Church through the power of the Holy Spirit. Sister Angela folded her hands in her lap and listened expectantly. While it all sounded a bit far-fetched, if what the priest said was true she didn't want to miss out on it. She loved God and welcomed any opportunity to be closer to Him. After singing a few songs, everyone who desired the filling of the Holy Spirit was directed to another room.

Sister Angela gathered her belongings and followed the group down the hallway. People began to encircle a single chair that had been placed in the center of the room. The priest asked Sister Angela to sit down in it before placing his hands on her shoulder. Several others did the same. Sister Angela shifted in the seat, fighting an urge to stand up and leave the room. As the group began to pray, however, her shoulders relaxed and her heart inexplicably filled with joy. Initially, she fought an unaccountable impulse to laugh out loud—or sing. At last, lifting her head, she smiled up at the priest. "I feel like I want to sing a song," she announced spontaneously.

"Go right ahead, Sister!" Father encouraged.

Sister Angela began a musical rendition of Psalm 150 that was familiar to everyone present. The room echoed with the melding of their strong voices, until it became obvious that something unusual was taking place. Sister Angela, who had never before been a singer, found herself leading an entire group in worship. The group sang several more songs, basking in the glow of God's presence.

On the ride home Sister Angela wondered aloud whether there

might be another prayer meeting sometime soon. She shared with Gloria that she wanted more of what they had experienced that night. Did that sound foolish? she asked.

"It doesn't seem foolish," Gloria reassured. "Father said you'd need another prayer meeting soon, or you might lose what you just received."

"Where should I go?"

"They have one every Thursday night in Ann Arbor," Gloria offered. "It's at St. Mary's Church. I think you'd like it."

Sister Angela glanced out the window at the freshly falling snow. *What am I getting myself into?* she wondered.

The following week Gloria drove the two of them to Ann Arbor for the meeting at St. Mary's—after which they attended regularly, every Thursday evening, for the next year. During that time the number of participants grew from a handful to more than 500. In the spring of 1969 the leaders of St. Mary's asked Sister Angela to consider starting a prayer meeting of her own in Detroit. She decided to ask Father Kosicki, the pastor at Gesu, what he thought of the idea. Father Kosicki, who had visited Ann Arbor several times, fully supported the Charismatic Renewal and gave Sister Angela his blessing, suggesting she join forces with a small prayer group already meeting at the church.

Within a few months more than 200 people were attending Gesu's prayer meeting. Many of the parishioners who had never heard of the baptism of the Holy Spirit welcomed the experience when it occurred. Sister Angela found herself, on a local level, at the epicenter of a movement that was simultaneously impacting the entire world. God had placed her in a key position for welcoming young people as they began filling churches in Detroit.

                                         ☙❦❧

"A Catholic priest came to Bethesda last week," Judith commented as she stirred a cup of coffee. She watched Jim munch on a piece of toast as he scanned the newspaper. "He invited everyone to a prayer meeting at his church in Detroit. Maybe we could go sometime."

Jim didn't look up. "How about next week?"

Judith nearly spilled her coffee. After so many years were her prayers about to be answered? Suppressing a smile, she rose to clear the dishes from the table. "Sounds good," she agreed.

The following week Jim and Judith stepped into the social hall at Gesu Catholic Church. Wooden folding chairs were arranged in circular rows around a young man who sat with a guitar in his lap. Several nuns and a couple of priests stood in the back of the room. Jim looked around somewhat furtively, his glance registering the realization that there would be nowhere to hide—there was not so much as a stray seat in the corner. Resigned, he seated himself in the circle, folding his arms across his chest. Judith slipped in next to him and watched as people filed into the room. There were college students, young marrieds, and even some older folks. Soon the room was full, and the air was charged with excitement as the guitarist strummed a few chords. As everyone stood Jim slipped his hands into his pockets. A young woman in the circle beat a tambourine on her hip and started to sing, and most of the group clapped in time to the music. Digging his hands deeper into his pockets, Jim edged a little closer to Judith.

After the third song the room grew quiet. Calm fell over the group as people hummed along softly before starting to sing *"We are one in the Spirit, we are one in the Lord. We are one in the Spirit, we are one in the Lord . . ."*

The woman on Jim's left felt for his hand, which he obligingly removed from his pocket, and held it firmly. Well outside of his comfort zone, Jim first glanced toward the door and then stared at the floor, waiting for the song to end. When his hand was free he turned to Judith and whispered in her ear. "You can stay if you want," he mouthed softly, "but as soon this next song is over I'm gone."

But the song didn't end. Instead it flowed into another melody, more upbeat and energetic, after which people broke into spontaneous worship that gave way to one long, continuous string of choruses. There was neither direction nor accompaniment when the exhalations of "Praise you Jesus!" and "We love you, Lord!" began filling the room. Even though no melody was introduced, the congregation seemed to know what to sing. Jim looked over at Judith, whose hands were raised in the air and whose eyes were closed. Dropping low in his seat, he simply listened. Jim listened . . . and was taken aback by his own reaction, because it sounded to him as though the space were filled with angels. More than an hour passed before the room finally fell silent and everyone sat down.

A young man rose to speak, and Jim forgot all about leaving. The man admitted to being an alcoholic, to cheating on his wife and leaving her alone with two small children. Jim shifted in his chair: this all sounded a little too familiar.

"Then I met Jesus," the speaker went on. "Everything changed after that. I gave up alcohol and moved back in with my family. I've been sober for more than a year now, and I just got a new job." His wife walked up to where he stood to give him a spontaneous hug, and everyone clapped.

Jim, longing for proof that his own life could be turned around, wanted to hear more. He was all too painfully aware that something was missing. Everyone in the room seemed to have figured out how to get close to God—everyone, it appeared, except him. He needed help.

The ride home was quiet. Judith prayed silently, while Jim wrestled with his thoughts. When they pulled into the garage Judith slipped into the house, leaving him alone outside. Jim sat down on the back porch and lit a cigarette. After several minutes he tossed the butt to the ground and snuffed it out with his shoe. Glancing around the yard for the unlikely possibility of an audience, Jim shrugged his shoulders, zipped up his jacket, and knelt in the grass to pray. "Jesus," he began, "I don't really know how to do this, but I'm asking you to come into my life like you did with Judith. I need you to do the same thing for me that you did for all those people tonight. I need a new life, God, and I'm asking you to forgive me for everything I've done."

He opened his eyes and gazed upward, transfixed, at the star-studded sky. A tear escaped his eye and zigzagged down his cheek, which he dabbed at with his sleeve. "Amen," he whispered. Jim took a deep breath before entering the house.

CHAPTER 19

The Psychedelic Nun

"**H**ey, Franko!" Jim poked his head around the corner of Frank's booth with a grin. "What's happening, man?"

"Not much, JJ," Frank replied. He took a puff from his cigarette and blew a stream of smoke at the ceiling. "What's up with you?"

"Got saved last night, man. Gave my life to Jesus."

"Aw, don't gimme that!" Frank moaned. "*You're* not gonna turn into a Jesus Freak, are ya?"

"No, man, this is for real. I met Jesus last night. Judith took me to a prayer meeting, and when we got home I knelt down in the yard all by myself. No priest, no confessional. Just me and God."

Frank reached for an ashtray and snuffed out his cigarette. "That's cool, JJ," he responded noncommittally, patting his friend on the shoulder. "I'm glad for ya. We're cool." On that note he turned and walked away.

"How about coming to the meeting with me next week?"

"Nah." Frank waved him off as he headed out the door. "It's cool for you, bro, but I'm not interested."

Jim nodded as Frank walked away. *All in good time, Franko.*

A week later Jim and Frank walked over to Kresge—a dime store situated at the west end of Tech Plaza—for lunch. Jim sat down on one of the swivel stools and motioned for Frank to join him. "C'mon," he beckoned. "We need to talk."

Frank sat down, ordered a Coke, and took a sip. "Okay, what's up?"

"I'm not here to talk to you about *religion*, man . . . ," Jim began.

Frank shook his head, chuckled, and exaggerated an eye roll. *Here we go . . .*

"What I wanna talk to you about is *Jesus Christ*—about having a personal relationship with Him."

"Mmm-hmm."

"I know what you're doing, Frank."

"What's that?"

"Shutting me down. You don't want to hear what I've got to say."

"C'mon, JJ. You know I'm listening. I'm just not into it."

"Well, you know I'm not turning into a holy roller—you know me better than that. All I'm asking is that you come with me to one meeting. That's it."

"Why?" Frank, riled now, flashed him an angry look. "What's the big deal? I told you, I'm not into it. Just drop it."

"I can't drop it, Frank." Jim bumped his hand softly on the counter. "I see the same thing happening with you as with me. Booze, drugs—they're going to destroy you."

"I'm not like you, JJ."

"Look, I'm telling it like it is. You know what I was like. Judith and I were ready to split. I'd come home every night, lipstick all over my shirt, and she'd still forgive me. That drove me nuts, man. She took away my whole reason for doing what I did. It was her love that drew me to the Lord, though—the love of God coming by way of my wife. Then, after she got filled with the Holy Spirit, things really started to change. She won me over, Frank. Loved me even though I didn't deserve it. That's what got to me."

Frank, his mouth set in a hard line, stared out the window. For the past week Jim had been harassing him daily about the prayer meeting. He couldn't take much more. "All right, JJ," he consented with a sigh. "I'll go this one time. After that you drop it, okay?"

"Okay, okay." Jim raised his hands in concession. "That's cool. Just check it out—that's all I ask."

Jim and Judith pulled in front of Frank's apartment, and Jim honked the horn. Frank—in the kitchen taking a hit of LSD—pulled on a Harley Davidson vest, grabbed a pack of cigarettes, and headed out the door. Jim watched Frank climb into the back seat and then glanced over at Judith. Both launched instinctively into silent prayer.

The meeting had already begun when they arrived. Frank's boots clicked on the tile floor as he walked across the room. Sister Angela, her interest piqued by the unaccustomed sound, glanced up momentarily and took in the bearded face, tight blue jeans, and black leather vest. Frank's arms were covered in tattoos, and a thin hoop earring hung from his left ear. As he pulled out a chair and sat down, Frank glanced around the group, his eye catching Sister Angela's. She nodded and gave him a smile.

When the music started, everyone rose to their feet and began clapping in synch with the music.

> *My glory and the lifter of my head,*
> *My glory and the lifter of my head . . .*

The unison voices echoed loudly across the room.

> *For thou, O Lord, art a shield for me,*
> *My glory and the lifter of my head.*

Sister Angela raised her own hands in the air and sang lustily, all the while continuing to smile.

That nun looks high! Frank thought to himself, adding with a start as a strange notion occurred to him: *Everybody in this room looks high.*

When the song ended everyone remained standing. Some kept their hands in the air and continued to sing, but in a language that Frank didn't recognize. He sat down to listen: this wasn't just an unfamiliar language, the sound was otherworldly. Leaning over, he whispered to Jim, as though his friend might not have noticed, "This don't sound like English to me, man."

Jim shrugged. He had grown accustomed to hearing people singing in tongues—he even joined in once in a while. Shaking his head, Frank leaned back in his seat. The LSD had kicked in, so he figured most of what he was seeing was part of the trip.

A priest stood up and began to read from the Bible. Frank couldn't focus on the words, so he closed his eyes and waited for the meeting to end.

Afterward Judith introduced him to Sister Angela. She took his hand and shook it firmly, gazing deeply into his eyes. "I'm glad you came tonight, Frank." Her voice was sincere.

"Yeah, well, I was watching you the whole time, Sister," Frank told her. "And you looked sorta high to me. Like a psychedelic nun!"

They both laughed, and Sister Angela assured Frank that she wasn't high—at least not on drugs. She invited him back for the next meeting and then kept him in sight as he left with Jim and Judith. She hoped she would see him again.

Frank had never before met anyone quite like Sister Angela. *That is no ordinary nun,* he reflected as they drove home. He couldn't put his finger on the difference, but this captivating young woman wasn't anything like the nuns he had grown up with. This one smiled all the time, and her eyes danced when she spoke. It was easy to get the impression she was high the way she walked around the room hugging everyone.

It was Frank who broke the silence. "I gotta say," he announced, "that was a pretty cool bunch of people. Those nuns weren't wearing regular habits, and the priests looked all right too." Judith smiled at Jim. "But I didn't go for any of that singing—or that jive talkin' either. Too weird for me, man."

When they arrived home Frank made a point of verifying that he wasn't expected to attend any more meetings. "We're square now, right, JJ? I told you I'd go this one time, so that's it."

The next week, though, Jim asked Frank to come along to another gathering, this one in Lansing. Frank cringed. "Lansing? I don't *think so,* man."

Jim put his arm around Frank's shoulder. "C'mon," he encouraged. "You'll dig it."

Frank felt cornered. Jim was his boss, and he needed the job, but prayer meetings had never been part of the deal. He didn't like the changes he was seeing in Jim. His friend was sober every day now and had stopped frequenting bars altogether. And all he ever talked about was God. It was getting on Frank's nerves. He knew that if he agreed to go to Lansing it would only make matters worse. Jim would never stop inviting him from that point on. He also knew that if he didn't go he'd feel like a chump. Jim had practically laid a career in his lap, and Frank owed him something for that.

If it'll make him happy to drag me to another meeting, I'll go, he decided. *But this is the last time. And if I go, I'm going stoned.* Frank knew he could handle anything as long as he was stoned.

This time, when Jim and Judith pulled up in front of his apartment, Frank hopped into the back seat with enthusiasm and patted Jim on the back. "Let's go, brother!" he trilled. "Time to praise the Lord!"

Jim glanced into the rearview mirror. He could tell Frank was high. "What's happening, Franko?"

"Not much, JJ—not much. Hey, how 'bout some *music*?" Judith turned on the radio to "Spinning Wheel" by Blood, Sweat and Tears. Frank laid his head back to listen.

Two hours later they were in Lansing, lost in a sea of happy faces. Thousands of people, from a variety of denominations and traditions, had gathered for the ecumenical event. On stage a group of musicians tuned up their guitars. When they started to play the crowd rose as one. Frank felt sure that he knew the routine: sing for an hour, praise a while, then people start speaking in tongues. *Here we go!* he thought, feeling ready for takeoff. This time, though, the program opened with teachings on the Holy Spirit, after which people gathered in small groups to pray. Frank sat off by himself, waiting for it all to end.

Before he realized what had happened, though, Sister Angela had slipped quietly into the seat beside him. "I'm praying for you, Frank," she intoned softly. "—praying that you'll meet the Lord."

Concealing his surprise, Frank patted the nun's hand almost condescendingly and laughed. "I appreciate that, Sister. You just keep on prayin'."

Several other people took a turn sitting next to Frank. Pleased with the developing pattern, Jim urged everyone he saw to speak with his friend. "Try to get through as best you can," he urged them. "He might be stoned, but he's still listening."

One man described to Frank how God had changed his life. Frank heard the words, all right, but the acid made it hard to concentrate. Driving back to Detroit that night, though, Frank started to sober up, and Jim took advantage of the opportunity to tell his captive audience yet again about Jesus—his life, death, and resurrection.

Frank gazed out the window, pensive. "There were a lot of nice people there tonight, JJ," he remarked. "Everyone seemed to care. Sister Angela said she was praying for me. I must be one tough nut to crack, man, for a nun to keep praying like that. How come they don't just give up?"

"God isn't giving up on you, Frank, so neither are we." Jim ended the conversation there. If the Holy Spirit was at work in Frank's heart, he didn't want to get in the way. It was growing late, and everyone was tired. The rest of the ride home was quiet.

Sam sat rigidly on the edge of a bed, a .32 caliber pistol in his hand. *Through the head*, he told himself, raising the gun to his temple, *or through the mouth. Either way, there's no turning back once I pull the trigger.*

He dropped the gun into his lap then and fingered the cold blue barrel. *But what if Jim's right? What if there really is a God?* Placing the pistol on the nightstand, he sighed. *Then I'm a loser again . . . on the other side.* Sam Spano had known Jim for most of his life. They had grown up in the same neighborhood and hung out with the same people. Jim was like a brother to Sam.

"God," he sobbed with his head in his hands, "If you're real—if you're there—you know what I'm about to do. *You gotta help me!*"

At precisely that moment the phone on the nightstand started to ring. Sam looked up, startled, and stared at it. *Is that you, God?* Who else could be calling him at a time like this? He sat stock still for several seconds before picking it up. "Hello?"

"Sam, are you all right?" It was Jim. "I had this urge to check on you, man. God told me to call you. What's going on?"

Sam started to tremble violently. "I was about to shoot myself in the head."

"No, you weren't. C'mon, what's happening?"

Pointing the pistol at the ceiling, Sam fired two shots. "I told you," he repeated, "I was about to take my life. *Now* do you believe me?"

"Okay." Jim spoke slowly. "Put the gun down and wait for me. I'm coming over to get you, okay? Don't do anything. I'll be right there."

A year earlier Jim and Judith had moved to the suburb of Troy, a 40-minute drive from Sam's apartment in Detroit. Sam had always lived in Detroit, and four years earlier he had opened a business at Six Mile and Woodward. It was a blind pig—a speakeasy for the purpose of selling hard liquor after the bars had closed. As long as the police department looked the other way—as long as they were willing to be "blind pigs"—his business was safe. Sam had felt secure; he'd even looked into the possibility of expanding to the southern end of Detroit. A surprise police raid, however, had left his apartment in shambles and his operation destroyed. Now he felt like a leper—no one wanted anything to do with him. Sam sat surrounded by broken furniture in his ransacked bedroom. Like a drowning man gasping for air, he loosened his collar and felt himself taking shallow, raspy breaths. His life played out like a newsreel in his mind as he thought of all the people he had hurt—of the people he'd loved. Sam's heart sinking under the weight of it all, he hung his head.

His hand was still resting on the .32 when the door burst open with Jim behind it; he hadn't bothered to knock. Gently he guided Sam's hand away from the pistol before leading the man slowly, like a docile child, through the apartment. Gathering in one arm a random handful of clothes, he steered his friend down to his car.

Judith was ready with a fresh pot of coffee. She hugged Sam tightly when he arrived and sat him down in a chair. Sam glanced at the Bible on the table and chuckled. He wasn't surprised—Jim and Judith were about to tag-team him. The three friends drank coffee and talked about God for several hours. When the sun began to rise Sam headed for the couch.

"He just needs somewhere to crash for a few days," Jim told Judith. "You know Sam. He's probably already got big plans brewing in his head."

The next day Jim told Sam he needed to think about finding a real job—not starting another speak-easy.

"I'll figure something out," Sam assured him, stuffing his clothes into a bag. "Thanks for saving my life, man. I'd be dead right now if it weren't for you."

The following week Jim stopped by Jade Lounge, Sam's favorite pool hall, to see how his friend was doing. Sam waved his cue stick in greeting before taking a shot. "Hey," he suggested casually as the eight ball slipped into a side pocket, "how about lending me twenty bucks?"

"I'm not giving you any more money," Jim stated emphatically. "You'll just use it for the devil's work."

Sam scowled. "You know, all that stuff you talk about—how concerned you are for my soul and all that—well, my soul ain't gonna make it if my body doesn't."

Jim didn't respond, so Sam tried a softer approach. "I'll tell you what," he suggested, his eyes smiling. "Here's the deal: we play a game of pool, and if I win, you give me twenty bucks. If you win, you tell me what I have to do. I'll do whatever you want."

Jim chuckled. "You got it. It's a deal. This is what I want, though: four days. One day a week for the next four weeks you come with me to the prayer meeting at Gesu's.

Readily agreeing, Sam racked up the balls. *I'll let him break*, he thought, *and then I'm gonna run 'em.*

Jim lined up his stick with the cue ball before lifting his eyes toward Sam. "I don't know who it is you think you're challenging, man, but it isn't me." His shot reverberated in the hall, and the balls scattered in all directions. The eight ball rolled toward the side pocket and dropped in. Jim laughed, reached into his pants pocket, and pulled out a twenty-dollar bill, handing it to Sam with a smile. "Even though I won, I'm still giving you this." He put on his jacket and pointed at Sam. "But I'm collecting on those four days, man. I'll be picking you up for the first meeting next week." Not waiting for a response, Jim turned and strode out.

Sam stuffed the twenty into his shirt, lit a cigarette, and racked up the balls for another game.

☞☜

Frank had never thought of himself as a serious user, so when he picked up a dime pack of heroin—his first—in Detroit he knew he had crossed a line. Tucking the pack into his shirt pocket, he made the drive home to his apartment. Everything was ready in his bedroom: a small electric burner, a spoon, a clean needle, and a tourniquet. Frank put on a Jimi Hendrix album before sitting down on the bed. A knock at the door gave him a start, breaking his rhythm. Dropping the packet onto the floor, he swore under his breath and hurried over to see who it was.

Frank let Jim in, then headed back to the bedroom to turn off the burner. But Jim spied the pack lying on the floor and reached down to pick it up. "What are you doing with this, Frank?" he asked, a stern edge to his voice. Striding purposefully over to the bathroom, he tossed the heroin into the toilet and flushed it. "You can't be doing that, man!"

"It's none of your business, JJ."

"It *is* my business. You're not shooting heroin if you wanna work for me. You're going back to Gesu's with me next week, and this time you're going straight."

Frank sat heavily on the couch and gazed down at his arm as though seeing it for the first time. He ran his finger absently over a large blue vein, thinking how close he had just come to shooting up, dropped his head into his hands, and heaved a ragged sigh. "H" was the only drug he hadn't yet tried, and mainlining was the preferred method. But he had never meant it to come to this. Frank looked over at Jim, the only real friend he had ever had. "I'm glad you stopped by, JJ," he admitted. "Thanks, man."

Jim sat down next to him. "You don't have to live like this, Frank," he pointed out. "God cares about you, and He's offering you a new start. Don't you think it's time to give the Lord a chance—see what He can do for you? What've you got to lose?"

"Not a thing," Frank replied. "What time's the meeting?"

1952, Little Flower Institute, Cape Breton Island, Nova Scotia. Frank and his brother, Chuck, lived for six years at an orphanage run by the Sisters of Saint Martha.

Adopted by the Majewskis in 1959, Chuck, eleven, and Frank, eight, started a new life in Detroit, Michigan.

Father Gibault Home for Boys, 1965. Fourteen-year-old Frank (center) endured tough discipline at the reform school in Terra Haute, Indiana.

1967. Sixteen-year-old Frank was arrested multiple times and sent to the Macomb County Youth Home in Mount Clemens, Michigan.

Jim and Judith Johnston, 1970. Jim took Frank under his wing, enrolled him in barber school, and then introduced him to Christ in 1969.

In 1968 Father Dale Melczek prayed over Frank in the hospital. In 1970 he opened the doors of Saint Sylvester Catholic Church, allowing hundreds of young people to attend Frank's Friday Night Meeting.

Sister Angela Hibbard played a pivotal role in Frank's conversion. In 1969 her prayers and persistence paid off when Frank surrendered his life to Christ. Sister Angela's bright smile and overflowing love for God inspired Frank to call her "the Psychedelic Nun."

"I was raised on the other side of the tracks, so to speak." Frank's message was the same whether he was preaching to a crowd or one-on-one with a customer at the barber shop.

Summer water baptisms took place in swimming pools or in one of the lakes at Stony Creek Park—a forty-minute drive north of Detroit.

More than 750 young people gathered each week in the social hall at Saint Sylvester Catholic Church in Warren, Michigan. They sang, prayed, and then sat spellbound as they listened to Frank's preaching.

Larry (MoJo) Wolf was Frank's loyal sidekick and "partner in crime" throughout their high school years. But when Frank introduced him to Christ in 1969, MoJo's life was dramatically changed.

Emil and Marge Cardamone graciously opened their home to dozens of teenagers, enabling Frank's meetings to continue.

As a college student Mike Cassady wanted no part of the Jesus Movement. But in 1970 he gave his life to Christ and became one of Frank's strongest supporters.

Randy Marcial, a despondent, heartbroken Vietnam vet, found salvation when he prayed in the sanctuary of Saint Sylvester Catholic Church. In 1970 he became Frank's preaching partner and helped lead hundreds of young people to faith in Christ.

When his family moved in 1968 from Southwest Detroit to the suburb of Sterling Heights, Alex Silva brought a little of the city along with him.

Alex gave his heart to Christ when he attended a Teen Challenge meeting in 1966. He recommitted his life when he was twenty and later became the pastor of Fisherman's Net Church.

In 1970 Joyce Todd read David Wilkerson's *The Cross and the Switchblade*, and her life was turned upside down. Gathering teens into the kingdom of God became her passion.

"So in walks this short, wiry, gray-haired little man," Joyce told her friends. Ed Maurer became the firebrand God used to launch the Todds' meetings in 1970.

Bruce Todd watched as dozens of young people committed their lives to Christ in his living room. He later became the associate pastor of Fisherman's Net Church.

In the spring of 1970, Bob Holt was a homeless, wandering hippie when he stumbled into a revival meeting in Sarasota, Florida. He gave his life to Christ and later moved to Michigan to help lead the Todds' prayer meetings.

In the early 1970s Frank and Randy visited high schools and colleges in order to share God's message of salvation with students.

Although the Friday Night Meetings ended in 1983, Frank's love for sharing the gospel never faded.

Frank's life continues to bear fruit more than forty years later as the Jesus People pass the torch of the testimony on to their children and their children's children.

CHAPTER 20

"If You're Real, Prove It"

October 17, 1969
Gesu Catholic Church, Detroit

Frank walked into Gesu's and looked around for Jim, finding him seated next to Sam, the tough Italian mobster he had met at the shop. Frank gave Jim a nod before slipping into a seat next to Sam. He was glad to be back at Gesu's. After that close call last week with heroin, Frank was ready to give God a try.

Sam had been attending the meetings for several weeks. After paying off his debt to Jim he still wanted to participate. Why not? He felt peace in his heart for the first time in his life. Sam looked over at Frank and recognized a mirror image of himself: hard, stubborn, and cold-hearted. He knew Frank was running from the Lord. If only he could know how freeing it is to surrender to Christ . . .

"What's going down?" Sam held out his hand, and Frank gave it a smack.

"Not much, man." Sam was easy to talk to and instantly put Frank at ease. He liked having him around.

Frank wasn't sure why, but he felt different tonight—not itching to bolt out the door as soon as the opportunity presented itself. When the music started he rose to his feet along with everyone else and began to sing. Jim glanced at Frank in surprise. Nothing seemed to bother his friend tonight—not the songs, the prayers, or the praise. And when people started to speak in tongues, Frank barely flinched.

After the meeting Sister Angela tapped Frank on the shoulder. "Why don't we go pray tonight?" she invited, nodding toward the empty classroom.

"What for?"

"You know what I'm talking about. Let's pray that the Lord will come into your life."

"Nah." Frank dismissed her with a wave of his hand, but there was no hint of real opposition in the gesture.

Sister Angela, keeping her hand on his shoulder, gazed into his eyes. "C'mon, Frank," she insisted. "Give it up."

Frank, knowing better than to argue with a nun, rose from his chair and followed her into the room. Several people had already gathered around two chairs. Following Sister Angela's gesture, Frank sat down in one and folded his arms. Sam strolled in and took the other seat, after which Sister Angela and the rest of the group formed tight circles around the men.

"So, what do we have to do?" Frank asked, trying to sound casual.

"All you have to do is repent of your sins," Sister Angela explained. "*And make it real!* Tell God you're sorry. Then ask Him to come into your life."

"All right," Sam announced agreeably, "I think I can do that." He closed his eyes and bowed his head.

"Okay," Frank consented. "Let's go."

Sister Angela, standing in front of Frank, lay her hand on his shoulder; others did the same, tightening the circle around him. Another group gathered around Sam and everyone began to pray. Outside in the hallway Jim knelt with several other people, imploring the Lord that his friends might receive the Holy Spirit.

The room resounded in prayer as those present called as one upon God. As Frank himself began to pray, an overpowering force—rising from the deepest recesses of his heart—seemed to break free and erupt inside his chest, spewing upward waves of rage and pain that had been buried for years. When the dam broke it burst like a floodgate, and tears streamed unchecked down Frank's cheeks. His body shook, and he sobbed raggedly, as though his heart would break.

Sam, after observing Frank for a long moment, shut his eyes again, only to realize with a start that he was having a vision of Jesus, hanging on the cross, blood pouring from his wounds. From behind closed eyelids he continued to study the vision as a gentle voice spoke to him: "As the blood runs down my body, so runs your sin. Go in peace." Sam too began to weep as an accumulation of foul waste, resulting from years of sinful living, was expelled from his heart.

Through his own tears Frank cried out to the Lord. "Jesus," he implored, "if you're really here, prove it to me. I'm doing what they said. I repent of my sins, and I'm askin' ya, if you're real, show me now. You know I'm doing it, Jesus . . . *This is it!*"

As Frank prayed the gathered crowd was astonished to witness him being tossed from his chair and then landing several feet away onto the floor. Transfixed, everyone stopped and stared. Just as startled to find himself lying on the ground, Frank began to laugh. He wasn't hurt; he was giddy. It was as if heaven and hell had just collided, and the force of the impact had launched Frank from his seat. Almost in comic relief, everyone else erupted in uproarious laughter as well; the room reverberated with it. Frank's tears had run their course; a celebration had begun.

Frank lay on the floor for several more minutes, allowing the cleansing laughter to wash away the sorrow and bitterness from his heart. He knew now for certain that Jesus is real—was so thoroughly persuaded of this in fact, that no one could have convinced him otherwise. No drug or alcohol had ever given him such an experience. He felt cleansed from his tarnished past—as fresh as a newborn baby.

"How did you end up down there?" Sam asked, mystified, after Frank had resumed a standing position.

Frank didn't have the answer. "You got me, man," he responded. "I was just sitting in the chair, and the next thing I know I'm on the floor."

At that moment, Sister Angela, in a clear, strong voice, caught the attention of all those present: "You will go forth as Isaiah," she declared, "and you will knock down many trees in the sight of the Lord."

Frank, no longer amused, glanced up in bewilderment. "What's that supposed to mean?" he asked, directing his gaze at the nun.

"I guess you'll have to find out," Sister Angela told him with a smile. She was as amazed as the rest of the group at what had just taken place. No one to her knowledge had ever been thrown from a chair at Gesu's. As she watched Frank exit the room, she had no doubt he would never be the same.

Frank, virtually brimming with new life, went about hugging everyone in the main hall. He had never before hugged a nun or a priest, but his joy could not be contained. It was contagious too. Everyone else at Gesu's began to embrace and to joyfully celebrate the goodness of God.

Jim rushed over to Frank. *"What happened in there?"* he asked, incredulous despite the fervency of his prayer. "I was praying for you out in the hall, that God would touch you so powerfully He'd knock you right out of your chair."

Frank stopped in his tracks and planted his gaze on Jim. *"Are you serious, JJ?"*

"Yeah, why?"

Frank draped his arm over his friend's shoulder. "Well, bro, that's heavy—'cuz that's exactly what just happened!"

CHAPTER 21

Knocking Down Trees

MoJo was stretched out on the couch taking long, slow drags from a joint. Blue bubbles floated like jellyfish inside the lava lamp near his head, and "Purple Haze" by Jimi Hendrix blared from the record player. His guitar lead was so loud the speakers rattled. MoJo leaned back his head and closed his eyes.

> *Purple haze all in my brain,*
> *Lately things just don't seem the same.*
> *Actin' funny, but I don't know why,*
> *'Scuse me while I kiss the sky.*[4]

The door flew open, and Frank burst in without a word, heading straight for his room. MoJo sat up. He could hear Frank in the bedroom, opening drawers and tossing things onto the floor.

"What's goin' on?" he called.

Frank didn't answer.

MoJo pulled himself off the couch and stumbled toward the bedroom, where pills and drug paraphernalia were being tossed into a pile on the floor. Leaning against the door jam, he brushed his hair from his eyes. "What're you doing, Frank?"

"S'cuse me, bro." Frank, all business, stepped around MoJo and headed for the bathroom with a handful of pills. Acid, uppers, and downers—he tossed them all into the toilet and flushed them down.

"Are you crazy?" MoJo yelled. "What are you doin' that for, man?"

"God saved me tonight, Moj," Frank told him. "I'm done doing drugs. I'm starting a new life."

MoJo grimaced. "Aw, *no!*" he countered, shaking his head. "Don't tell me that. You're not turnin' into a Jesus Freak . . ." He went back into the living room and threw himself sulkily onto the couch.

Frank followed him. "Look, bro, God knocked me outta my chair tonight. I can't just ignore that, can I?"

"But *not the dope!* You didn't need to flush the dope down the toilet."

"It's too late, Moj. I'm done with it. Don't want no part of it. No more."

MoJo slipped on his shoes and grabbed his keys. "I'm *outta* here!" he huffed. "I'll see *you* later." Glancing back through the open front door, he threw out a parting shot: "You're crazy, Frank."

Frank went back to flushing pills. Then he gathered pipes, needles, and his electric burner, tossed all of the paraphernalia into the garbage, and ripped down his collection of posters from the walls—pinups from his old life. When he was finished he hopped into his car and made the drive to Warren. Frank knew exactly where to find MoJo—crashing in his parents' basement, as usual. Pulling into the driveway of the small red-brick ranch, he let himself in. MoJo was smoking another joint and listening to Zappa on his record player. To get his attention Frank turned off the music and sat on the edge of the couch.

"Listen Moj," he began, "you gotta understand. This is for real. I'm not crazy, and I'm not making things up. Tonight I told Jesus to show me if he was real, and he did it, man. Knocked me right out of my chair. I'm not kidding, Moj, so don't tell me to shut up. You need to get down on your knees and repent like I did."

"You're nuts!"

"Just do it, Moj."

"Not me, man! Forget it."

Frank stood up. "All right, bro, I'm not gonna argue with you. Sooner or later you're gonna hafta give it up. That's what the psychedelic nun told me, and now I'm telling you. Think about it for a while, and I'll talk to ya later."

⌖

Jim set down a box full of pocket-sized New Testaments. "Here, Frank," he invited. "You can pass these out to your customers. Give one to MoJo too."

Frank set down the box in his head booth. When his first customer arrived he began to tell him about his conversion of the previous evening, describing how his life had been full of drugs and crime and how it had left him alone and miserable. Then he talked about the prayer meeting at Gesu's—how God had knocked him right out of his chair. "My mind got blown away by this psychedelic nun," he commented as he cut the young man's hair. "She told me all about Jesus, that He wanted to clean me up on the inside. All I had to do was ask God to forgive me. So I did it, man, right then and there."

"Aw, you don't believe any of that Jesus stuff, do ya?" his customer cut in with a cynical laugh.

"I do *now*, bro," Frank replied seriously. "I prayed, and the next thing I know the Holy Spirit tosses me right out of my chair. Threw me to the floor three feet away."

The client shook his head. He was used to hearing tall tales from Frank, but this one was the wildest.

"I'm tellin' ya the truth, man! God knocked me to the ground. Next thing you know I'm laughing my head off. Laughed so hard my sides almost split. It was like I was a little kid again. I couldn't stop. Then all of a sudden I start hugging everybody in the room. Now, bro . . ." Holding his scissors suspended in the air, Frank stepped around to face his client, "that's not something I normally do, you know what I mean? Nobody can say that's normal for me. God grabbed hold of me, man, and cleaned me up. I felt it in *here*, okay?" Frank tapped his chest. "On the inside, man. And now I don't need dope or booze. I'm living for the Lord now. I got a Bible right here if you want to take one."

Frank handed his client a Bible and asked whether he wanted to pray. "You need to live for Jesus, bro. And if you bring some of your friends back here to the shop, I'll give them a Bible too. It's free, man, just like God's forgiveness is free."

As word spread about Frank's sudden change, several regulars decided to stop by the barbershop to hear him speak. Every night that week, after the shop had closed, Frank shared his story with a captive audience sitting cross-legged on the floor. After each impromptu session everyone bowed to pray. Frank urged those in attendance to ask God for forgiveness in the same way he had. Next he prayed that God would touch each of them in a powerful way, and then sent each person home with a Bible.

Over the next several weeks Frank's story continued to hold his listeners' attention. He began to add details from his life: the crimes he'd committed, the drugs he'd experimented with, even the abuse he'd endured as a child. People sat spellbound on the floor. In each instance, by the time Frank was finished everyone wanted to pray. Bikers, dopers, and even gang members crammed into the barbershop each night to ask Christ into their hearts.

Frank never tired of telling his story. In fact, the more times he shared it the more convinced he became that God was calling him to preach. Frank wanted everyone to know that Jesus Christ had given His life for the world and that heaven is a free gift. "Just tell Him you're sorry for your sins," he directed, "and He'll give you a brand new start. God will wipe the slate clean."

Jim watched in amazement as young people continued to file into his barbershop each evening. Some who came by for a haircut ended up staying after to listen.

One night more than 30 individuals crammed the narrow shop, while others loitered outside. Junkers took up parking spaces intended for customers of Tech Plaza Shopping Center, and some of Jim's fellow retailers began to complain about the riff raff congregating in his shop. "Our customers are shying away," they complained, "because of all those kids in the parking lot. They're making people nervous."

Jim knew it was becoming a problem. "I own the business," he explained to Frank, "but I rent this space. The shop owners are getting uptight about all the hippies. People think we're running a drug house over here."

"What are we supposed to do, JJ?" Frank asked. "The kids keep coming. I can't turn away anyone that wants to hear about the Lord."

"Why don't we just do it one night a week instead of every night?" Jim suggested. "You keep talking while you cut hair, but tell everybody to come back on Friday if they want to hear more."

That sounded like a good plan to Frank. He spread the word about the meeting, then waited to see whether anyone would show up. That Friday more than 30 people arrived after hours at Plaza Barber Shop. They squeezed through the door and sat shoulder-to-shoulder on the floor. By the time the meeting was over many had given their lives to Christ.

"You're not gonna believe this . . ." began Mark, the bass player from Mike Cassady's rock band.

"What?" Mike asked.

"Frank Majewski found religion."

Mike laughed. "Yeah, *right* . . ."

"I'm serious. You gotta check it out. He preaches at the barbershop every Friday night."

Like many of his friends, Mike was a regular customer at the shop. But this was the first he'd heard of Frank's conversion. He decided to stop by to check it out.

Familiar faces greeted Mike at the door. Friends from high school and Macomb College were sitting in barber chairs, waiting for the meeting to begin. Mike found a spot against the wall and eased himself down to the floor.

Without introduction Frank launched into his message. "I gotta tell you guys," he began, "my mind got blown the other night by a magic nun." He pointed over to Jim, who sat near the door guarding the cash register. "And that dude there, he blew my mind too. He took me down to this place in Detroit called Gesu's."

Frank went on with the story, his "testimony," as people were now calling it. Though he listened with interest, Mike had no desire to get caught up in the Jesus Movement. Too many of his friends had turned religious, and he wanted no part of it. *I don't know if I believe what Frank's saying,* he thought, *but one thing's for sure — the guy has definitely changed."* There could be no denying it: Frank was a different person from the angry punk Mike had tried to avoid in school.

Matt, another friend from Cousino, sat next to Mike on the floor and nodded his head in agreement as Frank spoke. Matt was a lady's man, a good-looking guy with long, dark hair that hung past his shoulders. He was the life of the party too—always had some dope to share. But word had it that after Matt had heard Frank last week he had prayed with the rest of the crowd and given his heart to Christ.

When the meeting was over Mike invited a few friends to Peppy's to drink Cokes in the parking lot and listen to some music on his new speakers. Several teens hopped into his car.

The back passenger door swung open, and Matt climbed inside. "Hey, man," he blurted, addressing the entire carful, "What'd you guys think of the meeting? Are you going again next week?"

Mike cringed. He liked Matt but wished he would get out of his car. "Actually, no, *I'm* not," he responded, glad to have an excuse: "I'm leaving for Europe next week."

"You should give your life to Jesus before you go, Mike. Quit messing around."

"Listen, Matt." Mike was struggling to remain calm. "I'm not into that stuff, okay? I'm glad you guys found what you were looking for, but it isn't for me."

Climbing back out of the car, Matt leaned in for one last try. "Just come one more time, okay? Just once more before you take off."

"I'll . . . see what I can do," Mike replied noncommittally, waving him off. He had steered clear of Frank in middle school and later in high school, and still wanted nothing to do with the guy—especially now that he'd turned preacher.

In January of 1970 the barbershop meetings were still going strong. Every Friday night the place overflowed with young people. Jim faced a dilemma: they were running out of space. To top it off, motorcycle clubs were roaring in from Detroit. Word of Frank's conversion had hit the streets. His life as a fighter had long since earned him the respect of the bikers, who now made the trip to Warren in packs to check out for themselves the situation with Frank. One night a surly looking bunch pushed through the crowd and stood against the back wall with folded arms. Jim didn't want trouble; now he wondered whether Frank's past was about to catch up with him.

The bikers listened impassively as Frank spoke. His voice boomed across the room and even out the front door that had been propped open to let in some air. An overflow crowd had settled on the curb and peered in through the window as Frank preached. When the meeting ended several of the bikers bowed their heads to pray.

Sitting among the crowd, unnoticed, was Pastor Dick Bieber from Messiah Church in Detroit. Dick, who had heard the stories about a young, tough biker who was preaching to teens in a barbershop, wanted to see for himself. He got there early enough to find a spot on the floor, and soon was scooting to the back to make way for dozens of teenagers as they filled the room. By the time Frank stood up to read from the Bible, no one was paying attention to the young pastor seated in the corner. That night Dick Bieber went home with a renewed vision for his own church. On Sunday he invited his congregation to receive Christ at the altar. The aisles were jammed with parishioners making their way to the front. Pastor Bieber bowed his head in gratitude for a visitation from God.

Pastor Jim Beall was another barbershop visitor. As the eldest son of Myrtle "Mom" Beall and assistant pastor of Bethesda Christian Church, Jim had heard all about Frank's conversion. Several teenagers from his congregation who attended the meetings had stopped using drugs. It was hard for Jim to believe that a drug dealer like Frank could be called to evangelize. *No one just opens up the Bible and leads people to repent,* he reasoned. *It doesn't work that way. And why would God use a barbershop instead of the church?*

But as Jim listened to Frank speak the answer became obvious. No doubt Frank's handling of the Word of God was unschooled, and his preaching was coarse, but the results were undeniable. Frank, filled with the power of the Holy Spirit, was turning the neighborhood upside down. *You can't argue with results,* Jim decided.

When the meeting was over Pastor Beall made his way to the front to shake Frank's hand. "These young people need to be baptized," he remarked, going on to offer the use of Bethesda's baptismal. He also offered to teach Frank the fundamentals of the faith and went home that night marveling at the unforeseen turn of events.

Frank took the pastor up on his offer to study Scriptures together. Now that he was preaching once a week he wanted to know everything the Bible had to say. Jim Beall helped Frank gain a fuller understanding of the implications of Christ's death and resurrection. Now, each morning before work, Frank would read his Bible. At lunchtime he would read it some more. And he was still pouring over it late at night. He was hungry for understanding and yearned for an intimate relationship with Jesus. At times the words he read seemed to hit Frank between the eyes, while in other instances he found it necessary to mull over a passage for days. Pastor Beall explained that when that happened the Holy Spirit was illuminating His Word. Frank was beginning to learn how to listen to what God was saying.

"Unless a man is born again," he read from John 3:3, "he cannot see the kingdom of God." Frank paused to take that in. *He's talking about me,* he recognized. *I'm the one that couldn't see. I needed to be born again.* Sitting back pensively, he stroked his beard. He had never thought about this before, but he wondered now why no one had ever bothered to tell him about Jesus before. The nuns, the priests, his parents—did all of them know what the Bible said? The only time Frank had heard the Lord's name at home was when his parents had cursed.

Everything was starting to make sense. All of the anger, bitterness, and violence in his life seemed to have led up to this defining moment. *I just didn't understand it*, Frank marveled. *When Jesus hung on the cross, he was dying for me. I needed to repent for all the bad things I did, but I didn't know it.* Frank remembered praying after he'd been shot. Although he had hardly known what to say, he realized now that God had been listening. Now, after years of running from Him, Frank realized he was getting a second chance. At Gesu's, Sister Angela had announced that he would be knocking down trees for the Lord. Even that was starting to make sense.

The next evening Frank drove over to Peppy's with a bagful of Bibles in his backseat. In the past customers had known him as the dealer who peddled drugs from car to car. Now he carried a sack of Bibles and handed out tracts instead. Reaction varied: some spit in his face, while others rolled up their windows and drove away. No one had ever told Frank that knocking down trees would be easy, but those who took the time to talk to him were introduced to Jesus Christ.

∞∞∞

MoJo didn't think Frank's conversion would last. *"He'll be back selling dope on the street in two weeks,* he thought smugly—and told Frank so the next time he saw him.

"MoJo, you just don't get it." Frank shook his head. "This is for real. I gave the Lord my life, and I'm not taking it back. You got any idea what 'repent' means? It means you change your mind, change the way you're headin'. I got a new life now, Moj, and I'm not going back to the old one."

"Okay, Franko," MoJo shrugged. "That's cool. But it still isn't for me."

Frank sat down next to his friend and looked him straight in the eye. "Look, man," he begged him, "just bow your head right now, okay? I'm gonna pray, and I'm not taking no for an answer."

In his heart of hearts MoJo wanted what Frank had. He was just afraid that it wouldn't work for him. "So what if we pray and nothing happens?" he asked skeptically. "I'm not like you, Frank."

"Don't worry about it. All that'll happen is Jesus is gonna come into your life."

MoJo complied, bowed his head, and Frank prayed. Afterward he glanced up and looked around. "I told you, Frank. Nothin' happened."

"Look, man." Frank had developed patience. "You just need to come with me to the meeting at Gesu's, okay? You gotta get filled with the Holy Spirit—that's all."

"If I go, you gotta tell me what to do."

"You don't do *nothin'!*" Frank explained. "Just pray, that's all. And then you keep praying till all of a sudden you'll feel this electricity go through your body. You might see a blinding light or get thrown on the floor like I did . . ."

"Okay, bro," MoJo agreed, "that sounds cool. I'm into blinding lights."

The next week the pair drove to Gesu's and settled within the circle of chairs. After the meeting Frank introduced MoJo to Sister Angela, who gathered a small group of people around him to pray.

"All right, Moj," Frank announced. "This is it—your turn to get zapped."

MoJo bowed his head as Sister Angela started to pray. Others joined in by placing their hands on his shoulder and lifting their voices to God. Frank waited for something dramatic to happen. But when the prayer ended MoJo simply lifted his head, looked around, and smiled. He rose from his chair and exited the room with Frank. Frank was disappointed, but MoJo understood that something deep inside had changed.

〜

Emil and Marge Cardamone were starting to worry. Their teenaged son was using drugs; they were sure of it. Every Saturday Chuck would slip into the house before dawn, crawl into bed, and then spend the next day sleeping off whatever he'd been into the night before.

Emil took a sip of coffee and glanced over at his wife as she stood near the kitchen window. Marge was staring into the backyard, recalling happier times when the kids were young. "Chuck was out late again last night," she commented without turning around. "I'm worried about him."

"God only knows what he's doing every weekend," Emil sighed, and then wished he hadn't said it.

"Something's got to change, Emil, or he's going to get hurt."

Emil took another swallow. "I wish I knew the answer."

Marge sat down and pulled her housecoat close. Worry lines creased her forehead. "Chuck told me about a prayer meeting at the barbershop. He said Frank Majewski had some kind of religious experience, and now he's preaching. I told him he should go. Maybe it'll help."

Emil had been a regular customer at Plaza Barber for years. Jim had told him about Frank's conversion, but he had shrugged it off. As the city attorney for Warren, Emil was quite familiar with Frank Majewski's police record—in his opinion it would take more than a prayer meeting to change a guy like him. But according to Jim kids were giving up their drugs and turning over their lives to Christ every time Frank spoke. Maybe Marge's suggestion would help their son.

The following Friday night Chuck headed for the barbershop. Several of his friends from high school were there, and he found a seat on the floor. After a few songs Frank started to preach. He talked about his past life, the life he no longer lived. It was obvious to Chuck that Frank wasn't the same person he had been in school. Something had happened to change him, and Chuck wasn't leaving till he knew what it was.

Frank opened a Bible and read something from the Gospel of John. The words rang true in Chuck's heart: *"For God so loved the world that He gave His only begotten Son, that whoever believes in Him should not perish, but have eternal life"* (John 3:16).

When it was time to pray Chuck bowed his head. He had drifted far from God—and knew it. Frank offered to pray with anyone who was interested, and Chuck raised his hand. At Frank's prompting he closed his eyes and asked God to forgive him for messing up his life. He wanted a new start. Peace flooded his heart as Chuck continued to pray. Finally he lifted his eyes and looked around the room. Everything looked the same on the outside, but inside he felt brand new.

CHAPTER 22

No Room at the Inn

"NO MORE MEETINGS AT THE BARBERSHOP
Signed, the Management"

Jim tore the note from the door and stepped inside his shop. He should have seen this coming. Last Friday night nearly 50 kids had shown up for the prayer meeting. Even one night a week is bad for business, the manager had told him. Jim understood but didn't know what to do about it. Where should they go? Stymied, he dropped immediately into a chair and bowed his head. "Lord," he prayed, "if you want these meetings to continue, we need your help."

There was no doubt in his mind that God was up to something. It was as though someone had flicked on a switch and turned Frank loose. Whenever he preached, Frank's voice thundered and his eyes flashed. And when he relayed God's offer of forgiveness people gave their hearts to Christ. Then they kept coming back, week after week. Jim understood that an anointing from the Lord had fallen upon Frank.

The message he delivered each Friday night was simple: Jesus died on the cross for your sins, rose from the dead, and now offers you the free gift of eternal life. One thing Jim knew for sure: if the message had been any more complicated Frank could not have been chosen as the messenger. He only had one style of preaching—blunt and to the point. No one ever left his meeting confused about the choice they needed to make. Frank made sure the road to salvation was easy to find.

Jim looked down at the crumpled piece of paper in his hand. He didn't want the prayer meetings to end just because there was nowhere to meet. They had to find another place.

Frank offered to visit some churches in the area to see whether any might be willing to take them in, but he trudged back into the barbershop one afternoon downcast and discouraged. "Everywhere I went, JJ, all I heard was 'No way.' I went to three different churches, but none of them were interested. It comes down to this: there's no room at the inn."

St. Sylvester Church was a hub of activity for thousands of Catholics living in the Twelve Mile and Hoover area in Warren. Father Dale Melczek had joined St. Sylvester back in 1964 as co-pastor, along with Father Bob Bretz. He also served as the chaplain at South Macomb Hospital and had never forgotten the time he had encountered Frank lying on a gurney with a bullet in his head.

Frank walked into the rectory and pulled off his hat. A statue of Christ stood on a pedestal near the door, and a portrait of Pope Paul hung on the wall behind the reception desk. Frank looked into the eyes of the pontiff. He hadn't been to church in years and hoped that wouldn't count against him. *If the nuns at Little Flower could see me now . . .* he chuckled, *they'd never believe it.* The door swung open, and Father Melczek welcomed Frank into his office.

"Father—." Frank dove right into the reason for his visit. "I don't know if you remember me, but a few years back I was in pretty bad shape. You met me in the hospital just as they were wheeling me down to surgery."

"I never forgot it." The priest pointed to a chair. "Have a seat, Frank."

"You know, I did pray that night after they took me down the hall. I was sorry for what I did, but I'll be honest with ya, Father—once I got outta there I went back to my old ways."

The priest nodded.

"After that I got into even more trouble. Started doing drugs, and everything that comes with that. I knew I was messing up pretty bad, but I didn't know how to stop. Then my buddy JJ and his wife took me to a prayer meeting down at Gesu's in Detroit. Maybe you heard about them meetings before . . ."

He had.

"Anyway, this nun, Sister Angela, prays over me and asks God to fill me with the Holy Spirit. The next thing I know I'm on the floor, laughing. It was like God's Spirit grabbed hold of me and knocked me out of my chair. I was totally changed after that. Everything looked different to me. I started hugging people and could hardly wait for the next meeting. The next day I go to work at my barbershop at Tech Plaza, and I'm telling all my customers that Jesus Christ changed my life. Before I know it, Father, I got 30 kids coming by every night to hear me talk about the Lord. Most of them gave their hearts to Him, and now they're bringing their friends."

"I did hear about those meetings . . . ," Father Melczek acknowledged.

"I never planned any of this, Father. All of a sudden I've got people coming by and nowhere to put 'em. The manager at Tech Plaza is kicking us out. He don't like the crowd—too many hippies, I guess. So I asked a bunch of churches around here to let us in, but they all turned me down. So that's why I'm talking to you. I need somewhere to hold these meetings and thought maybe you could help. You know, after praying for me and all . . ."

Father Melczek replied that this wasn't something he could decide on his own; he'd need to talk to Father Bretz. A smile played over his lips, though, as he envisioned a roomful of hippies gathered at his church. The Charismatic Renewal was sweeping the nation, and he had to consider the possibility that the Holy Spirit was asking him to welcome this group. "I'll talk it over with Father Bretz," he promised, "and let you know if we can help. We may be able to find a room for you at the convent, but I'll have to check."

"Anything you can do would mean a lot to us, Father," Frank finished as he rose to leave.

Father Melczek shook his hand. "It's obvious things have changed since the last time we saw each other, Frank. I'll see what I can do. One way or another, we won't shut the door in your face."

Frank left the rectory and headed straight for the barbershop. He could hardly wait to tell Jim the news. "So Father says, 'There's no way I'm slamming the door in your face, man,'" Frank explained. "He says, 'the last time I saw you, you were pretty messed up. And after what I'm hearing now, there'll be a place for you here.' But check this out, JJ, we might be meeting in the *convent!*"

Jim laughed. Circumstances were coming full circle for Frank. Raised by nuns at an orphanage, battling with nuns all through school, Sister Angela praying over him at Gesu's—and now about to hold prayer meetings in a convent. *Unbelievable,* Jim thought, . . . *just like everything about Frank's life — unbelievable!*

⊂⊟⊃

Jim taped a note to the barbershop door announcing that the meetings had been moved to St. Sylvester Church. Heading over to the convent, he doubted many would show up this first night. By 7:00, however, more than 50 teenagers sat expectantly in the nuns' basement as Frank began to speak.

Father Melczek stood in the back, watching the scene unfold. The room had already been filled with high school and junior high kids when some hippies and bikers began to arrive as well. All were well behaved; Frank seemed to be in control of the crowd. Still, Father Melczek felt responsible for the gathering and kept a close eye on the proceedings. He had assured Father Bretz that the meeting would be well supervised.

Within a few weeks the group had outgrown the convent basement, so the meeting was moved to the cafeteria—only to outgrow that space in a short time as well. Father Melczek was beginning to wonder just how large this gathering might become.

Chuck Cardamone never missed one of Frank's prayer meetings. He had stopped going to parties, given up drinking, and was no longer taking drugs. When the meetings had moved to St. Sylvester's, Chuck had come along. His parents were thrilled to see the change in their teenaged son.

One day Chuck asked his father whether the prayer meeting could be moved to their basement. The convent was too small, he pointed out, and Frank needed more room.

Emil laughed aloud as he envisioned Warren's city attorney holding meetings for drug addicts and bikers in his home. The finished basement of the Cardamone's was big enough to accommodate a group of 50— maybe 60 at the most. Chuck assured his father that it was a temporary move until a larger space could be found. Despite some misgivings on this point, Emil agreed, feeling certain that his neighbors would approve of any gathering intended to help turn young people away from drugs.

The following week a stream of teens and young adults descended from a motley assortment of vehicles parked up and down several of the streets in the area and congregated at the Cardamones' front door. They wound their way through the living room and the adjacent kitchen all the way down the basement stairs. Marge, serving punch and cookies in the kitchen as they passed, greeted each as she would have her own son or daughter. Emil worked feverishly in the basement, continuing to set up more and more wooden folding chairs donated by his friend Don Temrowski, the owner of a funeral home in Warren.

When the meeting was about to begin Marge seated herself on a basement step to observe the goings-on. Trading locations with his wife, Emil stayed upstairs in the living room to keep an eye on the door. By 7:00, the basement was filled with young people. The Cardamones could feel the presence of God in their home and listened in amazement as Frank began to preach.

The next morning Emil entered the kitchen for a cup of coffee, only to spot through the sliders a teenager fast asleep on the patio. Opening the door, he called out to the boy. "Why did you sleep out there? You could have slept on the couch. Come on inside, and I'll make you some breakfast."

The meetings continued for months with a coarse, tribal feel to the gatherings. Frank didn't have a map to follow, so he navigated his way through every challenge as best he could. He was still a scriptural novice, and untrained in public speaking, but his heart burned with zeal for the Lord.

At one meeting a young man stood up to share. "I was at this party the other night," he began, "and I was reading my Bible. All of sudden somebody lit up a joint and started passing it around. I didn't know if I should take it or not, so I flipped open my Bible, and it opened right to this verse that said *"a sweet smelling aroma unto the Lord . . ."* So I figured *What the heck?* and took a hit." The kid sat down and grinned a little sheepishly, while several people nodded and said *Amen.*

Next, a young girl raised her hand. "The Spirit of the Lord came over me in English class yesterday. I started speaking in tongues, and the teacher told me to stop. But I couldn't, so she kicked me out of class and sent me down to the principal's office. When I got there I kept speaking in tongues and the principal got mad at me. *It was heavy persecution!"*

"Amen," several others called out. "Praise the Lord!"

Frank stood up. "Okay, everybody quiet down for a minute," he cut in. "Let's get something straight, all right? First of all, there's no verse in the Bible telling you it's okay to smoke dope, man." He glanced at the boy. "I'm sorry, bro, but it isn't in there. You have to give up your pot if you want to follow Jesus Christ. And you probably need to stop going to them parties too."

The room became quiet.

"And another thing . . . ," Frank continued. "That's cool, sister, that the Holy Spirit gave you the gift of tongues. It's a great gift, and you should use it. But you know, there's a time and a place—am I right? All's I'm saying is that English class may not be the time *or* the place for using that gift. My suggestion to you is this: go to school, and when you're in school just do your work, okay? Don't go blowing the teacher's mind by speaking in tongues or anything like that. I mean, she's over there trying to teach English, and you walk in speaking some foreign language. That's not cool."

Everyone tittered. With that Frank reached for his Bible and opened it to the Gospel of John. "Okay," he directed in a tone commanding respect, "now quiet down. Let's pull it together here and figure out where we left off last week."

CHAPTER 23

Under the Stars

Spring, 1970

Jim lit a cigarette and took a stroll over to the field behind Warren City Hall. Two abandoned farmhouses stood near the back of the lot. Other than that, the parcel was empty. His gaze panning the wide-open space, Jim nodded. *Plenty of room to stretch out,* he noted, *and to grow. With the weather turning warm this just might work.*

After outgrowing the Cardamone's basement, Jim had secured a permit from the City of Warren and spread the word that, starting next week, Frank's meeting would be moving outside. By the time everyone had convened at the field, the group looked more like a Woodstock gathering than a prayer meeting. Throngs of hippies milling around, music, and singing—it was all there, but without the drugs. Matt and another young man, Gerhardt, strummed their guitars as more than a hundred young people spread blankets and settled onto the ground. When the music began everyone jumped to their feet and broke into lusty singing:

> *"There's a river of life flowing out through me*
> *Makes the lame to walk and the blind to see*
> *Opens prison doors, sets the captives free*
> *There's a river of life flowing out through me . . ."*

As the numbers continued to swell, the singing grew louder and stronger. People held hands and swayed. More songs followed—upbeat, hand-clapping tunes that set many to dancing. An hour later Matt asked those assembled to take a seat while Frank made his way to the front. Several motorcyclists, pulling up just then, parked their bikes near a curb in the back.

Frank gazed out over the crowd, now more than 150 strong. Shaking his head, he smiled to himself, incredulous. *The Lord preached outside like this a few times,* he realized. *And there was no podium or microphone, either.*

"I came here tonight," Frank began, "and I brought nothing but what the Lord gave me to say. I just want to share with you a little bit about what Jesus Christ means to me. But before I do that, let me tell you about my life before I met the Lord."

The crowd grew quiet as Frank's commanding voice filled the area. The whoosh of cars speeding along Van Dyke Avenue receded into the background.

"If you're here today," Frank announced, with one eye on the bikers, "and if you don't know Jesus Christ, you need to know something: He's already claimed you. He died on the cross for all men—not just for me, not just for you, but for everybody.

"When I was born—when I was a little kid—I don't remember anybody jumping up and down and getting all excited. I really don't. Two years later—I didn't know it then but I found out later—my father committed suicide. Suicide does strange things to a family. My dad owned a taxicab company up in Canada. He called it Frenchy's Cab. It was one of the biggest cab companies in Nova Scotia, and it's still there to this day. But apparently he was bootlegging whiskey, and a cop—this guy made it his goal to take my dad down—was closing in. But anyway, before that happened my dad drove his taxi out into the woods and shot himself in the head. From that point on my mom was faced with a choice. What does she do? She's got three kids now, and no husband to care for them. So they took my brother Chuck and me and put us in an orphanage. Then my mom moved on to New York with my sister, and I never heard from her again."

Subdued, the crowd fell silent. The majority of those present knew their parents and had a place they called home. Frank had their full attention.

"So me and my brother Chuck are being raised at an orphanage, okay? No going to the park every week, man. No one to put you on their lap and hug you and say 'I love you.' I never got any of that. And if you don't get that, you become, like, some other person. You're not going to have very much love in you when people don't show you love. And while I was in the orphanage we had these dormitories to sleep in. How many like having your own bedroom?"

Hands flew up all over the field.

"Well, I never had one. All I had was this big dormitory with a bunch of bratty kids just like me. And once a week they would dress us up in clothes that people handed down to us. We didn't go to the store to get our clothes, man. We never got any new things; they were always donated. So they would dress us up and put us in a room so people could come by and check us out and maybe adopt us. My heart was getting pretty hard by this time already. I was a nice kid, but I was confused. I remember some lady coming up to me and saying, 'Would like to come live with me?' And I said, 'No! I don't wanna live with you.' I was a pretty good-looking kid too, and they all went for me. But I sure didn't go for them.

"So the nuns raised me in this Catholic orphanage. I have a whole lot of bad memories from that place too. One in particular: I don't even know what I did to deserve it, but the nun made me take off all my clothes. Stripped me down naked and beat me with a radiator stick. That was so humiliating. I don't care if you're a kid or not—when somebody makes you strip down, it's gonna get to you."

Frank's words startled his listeners. The bikers, hooked now, climbed off their cycles and settled down on the grass.

"I became withdrawn at the orphanage. I hid in the basement and stayed down there with a little stuffed donkey that I used to hold. That was my friend, this little donkey. In the orphanage we ate porridge all the time. It wasn't that much fun living there, believe me. My brother was older than me, and as close as I tried to get to him he'd beat me up instead. He just wouldn't let me get close. Apparently that was his way of showing me love—ha-ha—by beating me up. I'd go 'Geez man, you're my big brother. I want somebody here to love me, man!' But nobody would. Chuck would get me down on the ground and then start hitting me in the arm—*boom, boom*—I mean like 50 to 60 times and he wouldn't quit! In fact, I couldn't even cry after a while 'cuz it hurt so bad. That was my brother Chuck. But I still loved him.

"Finally we got adopted when I was eight years old and Chuck was eleven. We came from Nova Scotia over here to the U.S. And I remember when I first met my parents I didn't even want to see them. I ran away from them, climbed right up on the wing of our airplane, and they couldn't get me down. I was up there on this big old wing saying 'I ain't going. I ain't going.' Then some guy offered me an ice cream cone, and I says 'All right, give me the ice cream and I'll come down.' Heh, heh."

The crowd tittered.

"I needed to get hit with a hammer or something, 'cuz I had a hard head and a hard heart. So when Jesus finally breathed His life into me and changed me—this was years and years after—I became a new creature. My whole life was changed. Now, today, I'm following Jesus Christ wherever he takes me. I got baptized in the Holy Spirit, too.

"I can tell you honestly that I'm a totally new person. It's a miracle that God ever got a hold of me. He said that in the last days he's gonna perform signs and wonders—and, brothers and sisters, you're looking at one of them wonders right now. Ha, ha."

"We love you, Frank!" someone shouted.

"Yeah, thanks, man. I love you too. But Jesus loves you more than I ever could. His love is the only thing that's for real. Ok, now I'm gonna finish up here . . .

"My parents were really strict people, all right? In fact, at our house I couldn't refer to my mother as *she*. If I did I'd get slapped. That's the way we communicated back then. If Dad says 'Where's Mom?' and I go 'She went to the store'—WHACK! You couldn't say *she*. What's wrong with that? Is that a verb or a pronoun? I don't know for sure. I never made it too far in school. But anyhow, that's the way it was in that house.

"It just got bad, real bad. When they punished me I'd have to stay in for the whole summer. How many of you ever got punished by staying in the WHOLE doggone summer? And I mean it—that's no lie. Listening to kids outside the window having fun, and I'm stuck inside. So my brother and me used to climb down the telephone pole and run away from home. We ran away so many times I can't even remember. Sleeping in people's garages, sleeping in cars, you name it, the whole thing. And every time I got caught my mother would send me to the juvenile home. The cops didn't want me, so my mother would say, 'Take him. We don't want him either.'

"So I was in the Macomb County Youth Home for, I don't know, 11 months. I ended up breaking outta there. But Chuck, who was kicked outta the house at the time, came back to visit me once for my 14th birthday. It was about 11:00, and he took me out and got me drunk. When we came home my mom was waiting for us. She said to my dad, 'Call the cops on Chuck!' 'Cuz he wasn't supposed to be near the house. Anyhow, I told her, 'Why don't you just SHUT UP?' I mean I've had tons of abuse from her at this point: she scratched my face once with her wedding ring, hit me with doorbell pipes, and if she was plucking a chicken I'd get hit with the chicken. I got hit with shoes, belt buckles . . . you name it. And I got tired of it, you know? Real tired of it.

"At 14 years old I'd had enough. And I had a lot of alcohol in me too, and when you got alcohol in ya you become another person. Sometimes you get a little aggressive. So I remember when I told her to shut up she came up to me with a dishrag and threw it hard. That dishrag wrapped around my head, and the corner of it hit me in the eye. You know how that stings? I just lost it, and I jumped on her, put my hands around her throat, and started squeezing. I yelled, 'I hate you! I hate you! I hate you!' I could've killed her, and I'd be sitting in jail right now if it wasn't for God's mercy in my life.

They put me back in the juvenile home, and I spent like a year and a half in Indiana, at Father Gebault's School for Boys. The first day they made me eat a bar of soap. And I mean not just take a little bite. They took it and shoved that soap into my mouth, and I'll tell you I was blowing bubbles for the next four days. I can still taste it right now, in fact. That stuff was NASTY!"

Frank made a sour face, and the crowd broke into laugher. Across the grassy field the sun was beginning to set, and the temperature was falling. Several people drew blankets over their shoulders, while others pulled on jackets and zipped them up.

"Anyhow, the way they discipline you in reform school is they give you three whacks with a paddle. You have to stand on a line, and when they whack you they don't just hit you in the butt, they hit you *below the butt*—and, man, does that hurt! When you run away, or something like that, then they hit you with a 2 x 4 after they catch you. They shave your head and then hit you with this big piece of wood.

"Well, according to statistics I got more whacks than anybody in the history of Father Gebault's school. They were whacking me left and right, man! I would put socks in there when it was my turn to get whacked, but the prefect of discipline, "Big Willy," he knew if you had something in there, so he would say 'Get them socks outta your pants,

Majewski. In fact, I'm giving you two more whacks just for that.' Gee, *thanks*, Big Willy.

"The only way I could get outta that place was to straighten up, so I became an honor roll student. No kidding! I got the highest average in the whole school that year. I won medals in football and a plaque for the amateur athletic union that thousands of kids were competing for all over the state. Everybody said 'Aw, he's a good kid now . . . we're gonna let him go.' Well, I wasn't a good kid. I just figured this is what I gotta do to get out.

"As soon as I was free, though, I started doing bad things again. I remember breaking up a whole elementary school by myself with a sledgehammer. I busted every window and every light I could find. I mean I *demolished* three floors of this building. Another time I went around smashing car windows. Not just one, but everybody's. I threw matches into garages and watched them go up in flames. I wasn't an arsonist or anything; I was just a kid that didn't care about nothing. I figured if they don't love me, then I don't love them.

"I became a good thief, too. I was boosting everything. I remember when I broke out of the youth home I ended up at Kmart. I stole socks, shoes, a comb, Brylcreem . . . the works. Then I even stole a nice sharkskin suit from JCPenney. That's when I met my good buddy Larry Wolf – we call him MoJo. I was taking off some baggy pants and putting on the suit when he caught me behind Tech Plaza. He said 'Whatcha doin'?' I says 'Hey man, I'm hungry. I just broke out of the youth home. Can you take me home and give me something to eat?' Well, he did, and MoJo and me have been friends ever since that day.

"Anyway, my last time in high school I got into this big fight at a battle of the bands concert. Me and my brother and a few other friends were fighting everybody at the school. While I was down on the ground a teacher hit me in the nose, and one of my buddies said, 'Do you know who just gave you that bloody nose? It was Mr. Lichter.' So I went looking for him. I started smashing windows in the school until the cops nabbed me and took me away. I never went back to school again after that, other than barber college.

"When I turned 17, we were hanging out one night—me, MoJo, and my other friend Johnny. We were walking through a park, drinking beer and getting drunk. A car was in the parking lot, and somebody said, 'What're you kids doin'?' I said, "Nothin'." And he goes, "Let me see some I.D." I guess he was a cop or something. So I said "No, we're not gonna show you nothin'." So we took off and ran across 12 Mile. We were just catching our breath when another car pulled up and stopped. This guy said 'Hey! What are you kids runnin' from?' I went up to him and I said, "None of your business." I'm looking in the passenger side window, and all of a sudden he pulls out a gun! He puts the gun right in front of my face at point blank range. Two inches. And I go, 'What'd you hafta pull a gun on me for?' And he says, 'Well, I don't know what you got hiding under your coat.' So I pulled it open and showed him I didn't have a gun, and he starts accusing us of breaking and entering. I said, 'Has your place been hit or something?' And he says 'I haven't been home yet.' And just like that—BOOM! He pulls the trigger.

"Well, that bullet went up my nose and curved underneath my eye— right here, see—and got stuck in my temple. MoJo got shot in the stomach, and my friend Johnny got it in the groin. He shot all three of us down, man, and my nose has never worked right since then. I got sinus problems to this day. I'd like to get a hold of that guy that did it and say, 'Hey, I gotta sniff about two hours every morning before I can breathe! Thanks a lot!'

"So now I'm in the hospital, ready to die, and the priest comes to hear my sins. I couldn't even talk. My mouth was over here, my head was way up there, and I was bleeding outta my ears, my mouth, and my nose. I just prayed to myself, you know, like, 'Forgive me for everything.'

"Then, when I went in to get operated on, I thought I was dead. But I did wake up finally, and two weeks later, after another operation, they took the bullet out of my head. MoJo's still got his in his stomach, and Johnny's got one too, but they had to take mine out. My jaw was wired for a year and I couldn't eat nothing. All I had was milkshakes, man. That's why I didn't go into the army, because my jaw was still wired up when they called me for the draft. They figured they're not gonna put a guy like me that can't eat in a foxhole. You know, we're not giving him milkshakes and soft-boiled eggs . . ."

The crowd chuckled. It was growing late, but no one wanted to leave. The sky was black, and bright stars had begun to appear. Since the area was not equipped with floodlights, several people turned on flashlights.

"So even after I promised the Lord I would behave, me and MoJo started taking drugs. And I mean *a lot* of drugs. Like around three hundred and fifty LSD trips, man. STP, uppers, downers, pot, beer. We were just stoned and zonked almost every day of our lives. We would get high in the morning, high in the middle of the day, and we'd be high at night. We would literally pass out while sitting in the car at a red light. People would start beeping the horn, and we'd still be there, passed out on the road.

"After all this my friend JJ started going to a prayer meeting down in Detroit and asked me to come along. Of course I didn't want to go. You know, I was brought up, like I said, in the Catholic Church. Somebody had told me I was baptized. How many of you know that when you baptize little kids they usually don't know they're being baptized? You have to tell them when they're older. I remember them dressing me up in an all-white suit with a little bow tie to make my first communion, then a couple of years later, I remember lining up in front of the Bishop for confirmation.

"Anyhow, I went through all of these different things, but I'll tell you what—I never repented for my sins. I never gave my life to Jesus Christ. I just went through the motions. It wasn't from my heart. So, anyway, they brought me to this prayer meeting and I went, you know, two or three times and never would give in. But then there was a nun there—I call her the "psychedelic nun"—and she cared about me. After all the nuns that had mistreated me, this one loved me. She kept saying 'I'm praying for you every day, Frank, that you'll meet the Lord.'

"So one night I decided to put God to the test. I said, 'Okay, Lord, if you're really there come into my heart. I'm sorry for all my sins, man.' Well, when I said that prayer I got knocked out of my chair about three feet. Landed on the ground—and had the greatest feeling I've ever experienced in my entire life. No drugs, no alcohol—nothing of any kind could come close to matching it. This was being totally cleaned up, like I took a shower right there.

"Now a lot of people say, 'Well, geez, Frank, after hearing your story, you *needed* Jesus. *I'm* not like that. *I* was brought up in a good home where everybody loved me. And *I* never drank or took dope. *I* didn't do nothing.'

"Don't tell me you ain't never lied, bro. Did you ever tell a lie, Mr. Good Person? Miss Good Person? If you say you didn't, then you just told your first lie right there. Ha-ha. We're ALL sinners, man, every one of us. And Jesus says everyone who sins becomes a slave of sin. That's heavy, isn't it? But he also says that if the Son makes you free, you are free indeed. God won't leave you in sin, man. He made a way out, and that way is through Jesus Christ.

"I'll tell you what, my story might be kind of crazy and heavy and all that, but it shows you that when the Lord came into my life it was real. God is a wonderful God.

"I'm gonna leave you right here, right now, with the same choice I had. I'm talking to you motorcycle dudes back there too, man. If you don't believe God is real, I challenge you to ask Him to show Himself to you tonight. Jesus says He stands at the door and knocks. If any man opens the door, He'll come in.

"So what's it gonna be tonight? Are you gonna take that step? Right now Jesus Christ offers you a whole new beginning—a brand new life if you want it. Just ask him for it. Ask him to forgive you and become the Lord of your life. I don't want nobody leaving right now, all right? I'm gonna ask you all to pray that the Holy Spirit will just touch hearts. Ask Him to give everyone that little extra shove they need to make a stand for Jesus."

Stars twinkled overhead as the streetlamps along Van Dyke Avenue flicked on, casting a soft glow over the gathering as Frank began to pray.

"Jesus," his voice called out over the subdued crowd. "We come before your throne right now, Lord, asking that you speak to hearts here and let 'em know you're alive. And while we're praying, I'm gonna ask anyone that would like to meet Jesus Christ for the first time to stand right now where you're at, all over the place."

Two girls rose to their feet.

"Praise God. C'mon," Frank urged the others. "Stand up right where you are."

A few more people stood.

"Who else is gonna stand with them?" Frank asked. "All we're gonna do is take two seconds of your time, and pray with you, that you might meet Jesus Christ. If he's talking to your heart right now, man, I need you to stand. Thank you, brother. Thank you, sister."

All over the field people continued to rise, some wiping away tears.

"Praise God—that took guts," Frank acknowledged. "C'mon, the rest of you, stand up if want to meet Jesus Christ. You know God's tugging on your heart, man. Get a little guts. Thank you, sister. Stand for the truth, man. Jesus, just move upon their hearts. Hallelujah."

By the time Frank was finished more than 30 people were on their feet. Jim stepped forward and led the respondents to a grassy spot near a tree. *They're just kids*, he thought, glancing over the young group. *High school, maybe, but most of them look younger.* A few bikers followed the group as well. One held on to a can of beer as he listened to Jim speak about the need for repentance.

"You have to mean it," Jim explained. "Tell God how sorry you are for your sins, and then ask Him to forgive you. He'll come into your heart, and you'll know He's real."

Everyone knelt down and started to pray. Afterward Jim passed out Bibles, inviting each person to come back next week. "We'll be here every Friday," he shouted over the revving of motorcycle engines. The bikers nodded before roaring away.

Frank and Jim trudged slowly back from the field, headed to the barbershop. Jim lit a cigarette and blew a stream of smoke toward the sky. "Franko," he declared, "I never thought I'd see the day when you and me would be telling bikers to kneel down and pray. Things have taken a strange turn, man."

Frank laughed. Just a few short months ago he'd been getting high and selling dope. And Jim had been a hustler, on the brink of divorce. How had these unlikely converts turned into evangelists?

"It all started with the psychedelic nun," Frank remembered.

"No, man, it started with Judith," Jim countered. "She just never stopped praying."

"We owe her, JJ." Frank threw his arm over Jim's shoulder as they walked. "But I owe you the most."

"Yeah, well, you can thank me later. Right now we have to figure out how to keep my business open.

"What are you talking about?"

"My partner quit today. He says we're losing too much business with all this preaching." Jim unlocked the front door of the shop.

"People need to hear about the Lord, man."

"I know it. I'm not saying we should do anything different. God already told me not to worry about losing customers. 'What you lose in apples, you'll make up for in peaches.'"

"The Lord's heavy, man." Frank plopped down wearily in a barber chair. "And I know He's gonna take care of you, JJ."

CHAPTER 24

Next Step

Fall, 1970

"There's a group of hippies selling drugs behind city hall." Whether or not she had her facts straight, a neighbor was calling in a complaint to the Warren City Police. "Have you checked into it? I can see them right from my living room window."

Another call came in: "I heard that the ringleader of this group broke out of the youth home. Does the mayor know about this?"

Police Chief Charles Groesbeck's teenage daughter attended Frank's prayer meetings, making it awkward for him when the complaints came in. He decided the best way to keep an eye on the situation would be to assign some police patrols to monitor the gatherings. He also sent two undercover agents to slip into the meetings and report back to him.

"When we asked some of the kids what they're up to," one of the agents informed him, "all they said was that they'd come to learn about God. There were no drugs or fighting, and everybody carried a Bible. It all looked pretty harmless to us, Chief."

"Keep an eye on it," Groesbeck directed. "Swing by once in a while so the neighbors can see we're there. As long as there's no trouble, we'll just let 'em be."

The next week a squad car pulled up to the meeting just as Frank was preparing to speak. An officer stepped out, opened the back door, and pulled a youth to his feet. Every eye was on them as he pointed toward Frank and offered the boy an ultimatum: "Either sit here tonight and listen to this or come down to the station with me. It's your choice."

"I'll stay," the boy muttered, weaving his way through the crowd to the very front, furthest from scrutiny. He glanced back at the officer before turning his attention to Frank.

The next day a *Macomb Daily* reporter described what was taking place behind Warren City Hall:

> ... groups such as this one are springing up throughout the area. And a principle organizer is Frank Majewski, who has a criminal record and spent years on drugs.
>
> It is bitterly cold ... and the ... crowd seated close together on the ground [in front of] Frank doesn't seem to notice it ... "The love of the Lord will warm us," says Mike Osminski with a smile. [A large number] would eventually arrive, greeting each other ("praise the Lord, brother") with a special handclasp. Soon they would be singing and clapping to religious songs straight out of the old-time revival meetings.[5]

Over the next several months, Frank's meetings, benefiting from the free publicity, continued to grow, causing complaints from alarmed neighbors to escalate as well. Frank decided to pay a visit to Judge Roy Gruenberg. He and the judge had first become acquainted through numerous instances of posting bail for his brother, Chuck.

"Judge," Frank opened, laying it immediately on the line, "we're just trying to follow the Lord here. We been meeting in the field and studying the Bible. No one is causing any trouble. We got kicked out of the barbershop, we outgrew the convent, and now people want to kick us off public property. Isn't there something you can do?"

"Sure," the judge agreed. "there *is* something I can do." Scribbling something on a piece of paper, he handed the note to Frank. "You have this court's permission to use the field for as long as you like. No one is going to kick you off while I'm sitting on this bench."

Frank handed the memo to Jim with a wide grin.

"That's good news for now," Jim acknowledged, "but we still need to find somewhere to meet before winter. The nights are gonna get cold, Franko, and before you know it it'll be snowing."

Frank hadn't thought of that. The kids were already huddling beneath blankets when he preached. And the sun was going down a little earlier each week. As it grew dark Frank needed a flashlight to read his Bible. The field had worked great for the past few months but, while they had official permission to gather, they were running out of daylight . . . and warm weather. Last Friday night some of the teens had pulled their cars into a circle, turned on their heaters, and opened their doors in a futile attempt to heat the surrounding air. There was no doubt they needed to find a suitable, long-term meeting place, but where were they to go?

Part Three

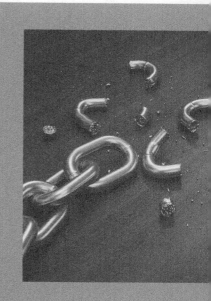

"EVERYONE
WAS MARVELING . . ."

LUKE 9:43

Part Three

CHAPTER 25
"Stay Out of Trouble"

Summer 1959
Mexican Town, Detroit

For as long as Alex could remember he had lived with his grandparents. His mother, Sylvia, a pretty Hispanic girl, had divorced his father in 1953. Soon afterward she'd moved with her three-year-old-son to her parents' small flat on Detroit's southwest side. While Sylvia worked in the offices at the Cadillac Plant, her parents took care of Alex.

By the time Alex turned five Sylvia had saved enough money to enroll him in the first grade at Saint Anne Catholic School—which boasted the incredible honor of having been a continuing congregation since 1701. The church, a stunning edifice constructed in the Gothic Revival tradition, is located in the heart of Mexican Town. Still buried beneath its original altar are the remains of Father Gabriel Richard, missionary to the Indians and founder of the University of Michigan.

Alex attended mass there with his family. Making his First Communion when he was six years old, he recited a prayer taught by the parish priest:

> *Good morning, dear Jesus, I give you this day*
> *My body, my soul, my work, and my play.*

His best friend, Roy, lived across the street. Roy and Alex did everything together: played ball, rode bicycles, and traded baseball cards. Nearly every morning Roy would park himself on the curb in front of his flat and wait for Alex to come out.

"Hey, Roy," Alex called this morning as he bounded down his front porch steps, "wanna go for a bike ride?"

"Sure." Roy hopped onto his bike and waited for Alex to join him.

The boys rode to West Grand Boulevard. "The Boulevard," starting at the river, headed north for several miles, turned east, and then went south before ending at Belle Isle, Detroit's beautiful island-park and the pride of the city. Today, however, the boys made a sharp left, and headed for Riverside Park. Dropping their bikes onto the grass near the water's edge, they ran to the swing set. Alex chewed on a blade of grass as he watched a pair of huge freighters roll down the river. The ships exchanged low, deep bellows that rattled in the boys' chests. A small postal tugboat edged up to one of the ships to hand off a sack full of mail.

Not far from this idyllic scene was the Michigan Central Depot, where passengers boarded a train and freight parts were loaded onto steel cars. A shrill whistle announced a train's approach and briefly turned the boys' attention away from the busy river. Gray, soot-covered cars lumbered slowly along the tracks before picking up speed and disappearing from view.

Alex lifted his eyes to the Ambassador Bridge to watch as hundreds of cars rumbled across the Detroit River into Windsor, Ontario. "Ever wonder where all those people are going?" Alex asked Roy, jumping from his swing and dropping onto his back in the grass. He twisted open an Oreo cookie and licked the cream-filled center. "I mean, what's so great about Canada?"

"I dunno," Roy mumbled, plopping onto the ground next to his friend. "Maybe there's gold."

"Yeah, right!" Alex, laughing, offering Roy half his cookie.

The boys returned home before dark. Waving goodbye to Roy, Alex put away his bike. Before proceeding into the house he gazed up at the skyline over downtown Detroit. His favorite skyscraper was the Penobscot Building, its red pinnacle shining like a beacon in the night. *When I grow up*, Alex sighed, *I'm gonna do something important.*

Sherry baby (Sherry baby)
Sherry can you come out tonight
(Come come, come out tonight)
(Come come, come out tonight)[6]

Alex and Roy lounged on the front porch listening to The Four Seasons on the record player. Alex had an impressive collection of 45s that he kept cleaned and stored in a black vinyl case. He stood up, snapped the case shut with a click, and picked it up by the handle. "I'm going down to the party," he announced. "You coming?"

"Sure." Roy grabbed his Pepsi and followed. Several doors down was the allure of food and music. Boys were pairing off with the girls and dancing to The Shirelles.

> *Mama said there'll be days like this*
> *There'll be days like this my mama said. . .* [7]

Alex and Roy sat cross-legged in the grass, watching. Everyone—Hispanics, whites, blacks— seemed to be in a good mood tonight; differences didn't much matter once the music started to play. The boys wished nights like these would never end.

A few days later Alex went over to Quica's house. Quica was a pretty teen-aged Hispanic girl who lived a few blocks further down, on 21st Street. She liked riding her bike, dancing to music, and drinking Pepsi. Alex liked all of those things too but was too young for the dancing. He hopped up the front steps and knocked at her door. When Quica came out she handed Alex a bottle of pop and sat down next to him on the porch. She tore open a bag of Ever Crisp Potato Chips and offered to share. Alex took a handful and watched as two small boys rode their bikes up and down the street.

"I'm gonna give you some advice, Alex," Quica commented. She touched his right shoulder with her finger. "You got an angel sitting here." Then she tapped his left shoulder. "And you got the devil over there." Quica took a sip of her Pepsi. "God is with the angel, so make sure you listen to him. Don't listen to the devil."

"Okay, Quica."

No se olvide. "Don't forget."

No lo haré. "I won't."

Summer 1962

Alex's grandmother frowned as she helped her husband toward the couch. Easing him onto the sofa, she plumped a pillow under his head.

Alex, rushing into the house and letting the screen door slam, was stopped in his tracks. "What's going on?" he asked. "What happened to Grandpa?"

Que ha sido herido! "He's been hurt," his grandmother replied. She stroked her husband's gray hair and patted his arm. *Descansa aquí, mientras yo pongo un poco de hielo.* "Rest here while I get some ice."

"Ohhhh . . ." Grandpa moaned and rubbed his temple. A knot was rising on his forehead, and a purple bruise encircled his eye.

Hombres malos! "Bad men," Grandma muttered as she returned to place a bag of ice on the knot. *Meterse con un anciano!* "Picking on an old man . . . !"

"What happened?" Alex asked again.

"Two men followed your grandfather on his way home from the restaurant. They attacked and robbed him." She shook her head. "Robbed an old man, and then beat him up."

"Eh, not so old . . ." Grandpa objected, trying to pull himself up.

Establecer, Grandpa, usted debe descansar. "Lay down, Grandpa. You should rest."

"*Ah, si.*" He lowered himself back onto the pillow.

While his grandmother called the police, Alex stepped over to the window and glanced down the street. His grandfather waved his hand, summoning him away from the window. "Alex," he invited, *Ven dime acerca de la escuela.* "Come, tell me about school."

Alex sat down on the edge of the couch. *Escuela estaba bien, Grandpa.* "School was fine, Grandpa, but I'm going to find out who did this to you."

No, vas a la escuela y simplemente olvidarse de él. "No, you go to school and just forget about it." Patting Alex's cheek, he closed his eyes.

ꞆꞀꞀꞀꞀꞀ

Things were changing in Detroit. Parents locked their doors at night, and many children weren't allowed to play outside after dark. Everyone knew the streets were no longer safe.

Gangs were becoming a fixture of nearly every inner city in America, and Detroit was no exception. The gangs around Mexican Town adopted tough-sounding names: the Hoodblades, Crows, and Bagley Boys. They divided southwest Detroit into turfs until every street west of the Ambassador Bridge was the sole property of one gang or another.

Nos estamos moviendo a un nuevo barrio. "We're moving to a new neighborhood," Grandpa announced one day. He had just located a home near 23rd and Bagley.

"It will give us more room," his mother agreed.

Alex headed out the door for Roy's house. After the boys rode their bikes along the familiar route of West Grand Boulevard, they plopped down next to the river, shared a cookie, and promised to always be friends.

⌖⌖⌖

Alex sipped on a Coke and leaned against the wall at a Catholic Youth Organization (CYO) dance held in the basement at St. Anne's Church. As the music played he looked up to see a group of teenage boys stroll into the hall. They wore creased pants, Banlon shirts and black fedoras with the brims turned up. Shiny black shoes clicked on the wooden floor as the boys made their way across the room. A crowd rushed over to greet the Bagley Boys.

Alex, still leaning on the wall, observed the excitement as teenagers gathered in a huddle around the young men. He wondered what it would be like to stride into a room and have everyone notice. *They're like celebrities,* he acknowledged, for the first time setting his own sights on joining a gang.

When Alex turned 13, riding bikes, playing catch, and attending Tiger baseball games began to seem like kid stuff. He wanted to go to parties and dances instead—do the things other kids his age did. His friend Carlos had just started a younger gang, calling it the Baby Bagleys. The older boys allowed the kids use of the name and even taught them the Bagley Code of respect, loyalty, and street smarts.

As soon as Alex heard about the new gang he set out to become a member. One day he pulled Carlos aside and asked him about joining. Carlos smiled, shook Alex's hand, and agreed that he could come around. Since the new gang was composed of friends from school and the neighborhood, he would fit right in.

One evening Alex waited for suppertime to end and then slipped out the front door to meet his friends. The neighborhood surrounding the Ambassador Bridge was all torn up; construction crews were working every day in preparation for the new I-75 expressway that would cut through the heart of Detroit. Many old homes had been demolished, while others sat empty, the ruins creating a dark and dangerous landscape. Cars and trucks whizzed overhead, drowning out the sounds from below. Spying Carlos and three other boys standing in the shadow of an abandoned house, Alex took a deep breath and strode toward them.

"Today," Carlos announced, "you get initiated. Can you take it?"

Alex nodded and braced himself for what was to come. They entered the house and someone put him in a headlock so he couldn't move. Next, all four boys descended on him with hard punches to the stomach. They pounded, kneed, and shoved Alex until he fell to the ground. Then, as suddenly as it had started, the initiation was over.

Carlos took Alex by the hand and presented him to the others. "Okay, man," he told his friend. "You're one of us now."

Alex wiped his mouth. "Thanks, Carolos."

The boys smirked and patted the new inductee on the back.

⊂⊖⊃

Alex hopped up the porch steps two at a time and knocked at the front door. A young black woman appeared in a bathrobe. "What do *you* want?" she asked with a sneer.

"Is Speers home?"

"Pa," the young woman called, ignoring Alex. "There's somebody here for you."

Alex drew three wrinkled singles from his pocket and smoothed the edges. It was a good arrangement: for a few sips of wine the old man would run to the party store on behalf of the Baby Bagleys.

Fourteen-year-old Alex had earned the money making tortillas with his friend Ralph, whose father owned a restaurant along Bagley Avenue. He had taught the boys how to roll flour tortillas, making them thin, round, and smooth. Each week Alex and Ralph worked in the tortilla shop so that by the weekend they would have cash to spend. Drinking had become a way of life for the boys—a way for them to fit in and have a good time.

The old man stumbled to the front screen and hacked a few times to clear his throat. Tucking his t-shirt into a pair of baggy brown pants, he pulled up the zipper. A week's worth of stubble covered his chin, and his hands trembled as he pushed open the screen. "What'll it be?" he asked, reaching for the money.

Alex laid the cash in his hand. "Two bottles of Lemon Smash."

Speers crushed the bills in his hand before making his way down the steps, and Alex sat down to watch as the old man shuffled down the street. When Speers returned he took a long glug, wiped the rim with his sleeve, and handed the bottles to Alex. Alex took a sip as well, screwed on the cap, and headed for the park to meet his friends. The gang drank, laughed, and strutted down the street, bottles lifted triumphantly in the air. When finished they tossed the empties into a vacant lot before heading for Vernor Avenue.

Swaying as they walked, the teens didn't notice a Chevy following close at their heels—Alex's mother. Sylvia had spied her son parading along with his friends and knew he had been drinking. She slowed her vehicle and followed quietly as the boys pushed and shoved each other along. At last she pulled ahead, rolled down the window, and called "Get in the car" in a tone that left no room for nonsense.

Chagrinned, Alex pulled up his collar, opened the passenger door, and slid down into the seat. As they drove away his friends broke into howls of laughter. Sylvia turned at the corner and headed for home. Alex loved his mother, yet as he stared out the window he sulked: *she has no idea who we are!*

◯─◉─◯

Sylvia resisted the urge to take the note in her hand and smack her son over the head with it. It was a notice from the Second Precinct Youth Bureau: an order to come in.

¿Por qué me quieres? Yo no hice nada. "Why do they want to see me?" Alex asked his mother. "I didn't do anything."

On the scheduled day Sylvia grabbed her car keys and pointed to the door. "Let's go," she stated brusquely.

"It's nothing, Mom, honest. No matter what they tell you, I'm innocent."

"Get in the car."

Detroit's 2nd Precinct was a busy place, the atmosphere punctuated by a cacophony of voices and the jangle of phones. Sylvia pulled into a parking space at 20th and Vernor and turned off the car. Inside the lobby an officer at the front desk took the notice from her hand. "Have a seat," he told them without looking up. "Someone will call you."

Thirty minutes passed before an officer appeared at the door, standing for a moment and scanning the waiting room. "Alex Silva," he called.

Alex stood, alone, and followed him down the hall. They entered a room furnished with desks, a few file cabinets, and some chairs. A policeman seated in one of the chairs leaned back with a cup of coffee in his hand. Not bothering with an introduction, he glanced at Alex and pointed to an empty seat. Alex sat down.

The officer leaned forward to study the boy's face. "So . . . ," he began, "tell me everything you know about the break-in at the Methodist church."

Alex rubbed his legs. "I don't know anything about it."

"Okay, so where were you at 9:00 last Wednesday?"

"At a friend's house."

"Does your friend have a name?"

"Ralph."

"Can Ralph vouch for you? I'll need to check your story."

Alex looked the officer in the eyes. "Yeah. We were at his house."

"What were you doing?"

"Just hanging out."

"Hanging out, huh? You're acquainted with some of the Bagley Boys?"

Alex looked down and rubbed his legs again. "Yeah, some of 'em."

"Seen anyone on the street last Wednesday? I mean, any Bagleys?"

"No. Like I said, I was with Ralph."

"So you have no idea what they were up to, right?"

Alex shrugged. "I didn't hear anything."

"Maybe you could listen a little harder next time."

The boy shrugged again.

"You're not a bad kid, Alex," the officer conceded with a sigh, pushing his chair back and rising. "Just keep your nose clean, all right? Don't get messed up with them. They're nothing but trouble. Your mother doesn't want you getting into trouble, does she?"

"No."

The officer opened the door and led Alex from the room. Sylvia rose as they entered the lobby, gazing anxiously from the officer to her son.

Alex smiled as he approached her. "I told you there was nothing wrong, Mom."

"So, why did they want to see you?"

"He's not in any trouble, ma'am," the officer assured her. "We're investigating a break-in from last week and needed to check some leads. Your son's clear."

Sylvia glanced at Alex as they walked to the car.

"I was at Ralph's that night, Mom," Alex told her. "I don't know anything about a break-in. I'm telling the truth."

His mother stopped and took his arm. "Alex," she stated flatly. "Stay away from those boys."

"What boys?"

"You know who . . ." She paused knowingly, eyebrows raised. "They're trouble, and I don't want you mixing with them. Do you understand?" *¿Entiende usted?*

"Yes, Mom. I understand."

"You're a good boy, Alex," Sylvia said. "Try to stay out of trouble."

Alex hopped into the car and thought about the advice Quica had given him years ago. An angel is on one shoulder, she had said, and the devil's on the other. It was a lot harder to follow the angel than he had thought.

Animosity among rival gangs began to intensify as fights broke out between the Bagley Boys and the Stilettos. Alex and his friends, commissioned as lookouts, listened to one of the older Bagleys as he explained their job. "You guys stay here on 23rd," he directed, "and keep an eye out for anybody you don't know. If you see Stilettos drive by, run down to Lambie Street and tell us. Got it?"

The boys nodded.

"So, what else do we do if we see them?" Ralph called hopefully over his shoulder as the older boy walked away.

"Brick 'em!" was the grim-faced response.

The boys gathered a pile of bricks and settled with them near the corner curb, positioning themselves to watch both Bagley and Fort. *No telling which way the Stilettos might come*, Alex reasoned. *We gotta be ready.* He had never bricked a car before and welcomed the chance to prove himself. He tossed a brick up and down in his hand, hoping the Stilettos would venture out tonight.

But no one came.

Bored and looking for action, Alex and Louie made their way to a party on 23rd Street. The house was packed with teenagers, both inside and out. Young men sipped beer and wine while girls line-danced in the living room. Sweet tunes from The Miracles sounded from a record player, and the air was stale with cigarette smoke. From the second floor Louie's older brother, standing near the railing, observed his younger brother's approach. "Hey Louie!" he called, pulling a quarter from his pocket and flipping it to the ground. "Go home, man."

Louie picked up the quarter and grinned.

"Get outta here, man!" his brother repeated. "Go on home."

Louie nudged Alex, and the pair headed for the kitchen. They had no intention of leaving; the party was just warming up.

Later, Alex was walking along Vernor Highway when he spied Lonnie, one of the Latin Counts, passing by with his girlfriend. Alex quickened his pace to walk alongside them.

"Listen, Alex," Lonnie commented. "When you turn seventeen we can have you join the Counts."

"*Really?* Thanks, Lonnie." Alex was flattered by the offer. The Counts were a classy group within the Bagley Boys. Their gang symbol included a top hat, gloves, and a walking cane.

"Catch you later, man." Lonnie turned down a side street, his girlfriend in tow, while Alex, suppressing a grin, headed for home.

CHAPTER 26

A New Start

Fall 1965

"**A**re you coming to the Quinceanera?" Alex was heading out the door as his mother called from the kitchen.

"Yeah, I'll be there."

"It's a special night for Rosie and her family."

Alex knew that a Quinceanera, a "coming out party," was a big event for a Hispanic girl—and with all the eating, drinking, and dancing he was sure to have a good time.

Upon his arrival Alex recognized several friends from Western High. Kids from the Catholic schools were there as well; the neighborhood had come together to enjoy the traditional festivities. A pretty young girl—someone Alex had never seen before—glanced up when he entered the room. Alex made sure the two were introduced before the evening was over. He jotted down Carol's phone number on a piece of paper and promised to give her a call.

The next evening Alex stretched the phone cord as far as it would reach from the dining room into the hallway. His insides quivered as he settled himself on the floor to dial Carol's number. Alex swallowed hard when he heard her voice on the other end. Not wanting anyone else in the house to hear, he spoke in quiet, clipped phrases: "Hi. This is Alex. Remember me? From last night."

"Hi." Carol's voice sounded even sweeter than the night before.

He swallowed again. "You wanna go riding around this Sunday?"

"I'll ask my mom." Carol set down the phone while Alex took a deep breath and blew out the air. He could feel his heart pounding in his chest.

"Okay," she responded easily when she returned. "I can go. What time?"

"I'll come by around one or one-thirty."

"Okay."

"See ya then. Bye."

Alex didn't notice his mother's knowing smile when he walked in to hang up the phone.

⚬⚬⚬

There was something special about Carol. Alex couldn't stop thinking about her. She was beautiful, but that wasn't all: the girl was kind and considerate, too. And Carol had plans for her future—she intended to study hard and do something with her life. None of his friends had ever talked like that. Carol didn't drink, smoke, or throw herself at the boys. She was one in a million.

One evening soon afterward Alex sat on the couch in Carol's living room. The two were headed to a dance, and he was waiting for her to come out.

Carol's mother walked into the room carrying a Bible under her arm and sat down next to him. "Alex," she told him, "you know I like you. And you know I don't mind you dating Carol. But there's something you need to know about her, something that makes her different from the rest of the girls."

Alex shifted in his seat.

"You've seen this before, haven't you?" She set down the Bible on the coffee table.

"Sure," he replied. "My grandmother has a Bible."

She opened it to the book of Psalms. "I want to read something to you," she announced, turning to Psalm 119 and locating verse 9: "'Wherewithal shall a young man cleanse his way? By taking heed thereto according to Thy word.'"

Alex explained that he was a Catholic.

"Yes, I know," Carol's mom agreed as she closed the Bible. "But it doesn't matter what church you go to, Alex. It matters what's in your heart. That's why I wanted to show you this verse. I want you to know what's in Carol's heart, too. She wants to stay pure—to follow God. You understand what I'm saying, don't you? Please think about that verse when you go home."

Carol appeared in the doorway. "Ready to go?" Glancing down at the Bible on the table, she smiled knowingly.

Alex turned toward her mother. "I'll think about what you said," he promised, standing up to leave.

Carol slipped her hand through Alex's arm as they stepped outside. "She's been wanting to do that for a while," she explained in an apologetic tone.

Tossing his arm over her shoulder, he pulled her close. "That's okay," he assured her. "It's no big deal."

Carol felt her heart was caught in a tug of war. She liked Alex and liked being his girl. It was fun going to parties with him and hanging out with his friends on Friday nights. On Sundays, however, she was filled with regret as she sat next to her mother in church. It seemed as though the longer she dated Alex the farther she felt from God. Her mother, observing with concern her daughter's attempts to lead a double life, prayed that Carol would make the right choice.

One night, after spending the evening with Alex, Carol arrived home with tears stinging her eyes. Dropping into a chair at the kitchen table, she began to cry. Alex had just announced that he and his family would be moving to a new neighborhood. His mother had bought a home in Northwest Detroit near Mackenzie High School, the school Alex would be attending in the fall. Carol blew her nose into a napkin and sighed. How would she be able to see him after the move? Alex had promised to visit on the weekends, explaining that he would ride the bus every Saturday afternoon, spend the evening with Carol, and take the late bus back.

Things transpired just as Alex had said. Carol had to admit that it was the best of both worlds: she could focus on her schoolwork during the week and see Alex on the weekends. For his part, Alex enjoyed having a beautiful girl on his arm and old friends to hang out with. Most importantly, in a few short months he would be old enough to run with the older guys.

But things were changing in Detroit. Teens, no longer content to occupy their weekends dancing or drinking beer in the park, wanted bigger kicks. By 1966 drug use had exploded, with dealers transforming houses into drug dens. For a generation hooked on pleasure a new age had dawned, and in the wake of the other changes crime and violence continued to escalate in the city of Detroit.

One afternoon Alex found himself in the backseat of a car as he and a group of friends headed for a pre-arranged fight; they were meeting a gang of rivals at an intersection along Grand River Avenue. Someone pulled out a joint and passed it around. As the car reeked with the smell of marijuana, Alex held the joint in his hand and took a drag. An unfamiliar burning sensation traveled down his throat, and his head soon felt lighter than air. This was his first taste of reefer, and he liked it.

Approaching the intersection, the car veered sharply left, careening toward a crowd of youths gathered on Grand River. Alex gripped his seat as the rival gang members, caught off guard, scattered. The driver wove back and forth, deliberately trying to pick off some of them, before turning down a side street and coming to a stop with a squeal of brakes. The occupants jumped out, their anger and yelling giving way to uproarious laughter as the boys realized how close they had come to disaster. Their adversaries had run off, so they hopped back into the car and headed home.

Seventeen-year-old Alex and his friends arrived at a small house party. Several of the older Bagleys glared at the boys as they entered the home.

"*Leave*, man!" one of them barked out. "I don't want to look at you. You guys think you're something, don't you?"

Alex and his friends headed for the back door, with several of the older guys shoving them from behind.

"Hey, take it easy!" Alex complained, knowing they were high. "Look man, everybody's cool."

"Naw. Get outta here!"

Someone threw a punch, and more shoving erupted. Alex and his friends exited down the alley without looking back, climbed into a Mustang, and drove away.

"Man, what was *that* all about?" Alex exclaimed.

"Yeah," his companions put in. "That ain't cool."

What's happening to everybody? Alex wondered. *It never used to be like this*. The older guys had begun turning on the younger set. As the strife continued, drugs brought not only darkness but also division: the loyal gang that Alex had admired all his life was coming apart.

Weeks later Alex was walking toward the bus stop near Clark Park.

Up ahead several people milled around on the sidewalk, handing out small black booklets prominently titled "Chicken." A young man thrust one of the booklets in his direction. "Hey, take one," he invited. "It's free."

"Thanks," Alex mumbled, stuffing it into his pocket.

Sitting down on the bus he pulled out the booklet—a gospel tract. To pass the time Alex started to read: "Young people drive cars at each other, just to see who's chicken . . ." He flipped the page and continued to read: "They end up getting hurt just because they don't want to be called a chicken. Young people, God is speaking to you right now. The nations are stirring. There's threat of nuclear war. But the question is: what will you say to God when you stand before Him? What will you say when His Son returns?"

Alex was shocked to find tears welling up in his eyes. His heart felt heavy, like a rock. Folding the tract, he stuffed it roughly back into his pocket as though it had offended him. He didn't want to think about God right now. Alex gazed vacantly out the window, watching street-lights and buildings whiz by in a blur.

⊂━⊃

Across the street from Mackenzie High School stood a Methodist church. The new minister, a tall, lanky young man fresh out of Bible college, stood in the parking lot bouncing a basketball. "You guys interested in a little two-on-two?" he called out as Alex and his friends ambled by.

The boys looked at each other and shrugged. "Sure, why not?" one of them responded.

The minister tossed the ball to Felipe, who immediately sprang into action. Weaving his way around his friends, he dribbled toward the basket, shot, and scored.

Teams were formed, and an hour later the players were hot and thirsty. "Can I offer you boys something to drink?" the minister asked. Trailing behind him to the porch, they sat down on the stoop.

"Thanks, Reverend." Alex took a bottle of pop from his hand. "You're pretty good out there."

The minister smiled, took a sip, and wiped his brow. "Listen, guys," he offered. "We're having a guest speaker this Sunday. How about you stop by to hear him?"

No one responded.

"He's from New York, and he was an addict. You might want to hear what he's got to say."

"Sure, Reverend," Alex put in noncommittally, picking up his jacket, "We'll try to make it."

"You're not serious about going to that, are you?" Felipe asked as they trudged away.

"Nah, but I didn't want to hurt his feelings. He's all right."

A few nights later Alex and two other friends, Mickey and David, headed for the church. As they entered the foyer a teenager placed a flier in Alex's hand. "This cat from New York is going to talk about how God changed his life," he commented.

"Cool." David smiled and grabbed his own paper.

"Thanks, man," Alex answered. "We'll listen."

"Teen Challenge—what's that?" asked Mickey, glancing at the flier.

Alex nodded toward the east. "They got a building over near Western," he recalled. "They're trying to get the fellas in Clark Park to come to their meetings."

"We're going in?" David asked.

"Yeah. *C'mon.* We'll have a few laughs."

"I don't want any religion shoved down my throat."

"What's the matter? Afraid you'll get saved?" Alex smirked and punched David in the arm.

The young men entered the sanctuary just as the meeting was getting underway. Slipping into a pew, they removed their hats and then folded their arms in a defiant pose.

The young minister stood near the front, looking winded and flushed, as though he had just breezed in from the basketball court. He smiled his acknowledgment as the newcomers filed in. "I want to welcome everyone here tonight," he opened. "The man coming to speak to us has quite a story to tell. He ran the streets, became a drug addict, and lived for only one thing. He came all the way from Brooklyn to talk to us about God. Brother Steve, welcome to Detroit. Come on up and tell us what God's been doing in New York City."

The speaker, younger even than the minister, made his way to the podium and adjusted the microphone. His eyes panned across the room with an expression that made him appear much older than his 19 years. Clearing his throat, he began: "I got nothing but gratitude in my heart tonight for what God has done in my life. Growing up in a family on the east side of Brooklyn, as soon as I could get out I made sure I was never home. There were too many rules living in that house, man, and too much fighting. I never had a real family; you know what I'm saying? So I ended up on the street. That became my family. Fourteen years old— drinking, smoking reefers, and hanging out with the fellas. By the time I turned 16 I was shooting heroin. Some of you know what I'm talking about." His glance took in Alex and his friends.

"I got hooked on drugs pretty quick," Steve continued, "and things got worse. I stole my mother's wedding rings so's I could cop some 'H'. What kind of a son steals his own mother's wedding rings? But that's how bad it got. I did it for 'H'. Everything I did was for 'H'. There was only one thing I cared about, and that was getting high. After that, it was all about finding more money to get high again. Nothing else mattered. But I found out that drugs are dangerous, man, because they can separate you from your soul."

Someone snickered, but Alex stared straight ahead. He could feel his heart beating in his chest.

"I'm gonna tell you the truth," Steve went on. "Everything changed one night. People from Teen Challenge invited me to come in and check out the program. I called out to God in prayer, and through Jesus Christ I was saved. He gave me a brand new start. The old habits are gone, man. God wants to save you too. He wants to set you free from sin—from doing drugs, stealing, or whatever else you're into. It's sin that keeps pulling you down. Turn to Jesus, and he'll give you a brand new life—a life free of drugs, alcohol, lying, and stealing. You can have a new start with God, man, and you can have it tonight. All you have to do is tell Him you're sorry and ask Him to forgive you."

A hush fell over the room.

"Now, what I want to know is this: is there anyone here tonight that'll stand up right now and ask Jesus to come into your life? Don't look at the guy sitting next to you. This is between you and God. Stand up right now, if you want a new start."

Alex rose to his feet, while Mickey, incredulous, yanked on his arm, hissing, "*Sit down*, man! They're gonna think you're a sissy."

Alex shook off his hand with a shrug and continued to stand. David, uncertain what to think, bowed his head.

"I'd like to pray with you," Steve announced. "So everyone who stood, come on up here in front, and I'll say a short prayer, all right?"

Alex headed up the aisle. Steve led the assembled group into a small room where some men from Teen Challenge were waiting to pray with them.

"What did you do in there, man?" his friends asked as they walked home.

"Not much," Alex replied. "Just prayed. But I gotta tell you fellas, I'm feeling pretty good right now. Lighter than a feather. Like a huge weight just fell off."

"That's cool, man." Mickey nodded. The three young men trekked the rest of the way home in silence.

CHAPTER 27

Recommitment

Carol was thrilled when Alex told her that he had accepted the Lord. Her mother invited him to come to Cobo Hall to hear a popular minister speak: "Oral Roberts is coming to Detroit. Why don't you come with us?" Alex agreed but hoped he wouldn't see anyone he knew. He wasn't ready to go public.

The auditorium at Cobo was packed. Alex did spot someone from Mackenzie sitting a few rows over. *I never heard that guy talk about God before*, he thought, mildly surprised, *but it's cool that he's here*. When the collection plate came around he emptied his pocket, tossing in his bus fare as well. That would mean a long walk home later tonight, but somehow he didn't care. After the meeting people began to make their way down to the main floor for prayer. Carol took Alex's arm, and they went down together.

Later that summer Alex phoned Steve, the speaker from Teen Challege. He was easy to talk to and understood how hard it was to give up the old ways, drinking, and gangs. He tried to encourage Alex: "Don't tell me how many tubes of glue you been sniffin', brother. Tell me how it's been since God's come into your life."

"Becoming a Christian was easy," Alex admitted. "But *staying* a Christian is harder than I thought."

"Bring your girlfriend by," Steve offered. "We'll eat dinner and then go to a church to worship together. You just need time to grow, man."

"Sure, I'll do that," Alex agreed.

After hanging up the phone Steve prayed that Alex's commitment to Christ would stick.

⊙⊙⊙

Alex slipped on a pair of dark sunglasses and headed down the steps. The party was in someone's basement tonight; he followed the scent of marijuana down a narrow stairwell and ducked his head underneath a beam as he entered. A Gladys Knight album blared on the stereo, while a fan bounced light shadows on the ceiling. The couch was occupied by a couple locked in a long and oblivious embrace. Alex nodded to some friends in the smoke-filled room. Most of the guys were high, as were some of the girls.

Alex had broken up with Carol. It was all his fault, and he knew it. Carol had heard rumors that he was playing around. When he didn't deny it she just walked out of his life. He didn't blame her—just wanted to forget. And he never wanted to think about God again.

Another night, another party . . . this one on somebody's front lawn. The music was loud, and young people began shouting and dancing in the street. A neighbor first complained loudly and then called the police; moments later, when he tried to back out of the driveway, someone threw a rock at his car, followed by a bottle. The man, thoroughly frightened, peeled away down the street. Sirens sounded in the distance, and several patrol cars arrived in short order. Officers immediately began looking for suspects. Alex, his friend, and two girls were getting ready to drive away when an older bystander pointed to their car. "Those people," he insisted. "They were part of the group that committed the assault. They threw the bottles."

Alex, livid with rage at the unfair accusation, lunged toward the man, while an officer grabbed him from behind and cuffed him. He held Alex's head down as he shoved him roughly into the patrol car, and headed for the McGraw Precinct.

Alex and his friend were released on bond and scheduled to appear before Detroit Recorder's Court in June. Their seasoned attorney cautioned them not to get on the judge's bad side: "She's a force to be reckoned with."

Judge Geraldine Ford, the granddaughter of a former slave, held the distinction of being the first black woman ever to be elected to judgeship in the United States. Pulling off her reading glasses, she watched as the two young men approached the bench with their attorney.

Sylvia sat near the back of the courtroom, concerned about the stern expression on the judge's face. She watched the lawyer shuffle a few papers before beginning his defense. Felonious assault was a serious charge, he had informed Sylvia before the trial. Even if Judge Ford were to agree to a lesser count, Alex most likely faced court costs, probation, and a criminal record.

The judge placed her glasses on the tip of her nose and studied Alex's face. "You like running with your friends, don't you?" She didn't wait for an answer. "Let me tell you something, Mr. Silva—you're not thinking clearly. Gangs, drinking, and big egos are a recipe for trouble." She looked over the papers in her hand. "Every day in this courtroom I tell young people the same thing: maybe you don't like people telling you what to do, but I don't want to see you in my courtroom again."

Alex's face turned red. He swallowed hard and met the judge's gaze.

Judge Ford leaned forward. "One year probation," she announced, pounding the gavel.

Sylvia took Alex's arm and led him quickly from the courtroom. She wasn't about to let her son throw his life away. "You've been making some bad choices," she reminded him as they drove home. "Young man, you're leaving gangs and all this trouble behind."

Alex hurried into the house, slipped into his bedroom, and closed the door.

Sylvia had recently re-married. Eric Ross was a solid, decent man who was also a federal agent. After Alex disappeared into his room, his stepfather knocked at the door. "From now on," Eric announced, "you're going to focus on your schoolwork. You can forget all about dances and parties, too."

This was precisely what Alex needed to hear. Standing before Judge Ford had diminished, for the time being, his desire for alcohol and drugs. He started to apply himself to his studies and set his sights on high school graduation.

Alex hunched low in the passenger seat, staring out the window. The landscape changed as they drove: skyscrapers were replaced by open land and flat-roofed shopping centers. Sylvia smiled and pointed out several new building projects along the way. A new grocery store, Farmer Jack, was coming to the corner of Chicago Road and Van Dyke. Every side street had brick houses lined up in neat, straight rows, as

acres of farmland were being converted into bustling new neighborhoods. Sylvia and Eric felt certain they were doing the right thing. Their
new house would be completed in a few months, and Sterling Heights
would be a much-needed change from inner city Detroit.

Driving past Cousino High School, Alex broke into a grin. "This
is looking a little better, Mom," he enthused, turning to catch the eyes
of two pretty girls walking near the school. He nodded his head in approval, and the girls smiled.

When Alex started school in the fall he found a few friends among the
Italians who had recently moved up from Detroit. His niche was somewhere between the frats and the greasers. Frats, who grew their hair long
and wore bell-bottom jeans, were easy to spot. Some, he learned, smoked
pot, partied at the Grande Ballroom on weekends, listened to Uncle Russ
on the radio, and played psychedelic music.

Greasers, on the other hand, slicked back their hair with Brylcreem
and wore tight black jeans with pointy leather shoes. The girls wore
mini-skirts, penny loafers, and scoop-necked tops. Greasers rode around
in muscle cars, drank, and listened to cool music.

Alex found a job at the Great Scott Supermarket and began saving
his money for a car. He had his eye on a '58 T-bird, a pale blue number
with a custom steering wheel. For the rest of his senior year he worked,
drove his new car, and stayed out of trouble. It didn't take long for Alex
to realize that it was time to tuck away his days of running the streets.
After graduating from Cousino he enrolled at Macomb Community College, hoping to later study law and maybe return to Detroit. Even though
Alex had left the city, the city had never really left him.

On a cold winter night in 1970 Alex and his friends Chuck and Dan
sat in his car drinking bottles of Ripple Wine. When they finished drinking they drove over to Peppy's to grab something to eat. After ordering
food from the car, the boys were startled by a sharp rap on the driver's
side window. Matt, with his wild, long hair, pressed his face close to the
glass, laughed, and signaled for Alex to roll down the window. Cold air
rushed in.

"What's going on?" Alex asked.

"Can I come in?" Matt opened the back door to let himself in. Leaning forward, he jabbed Alex's shoulder. "Did you guys hear about Frank Majewski?"

Alex had heard the name before. "That guy who rides a hog?" People knew about Frank's jet-black, hard-riding Harley Davidson.

"Yeah, but even crazier—he got saved, man. Gave his life to Jesus, and now he's telling everybody about it." Matt pointed toward Tech Plaza Shopping Center. "He preaches every night at the barbershop and people keep coming and coming. Everybody's getting saved."

Alex looked at his friends and shrugged.

"I just gave my life to the Lord too, man," Matt continued. "I was sitting there listening to Frank when all of sudden I knew I had to repent. I was screwing my life up pretty bad, so I asked Jesus to come into my heart. You guys gotta hear this guy. It'll blow your mind." Matt climbed out of the car again and left his friends in a bewildered silence.

A nervous laugh broke the spell. "That's crazy about Majewski," Chuck put in.

"Maybe we should check it out," Alex suggested.

The car grew quiet again. Alex decided on an impulse to share with his surprised friends all that he himself knew about Jesus Christ, going on to describe his nearly forgotten experience at Teen Challenge and how he knew Jesus was coming back.

Later that night Alex sat in his living room with a phone in his hand. He dialed the number for Teen Challenge in Detroit, wondering whether anyone would be available so late in the evening. The truth had hit him like a thunderbolt: he needed God back in his life—he knew that now but didn't know where to start. The phone rang several times before someone picked up. The man assured Alex that it was fine that he'd called. They prayed together, and Alex promised to call back in the morning. He also decided to check out Frank's meeting the following week—with or without his friends.

Chuck Cardamone and his sister Karen wanted to go too. They had heard all about Frank's meetings and were just as curious as Alex. On Wednesday evening he picked up the siblings in his T-Bird and drove to the barbershop. A small group of people gathered around Frank in the parking lot, Alex near the back. "Look man," Frank was telling everyone, "we can't have our meeting here tonight, so if you guys want you can follow me down to Gesu Church in Detroit. We'll go to their prayer meeting instead, okay? What d'ya say?"

Everyone agreed and headed for their cars. As the crowd dispersed Frank, dressed in a long blue wool coat, walked over to Alex and shook his hand. Frank was slim, but his handshake was firm. His eyes locked with Alex's. "So man," he asked, "are you comin' too?"

"Yeah, we'll come," Alex replied.

"Just follow me and MoJo." Frank climbed into his car and started the engine. The procession traveled down Van Dyke Avenue all the way to Detroit. Once at Gesu's the growing crowd quickly filled the empty seats in the meeting hall. Alex watched a nun walk over to Frank and greet him with a hug. *Now that's something you don't see every day*, he thought to himself as he took a seat.

A young man studying for the priesthood stood up to speak. He had struggled with sin, he shared, for most of his life, but the conflict ended when he gave his life to Jesus Christ. Alex's thoughts were racing: *If this guy, who's practically a priest, has sinned, where does that leave me?* His hands were starting to sweat as he closed his eyes and once again opened his heart. "Jesus," he prayed, "I asked you to come into my life a while ago, and now I'm asking again. I know I'm a sinner, and I need you to forgive me for my sins. Jesus, please help me to live again for you."

A tear made its way down his cheek. Alex opened his eyes and looked around. No one had noticed. He could feel God's presence in the room and felt certain God had heard his prayer. Then and there, as his guilt and shame melted away, all that remained was joy.

CHAPTER 28

Dark Clouds over Da Nang

October, 1967

Turning on the television, Randy dropped onto the couch with a bag of Oreo cookies and a glass of cold milk. The news was on and, as usual, it was all about the Vietnam War. A reporter shouted into a microphone, while protesters behind him lifted signs in the air and chanted: "Hell no, we won't go!" and "Make love, not war."

"An enormous crowd has assembled here today for an unprecedented event at our nation's capital," the reporter began. "As you can see, tens of thousands of marchers have gathered in front of the Lincoln Memorial. Riot police have been called to the scene, but so far no arrests have been made."

"Shut that thing off," Randy's father yelled from the kitchen. "Buncha communists . . ."

Turning off the TV, Randy headed back into the kitchen, still munching a cookie. At 19 years old he was tall, blond, and handsome. Randy leaned against the counter and watched his dad twirl a forkful of spaghetti. Edi Marcial's hair was growing thin, and the muscle shirt he wore accentuated the paunch across the middle. He looked nothing like the smooth saxophone player of 30 years earlier. Pausing with his fork in the air, Edi scowled at his son. "What are *you* looking at?"

"Nothing." Randy pulled up a chair and stuffed the rest of the cookie into his mouth. Washing it down with a gulp of milk, he went back to watching his father eat.

"Something on your mind?" Edi asked without looking up.

"Not much."

Edi scowled again.

"I been thinking . . . ," Randy put in finally.

"What about?"

Randy nodded toward the television. "About the war."

His father dismissed the Vietnam War with a wave of his hand. "Just a bunch of politicians in Washington getting a whole lot of people killed." Edi pointed his fork at Randy. "All you need to think about right now is finding a job."

"Kind of a narrow-minded view, isn't it, Dad?"

Edi laid down his fork. "Look, Randy," he stated flatly, "I'm all for defending this country, but I didn't start this war, and I don't see any reason someone should go over there and get himself shot. So, unless a draft notice has turned up at this house, I got nothing more to say."

Randy took a deep breath, held it, and then exhaled. "I enlisted today."

Edi sat back in his chair and threw up his hands. "Just like that. 'I enlisted.' No warning, no 'let's talk this over'! Just go behind your old man's back and enlist."

"It's not like that, Dad. I put a lot of thought into it."

"You thought about it. That's supposed to make me feel better? I don't even get a vote?"

"I figured you wouldn't be happy . . ."

"You got that right, bub. Who'd you enlist with—the Army?"

"Navy. I'm gonna be a Medical Corpsman."

Edi grew quiet. There was a long tradition of Navy men on his wife's side of the family. He stared at the clock on the wall for several moments. Who was he to tell his son that he couldn't join up? "All right Randy," he conceded, pushing his plate away. "Sounds like you've made up your mind. You better go tell your mother, though. It's gonna break her heart."

Randy left the room. He had expected stronger opposition—a plate thrown against the wall or a punch in the arm would have been more like his dad. Reluctantly he climbed the stairs to find his mom.

For the next several months Randy trained at the Great Lakes Boot Camp in Chicago, after which he worked at the San Diego Naval Hospital and then at a recruit depot on Parris Island. It wasn't until the fall of 1968, while stationed on the island, that he received his orders for

Vietnam. Randy flew home to spend Christmas with his family before packing his bags for Da Nang.

It was a cold morning in February 1969 when the Marcials gathered at Detroit Metro Airport to bid farewell to their eldest son. Randy's mother buried her face in his blue pea coat and sobbed. "Your dad loves you, Randy," she assured her son. "He just doesn't know how to show it."

Edi stood at a distance, watching Randy kiss his mother goodbye. It all seemed like more than he could take. On a last second impulse he strode up, grabbed his son by the arm, yanked him backward, and wrapped him in a bear hug. Both men choked back tears as they parted. Randy headed for the plane and, once inside the jet bridge, hung his head and allowed the hot tears to flow unchecked.

Twenty-six hours later Randy gazed out the window of a Boeing 707 as it circled at 38,000 feet over the South China Sea. Below them stood Da Nang Air Base, the largest U.S. military base in Vietnam. Situated some 50 miles south of the demilitarized zone, Da Nang had become one of the busiest airstrips in the world. It was also a strategic target for the Viet Cong.

As the plane hung low in the sky, Randy looked down at the airfield below. It was under heavy attack from the North Vietnamese, and enemy fire was making it impossible to land. For 40 minutes the plane circled above the gray billows of smoke. When at last permission was granted to land, it taxied onto a large concrete hangar bay. Randy watched as a fighter jet streaked off the runway, leaving in its wake a bright pink fireball. Bombs exploded at a distant airfield, shaking the earth with a low, deep rumble. Randy threw on his helmet, holding it in place with both hands, and ran toward a waiting cattle car on a set of train tracks. Vietnamese workers scurried about in bamboo hats and shouted at the explosions: *Mất bao! Mất bao!* "Take cover! Take cover!"

Randy hopped onto the train and leaned against the door as the engine lurched forward with a groan. For several miles he saw nothing but foliage spread over the plains like a lush green carpet. Eventually the plains merged into foothills at the base of the Annamite Mountains. The train rambled past the charred remains of several homes and villages— ghost towns on the outskirts of Da Nang. Hovels still smoldered from recent rocket fire, while the remains of stables lay half buried in ash. Several children splashed in a mud puddle; another squatted to defecate along the road. Randy waved to a small boy, who shook his head *no* and raised his middle finger in response.

So that's what I traveled 14,000 miles for? Randy thought ruefully. *Just to have some kid give me the finger.* He dropped onto the floor of the cattle car, pulled his helmet down over his eyes, stretched out his long legs, and tried to fall asleep.

⊂⊃⊂⊃

"Let's go, sailors—move it, move it!" the lieutenant barked as Randy and his medical team ran out onto the field. A helicopter had landed, the first of several to arrive that day, with a delivery of wounded men.

A heavy ramp on the chopper dropped to the ground with a thud. Randy and his team waited for the signal to advance before moving quickly to lift bleeding soldiers onto stretchers and carry them into the hospital. Each stretcher was positioned atop two sawhorses while the medics went to work.

Randy's hands shook as he cut away the first soldier's sullied uniform and tossed it to the ground. He had practiced this procedure hundreds of times in basic training, but nothing could have prepared him for what lay beneath the clothes.

The soldier had stepped on a land mine, and all that remained of his right leg was a bloody stump. The stench of burnt flesh turned Randy's stomach, and he fought an urge to bolt from the room; instead he applied a tourniquet and started an I.V. He had been taught to respond, not react, to perform without question whatever was necessary to save a life. Once his patient was stabilized Randy hosed down the cement floor, sending a stream of blood to the drain. When another chopper arrived he hurried again out the door with a stretcher. It was 7:30 a.m., and they were just getting started.

Physically and emotionally drained, Randy perched outside his barracks on a campstool and lit a cigarette. No matter how fast he had worked, he hadn't been able that day to keep up with the new arrivals. All day long the helicopters had brought more loads—more soldiers, more broken bodies than even their highly efficient medical unit could handle. Randy wondered how he would survive another day.

A fellow corpsman pulled up a stool and plopped down next to him. Gary had been in Da Nang for several months and knew how Randy must be feeling right about now. Reaching into his pocket, he pulled out a joint. "Here, man," he said softly, placing it in Randy's hand. "It's the only way to survive."

"No, thanks." Randy had never taken drugs before and didn't want to start now.

"Go ahead. Just to get through the first few days. You won't last a week without it."

Randy thought for a moment before nodding. Accepting the joint, he pulled out a match. "Thanks, man. Guess I could use a little help tonight . . . just to calm my nerves."

Gary patted him on the back, and Randy gazed up at the stars while he took a long, slow drag on the joint. He shook his head and laughed. "Turn on, tune in, and drop out—isn't that what they told us?"

"Pretty hard to drop out when you're stuck here in one of these uniforms, man."

Randy took another hit and passed the joint back to Gary. He was already starting to feel the effect.

Life at Da Nang Naval Hospital settled into a routine of chopper landings, hauling stretchers, and bandaging wounds. All day long the whir of twin blades announced the arrival of yet another shipment of broken bodies. At night Randy trudged back to his quarters with burning feet and a heavy heart. Gary usually met him in front of the barracks, lit a joint, and passed it to Randy before he could even sit down.

He's right, Randy acknowledged. *This is the only way to survive.* He could no longer imagine living a day without weed.

By now it was more than torn flesh and broken bones that were troubling him. Some soldiers, as they lay dying on stretchers, wanted Randy to take on the role of a parent or priest. No matter how clumsy he felt or how hard it was to find the words, he realized he was being called upon to dispense comfort to dying men.

"Doc, can you find me a drink?" a young soldier asked. He had lost the right side of his body and didn't have long to live. Randy was busy starting the I.V.

"Can I get some whiskey?" he asked again.

"Sorry soldier, there's none here on the base." *Poor kid*, Randy thought.

"How bad is it, doc? Am I dying?"

Randy pulled up a chair. "Look, I'm not a priest, but one thing I know: if there's a God in heaven, He knows what just happened to you."

"You think so?" the soldier asked wistfully.

"Yeah, I do." Hardly believing his own words, Randy touched the boy's shoulder and looked him in the eyes. "Do you want me to sit with you for a while?" The kid nodded before closing his eyes. *God,* Randy implored, *if you're up there, you gotta help this kid.*

When he had first arrived in Vietnam Randy had written to his mother every week, describing in great detail the incessant heat, the mosquitoes, and the grueling workload. But as the weeks turned into months he sent fewer and fewer letters home to Michigan. It wasn't that he had nothing to say; he just wanted to shield his mother from the agonies of war. How could he explain that his days were filled with mutilated bodies and soldiers begging to die? Morphine couldn't touch their pain, and Randy's nights were haunted by the sound of men screaming in agony. His mother could never begin to imagine the horror that was Da Nang, nor bear to know that her son's sleepless nights were peopled by haunting images of decapitated bodies on cold cement floors. So, in lieu of writing, he looked for ways to deaden the pain.

Randy spent his weekends in a nearby village, frequenting the kinds of places he would never have visited back home. His life revolved now around drugs, alcohol, and sex. Drugs calmed his nerves, alcohol dulled his senses, and contact with the ladies of the night in some sense satiated the emptiness in his heart. After a long week at the hospital the village offered some relief. A hit of speed, a bottle of whiskey, and an evening at the neighborhood brothel: these were the tools he needed to face yet another round of weekdays.

By December of 1969 Randy's tour was drawing to a close. Ready for a return to civilian life, he anxiously anticipated the return flight home. On his last night he stood guard outside the barracks. Weary from the day's work, he found himself struggling to stay awake. Finally, squatting next to a sandbag, he rested his rifle across his arm and dropped his head to his chest. His breathing slowed, and in seconds he was fast asleep.

What if you never make it out of here alive? A voice asked matter-of-factly in his dream. *What if you're killed just as your tour is about to end?* Randy lifted his head with a start and glanced around the sleeping camp. Straightening his helmet and scanning the empty yard, he instinctively pointed his gun into the shadows. *Must have been dreaming,* he assured himself, but he had heard stories about soldiers, ready for discharge, being blown to bits by enemy fire.

Who's to say it won't happen to you? It was that voice again, but this time he knew he wasn't asleep.

Randy's heart started to pound. His chest heaved, and he felt as though he were suffocating. Unzipping his flak jacket, he forced himself to take slow, deep breaths until he started to relax.

You're almost there, he told himself. Gazing up at the stars, his only immediate companions, Randy wondered whether anyone was listening. "God," he uttered, half aloud, "if you get me out of this place alive I promise I'll go straight. I swear I'll never touch another joint."

When the morning of departure dawned, Randy boarded a plane for California and never looked back, forgetting all about his promise to God. As the plane rose into the clouds and banked, he watched Da Nang shrink to the size of a postage stamp, then disappear from view. Leaning his head back against the seat, he closed his eyes. *It won't be easy,* he told himself, almost fiercely, *but I'll have to forget this year if I ever want to get my old life back.*

The plane had a three-hour layover in Los Angeles before heading straight to Michigan. A stewardess handed Randy a Coke, and he thanked her, took a sip, and looked out the window. Vietnam had been horrible, but it was the thought of landing in Detroit that now filled Randy with dread. He couldn't expect his family to understand. He had stopped writing, so how could they know that he had just been to hell and back?

As the plane began its descent into Metro Airport, he finished his Coke and took in the scene below. Gray February clouds hung low, and the tree branches had been stripped bare. This was just what Randy had been expecting—a dark, gloomy welcome for a war-weary returning vet.

CHAPTER 29

Another Chance

Randy's family was waiting for him at the terminal. His mom, dad, sister, and two brothers smiled when he stepped from the plane. His mother wrapped her arms around his neck and kissed him several times, while his dad shook his hand. Everyone looked happy, but Randy felt numb—neither happy nor sad, like a stranger entering a foreign land.

The reunion felt awkward for his family as well. His mother immediately sensed that something was amiss. Randy had changed; she could see it in his eyes and feel it in his hug. When he hefted his seabag and flung it over his shoulder, she shot a worried glance toward her husband.

When they arrived home Randy proceeded straight to his room and shut the door. Tossing his bag in a corner, he stretched out on his bed. Then, sinking into the unaccustomed comfort of a thick, soft mattress, he closed his eyes and fell immediately asleep.

Six hours later Randy sat up and gazed out his bedroom window. An old friend, Mike Cassady, still lived across the street with his parents. Randy watched Mike exit his house, lower himself into a sports car, and start the engine. Mike had changed over the last two years. His dark brown hair reached his shoulders, and he sported a full beard, long and thick. His friend looked to Randy like the kind of guy who might have a bag of weed stashed underneath his mattress. Before standing up to put on his coat, Randy watched Mike drive away.

Randy's mother glanced up, watching her son button his coat as he entered the kitchen. "Where are you off too?" she asked as casually as she could, though there was a catch in her voice.

"Can I borrow the car?"

She pointed to a set of keys on the table. "Where are you going?"

"I'm gonna go pick up a set of wheels."

His mother wiped her hands on a dishtowel and untied her apron. "I'll go with you," she announced. "You'll need someone to drive the car home if you buy something. Do you have enough money?"

"Yeah, I'm good."

They drove in relative silence the two miles down to Rinke Chevrolet, where they pulled into the used car lot. A white '65 Corvette with a black convertible top was parked out front—the exact make and model Randy had envisioned while stationed in Vietnam. He took it for a test drive before counting out the cash for the salesman. Ten minutes later he slipped on a pair of sunglasses and headed down Van Dyke toward Detroit. *The only thing missing now,* he thought to himself, *is a bag of weed.*

Randy pulled into the driveway of a small brick home on Detroit's east side, got out of the car, and knocked at the back door. No one answered, so he let himself in. Making his way down the basement stairs he was met by the familiar smell of marijuana. His old friend Dennis, also recently returned from Vietnam, was seated on the basement floor listening to Led Zepplin and getting high. A stream of incense wafted up to the ceiling, while a green lightbulb cast an eerie glow over Dennis's face. Looking up at Randy, he grinned. "Hey, man, what's happenin'?"

"Not much." Randy dropped down onto a beanbag. "How you doing, Dennis?"

Dennis shrugged. "Doing alright. When'd you get back?"

"Just today. I picked up a new set of wheels, and now I'm looking for a party."

"It's right here." Dennis laughed, made an expansive gesture with his hand around the room, and tossed a small bag at Randy. "The party's here, man." He pointed to the coffee table. "Some papers over there—help yourself."

Randy rolled the weed into a thin paper cylinder, twisted it together at both ends, lit it with a match, and dropped to the carpet to join Dennis. Familiar sensations returned as he took several long, slow drags. Sighing, he leaned back his head.

Whole Lotta Love blasted from the stereo, and Randy turned it up even louder. For the first time since leaving Nam Randy felt relaxed. Da Nang and all he had experienced there began a slow fade into the past.

After several minutes, though, the music started to change, the melody giving way to a screaming guitar lead that gripped Randy's heart with fear. Sitting bolt upright, he grabbed his chest; his heart was pounding, and a cold chill was running up and down his spine. Frantically he scanned the room for the demon that must surely have infiltrated the space. Dennis was fast asleep on the floor, so Randy reached for his keys and scrambled to his feet. Bumping into a chair and stumbling up the steps, he bolted out the back door.

The next evening Randy was sprawled on a chair in Mike Cassady's bedroom listening to music and admiring the pinups on his wall. Mike was stretched out on the bed, flipping through the pages of *Rolling Stone* Magazine. He looked nothing like the fresh-faced kid Randy had known back in grade school. Bell-bottom jeans and a Nehru shirt had replaced corduroys, penny loafers and cardigan sweater. A peace necklace hung from his neck, and a pair of sunglasses rested on the tip of his nose. Tossing the magazine to Randy, Mike stood to turn over the record. Randy flipped a few pages before throwing it down on the bed. "So, Cassady," he broke the silence. "I hear you got pretty heavy into the music scene while I was gone."

"You could say that." Mike reached into his wallet, pulled out a press card, and handed it to his friend. "That's a backstage pass for the Grande Ballroom. I've met some pretty cool bands: MC5, Cream, even Ted Nugent. You should come with me sometime. I could probably get you in."

"Cool, man. Sounds like you got connections. You got'ny more? I mean, when I was in Da Nang we used to smoke these little Thai sticks over there. Really tripped out on those things. You know where I can find some dope? Nothing heavy, man, just grass."

"I'm not into that scene anymore," Mike informed him. "But I might have one last joint stashed somewhere if you want it." He reached onto a shelf in his closet and pulled down a tin box. Mike rummaged through it, pulling out some eight-track tapes and a pipe before finally locating the reefer, which he handed to Randy. "That's my last one," he announced with some finality, putting the box back up on the shelf. "You're on your own after this."

"Thanks, man." Randy took the joint and slipped it into his shirt pocket, raising his eyebrows at a paperback book sitting prominently on Mike's desk. Its cover displayed a curious title: *Good News for Modern Man*. "So, what's with the book, Cassady?"

Mike glanced at his desk. "Oh, it's kinda like a Bible. You heard about Frank Majewski, right?"

"Who?"

"You remember Frank, that crazy guy that got kicked out of Cousino so many times. He busted out of jail and then started dealing dope. Last year he found religion and turned into one of those Jesus Freaks. Now every Friday night he preaches over at the social hall behind Saint Sylvester's. That's your folks' church, isn't it? Maybe they heard about it."

"I don't think so . . ." Randy decided it was time to leave. Thanking Mike for the joint, he headed home.

Hopping into his convertible, he picked up Woody and Grant, two more old friends from high school, before heading to Detroit. The three passed around the joint while listening to The Who on the radio. By the time they arrived at Trainer's Bar at Eleven Mile and Woodward, all three were stoned. Inside they found a table, ordered a few drinks, and settled in to watch the girls dance.

As the music played someone slipped into a chair behind Randy and scooted close. Randy could feel hot breath on his neck as the man spoke directly into his ear in a hoarse whisper: "You're a dead man!"

Randy froze, wanting to bolt from the room but feeling glued to his chair. A dark, demonic presence, like the one he had sensed in Dennis's basement, had returned.

"I'm not going to wait all night to do this," the voice continued. His breath was like fire. Randy knew there were people in the world who killed just for fun. This guy was one of them—he was sure of it. Satan's hit men, they were called. He wished he could see whether his antagonist had a gun.

Randy realized in that moment that he'd been playing God for a fool. He had vowed never to return to drugs, yet here he was back in the thick of that scene. Images of the opium dens and whorehouses he had visited in Vietnam flashed before his eyes. He had sold his soul in Saigon—and now the devil had come to collect.

Randy glanced down in consternation at the shaman beads around his neck, a psychic talisman he had worn for the past year. Tearing off the necklace, he flung the beads to the ground. The moments passed in slow motion as he waited to see what his adversary would do next. *You're telling me*, Randy thought to himself, *I survived Vietnam just to die in a rotten, stinkin' bar?* He raised his eyes to the ceiling and prayed silently.

God, I'm asking you to help me again. Please don't let this be the end. Give me another chance, God, please. He bowed his head. *What more can I say, God? What more can I do?*

A voice, restrained but strong, spoke in his heart. "Go, and sin no more."

Randy opened his eyes with a start. His knees were shaking and his palms were wet. Summoning all his courage, he turned around at last to look at the man—who was gone. Jumping to his feet in a panic, Randy threw on his coat and announced to his dumbfounded friends, "I gotta go, man. I gotta find a church."

"*What?*" Woody looked up from his drink. "What are you *talking* about? It's after midnight. Churches aren't open right now."

"I have to," Randy insisted. "I just talked to God. I gotta go."

Woody shot a meaningful look at Grant, then back at Randy. "You can't go to church, man."

"Why not?"

"Churches are locked up at night."

"Why are they locked?'

"I don't know! Maybe people steal stuff."

"Steal from God? *Are you nuts?* You don't mess with God, man! He's got the power to . . . to *dispatch* you!" Randy headed for the door. "I'm leaving, with or without you guys."

"You're freakin' us out, Randy," Grant stated coolly as he and Woody followed their friend out the door. "Calm down, all right? Just take it easy."

Randy climbed into the car. "You guys don't understand. Something happened back there. That place is evil—it's wicked." When he started the car the radio came to life—Sly and the Family Stone:

> *Looking at the devil, grinning at his gun*
> *Fingers start shakin', I begin to run*
> *Bullets start chasing, I begin to stop*
> *We begin to wrestle, I was on the top.*
> *I want to thank you falettinme be mice elf agin*
> *Thank you falettinme be mice elf agin.*[8]

Randy's hands froze on the steering wheel. He stared straight ahead while focusing on the strange lyrics. Woody and Grant exchanged a look. "What's wrong now?" Woody asked.

"Nothin'." Putting the car in gear, Randy pulled out of the parking lot. He hadn't thought about God in a long time. What little faith he'd had before Vietnam had been lost on the battlefield. But tonight he knew for sure God had spoken to him. He also knew his life had just been spared. *This is crazy!* he thought. *Did God just offer me another chance?* Dropping off Woody and Grant, he headed for home.

⊃⊖⊂

Mrs. Marcial picked up her purse and stepped into the living room. Randy was hunched on the couch, drumming his fingers on the cushion and tapping his feet on the rug. He had sat in virtually the same spot for three days. The curtains were drawn, and the room was dark.

She didn't like leaving him alone. What with his feet tapping and his eyes darting about the room, he looked as jittery as a jackrabbit.

"I'm going out for a bit," she announced as casually as she could. "Why don't you come along?"

"Where you going?" Randy asked, his feet bouncing furiously at the very thought of leaving.

"To the grocery store. It might do you some good to get out of the house, Randy." She held his coat out to him.

Reluctantly her son pulled himself up from the couch. At six-foot-two Randy towered above his mother, but his drooping shoulders and the lost look on his face made him appear much smaller and weaker. Slipping on his jacket, he followed Mrs. Marcial like a docile child.

On the drive to the store Randy began to recall his tormentor's hot breath and to hear again his threats—the low, dark murmurings as he had vowed to kill him. Randy wished he could wake up and realize, as he had once before, that it was all a nightmare. Staring out the window, he felt convinced that he was losing his mind.

As the pair made their way down the cereal aisle at Farmer Jack, Randy grabbed a box of Wheaties and tossed it into the cart. He wondered how it was he had come to this. How did a grown man wind up following his mother around like a little kid? Turning abruptly, he made a beeline for the exit, calling over his shoulder, "I'm gonna go wait in the car, Mom."

On the drive home he broke into a sweat, and back in the house he loosened his shirt collar and forced himself to take slow, cleansing breaths on his way to his room. Closing the door behind him, Randy dropped onto the bed. *Something is terribly wrong,* he recognized. *I'm either going to hurt somebody or kill myself. One thing I know for sure: I can't live like this another day.*

Randy's thoughts returned to his burning desire of a few nights earlier to find a church. Woody had told him all the churches would be locked. Now Randy aimed to check that out. Hurrying past his mother in the kitchen, he mumbled something about going for a ride. Moments later he had backed the car out of the driveway and was headed for Saint Sylvester Church.

To his immense relief he found the church door unlocked. It was heavy but swung easily in Randy's hand. Stepping into the sanctuary, he gazed around. Two tall candles flickered in the front, casting a warm glow over the altar, above which was suspended an enormous crucifix. The sculpted body of Christ was attached to the cross by three nails— one at the feet and one each at the hands. Randy groped his way to the front of the sanctuary and seated himself in a pew. Dropping from there to a kneeler he got down on his knees, folded his hands in a vice grip, bowed his head, and began to pray. "Oh God . . ." It was almost a whimper. Then a dam burst. Tears gushed from his eyes like a river, streaming down his cheeks and falling to the floor like rain. Randy bowed his head lower and doubled over, wrapping his arms around his middle. "Oh God," he cried again, his voice rising in decibels till it echoed off the cathedral ceiling. "Oh God, God, God. Ohhh . . . ohhh . . . ohhh!"

With each groan he bowed a little lower. His chest heaved, his limbs shook, and his cries reverberated throughout the sanctuary. His heart felt crushed. "Oh God, please help me," Randy implored. "If you're here, God . . . if you're really here. Please help me. *Ohhh* God . . ."

Randy felt suddenly as though a prison door had been flung open and a demon had relinquished its hold. As peace poured into his heart, something dark and sinister almost palpably departed, and Randy felt himself to have been set free. His anxiety vanished as liquid waves of love washed over him. The feeling grew so intense that Randy wondered whether he would survive the surging presence of God that threatened to overfill the room. As wave after wave continued to wash over him, Randy dried his eyes and lifted his head.

Gazing up at the crucifix above the altar, he gasped. The Christ figure was glowing and pulsing with a bright, unnatural light. *Did I just see that?* Rubbing his eyes, he looked again— the cross still glowed. Randy stared for several moments as the light moved steadily upward toward the ceiling, before disappearing altogether. Steadying himself in the pew, he fought to catch his breath.

CHAPTER 30

The Volunteer

Walking out of the church, Randy still felt strangely exhilarated; for the first time in his life he knew himself to be fully alive, aware that he would never again doubt the existence of God. An unexpectedly brilliant February sunshine greeted him on the steps, warming his face like a kiss from heaven. Smiling up at the sky, he walked briskly to his car. Everything had changed. Randy understood for the first time that God was full of mercy and forgiveness: He had just touched a broken, wounded soldier and given him a brand new start. No longer a prisoner to his grief and pain, Randy could hardly wait to tell his mother.

Despite the sunny day, a biting wind whipped his exposed cheeks as he climbed into his car. He drove home, parked in front of the house, and walked briskly to the front door. *I'm alive,* he thought, as another gust of wind hit his face. *I'm alive!* The wind, the sun, the pulsating joy in his heart—all provided tangible proof that he was indeed intensely alive, more vital than he'd ever been before. Opening the front door, Randy strode straight to the kitchen, calling out "Ma!" His mother, washing dishes at the sink, glanced up in surprise as her son—the same son who'd been acting so strangely since his return—now approached her from behind, slipped his arms around her waist, and planted a kiss on her cheek.

"Where have *you* been?" she asked, mystified.

"You won't believe it when I tell you."

Mrs. Marcial sat down in a chair, dried her hands with a towel, and looked up, a combination of amazement and hopefulness playing across her features: "Try me."

"Mom, I know I haven't exactly been myself since I got back. I've actually been pretty messed up, and have been for a long time. But something happened just now at the church. I went over to Saint Sylvester because I needed to talk to God. I had to get all this garbage out of me, Ma. I've been carrying it around for so long."

"So what happened?"

"It's hard to explain, but God was there, and He touched me. I could feel Him. All around me. I've never experienced anything like it. It was more real than I can describe."

Mrs. Marcial cautiously studied her son's face. His eyes, she noticed, were unnaturally bright, his breathing fast.

"I'm happy for you, Randy." His mother kissed the top of his head and patted his shoulder reassuringly. Overcome by her own emotion and not wanting him to see, she left the room.

That's good enough for me, he thought, and proceeded to walk across the street to Mike Cassady's.

Randy told Mike about his week—the terrifying experience at the bar; the anxiety that had overtaken him; and finally, the heavenly encounter in church. Mike listened politely before reaching for the New Testament on his desk. "Here," he said, "you can have this."

"What for?"

"Just read it, man." Mike was glad to be rid of the book—didn't know why he'd hung onto it for so long. He'd listened to Frank and watched most of his friends become Christians. Part of him wanted to believe in Jesus like everyone else, but he just couldn't do it. He fingered through the pages and marked the Gospel of John with a scrap of paper. "Start here," he said.

Randy took the book from his hand. "Okay. Thanks, Mike."

"You might want to check out that prayer meeting sometime too."

Randy hurried home to his bedroom and shut the door. He had never before opened a New Testament and turned to the spot Mike had marked. Propping his head on the pillow, he read all the way through to the account of Jesus' crucifixion. Randy bowed his head, saddened and sorry for all that Jesus Christ had to suffer. Learning what Jesus had gone through—his agonizing death on behalf of sinners—humbled Randy. Thinking back to the glowing cross, his heart was once again flooded with peace. Tears started to flow all over again, only this time they were tears of gratitude. All of the grief and pain were gone—had simply dissipated, as though into thin air.

That Friday evening Randy pulled into the parking lot at Saint Sylvester and made his way toward the social hall, a single-story building situated behind the church. The hall was used during the week for bingo and church board meetings, but tonight it bustled with an unlikely mix of teens, hippies, and bikers. The parking lot overflowed with high schoolers gathered outside to smoke cigarettes. Noisy junkers and motorcycles rumbled in and out, some pulling into parking spots and others simply checking out the scene. Slipping through the crowd to enter the building, Randy was struck by an even less likely assortment of individuals on the inside. Nuns and priests were seated in folding chairs, while dozens of younger kids sat cross-legged on the floor. Two men stood near the front tuning their guitars as people continued to file into the hall. Randy, leaving open the option of an early exit, stuck his hands in his pockets and leaned against the back wall.

The song leader, Matt, approached the microphone and got the evening underway. "Hey, everybody," he announced in an apologetic tone, "I'm sorry, but Frank can't be here tonight . . ." The crowd groaned with one voice. "*But Jesus Christ is here*, man, so let's all stand up and praise the Lord!"

Everyone rose to their feet. Never before having attended a prayer meeting, Randy had come with no idea of what to expect. One thing was certain, though: whatever scenario he may have imagined, this wasn't it! People clapped, smiled, and sang with gusto. The room felt energized, the lyrics and tunes were easy to pick up, and Randy soon found himself singing along.

I found a new way of living, I found a new life divine . . .

He watched several people lift their arms and wave their hands in the air as they sang. The atmosphere seemed electrified, and once again he could feel the presence of God. When the music ended everyone sat down. Randy remained standing—impressed but still noncommittal— in the back.

"All right," Matt invited, rubbing his hands together expectantly, "who has a testimony to share?" The room grew quiet as participants craned their necks to pan the audience in search of a volunteer. "Who would like to tell us what God has been doing in their life?"

No one spoke up.

"I know God did something in your life this week," Matt prompted, "but the devil wants you to sit there and not say a thing."

"I've got something to say," Randy called out—surprising no one more than himself! All eyes turned to take in the tall young man making his way to the front. His face and arms were bronzed; his hair was buzzed short, military style; and he sported a Fu-Manchu mustache. Matt raised the microphone several inches and stepped aside.

The unlikely volunteer took a deep breath and cleared his throat. "I just got back from Vietnam . . . ," he began. His commanding baritone instantly captivated the crowd. "And I gotta tell you that when you spend a year there like I did—all the suffering and torture of that place—all I can say is something happens inside. You're never the same. And you wonder if you'll ever pick up the pieces of your life again."

Randy's voice and presence carried the room. He didn't really need the microphone but bent over it anyway as he went on to describe his stint in Da Nang. Next he talked about the demonic presence that had met him in a bar on the day he returned home. "But God was waiting for me, too," Randy went on. "He was waiting for me to come to the end of myself. And when I finally did . . ."—he turned and pointed at Saint Sylvester's main building—"I ended up in that church right over there, down on my knees."

Randy described the tears that had gushed from his eyes and the waves of love that had repeatedly washed over him from the glowing, pulsating cross. Every eye was on the returning soldier as he spoke, and several people wiped away tears. A crowd gathered around him after he had finished speaking and stepped down. They wanted to hear more. Randy stayed behind to bask in the love and acceptance of the people God had seemingly assembled for his benefit.

Later on, as he walked to his car, it occurred to him that God must have been looking for him all his life. Yet He had deemed it necessary for Randy to cross the ocean and come back again to find out that his greatest need could be met right here—in Jesus Christ. Randy gazed up at the stars and thanked God for the gift of new life.

CHAPTER 31

"Joyce, What Have You Done?"

Spring 1970

Joyce was curled up on the couch with a cup of coffee and a good book. This one wasn't a romance novel like the ones her lady friends were reading. This was a true story—a tale of drug addicts and teen gangs living on the streets of New York. *The Cross and the Switchblade*, written by David Wilkerson in 1962, had become a best seller. It is the story of a small-town pastor who had left his home in rural Pennsylvania to preach on the streets of Brooklyn. Wilkerson describes how he shared God's love with street gangs and how this endeavor led to dozens of teens giving their hearts to Christ. When Buckboard and Stagecoach, leaders of a notorious gang called the Chaplains, knelt down on a street corner to pray, Wilkerson knew he was witnessing a miracle. His willingness to go wherever God sent him helped launch a spiritual awakening among gang members in New York City.

The Cross and the Switchblade sparked revivals in churches across America, as people began to gather in small groups to pray. The book challenged Christians to believe once again in the life-changing power of the gospel and of the Holy Spirit's ability to apply that gospel to hearts. Joyce decided to pick up a copy to see what the fuss was all about. Once she started reading, she couldn't put it down.

Joyce Gramm was a bright, witty, and attractive woman, born in 1928 and raised in New Rochelle, New York. The only daughter of a wealthy socialite couple, Joyce enjoyed a carefree life filled with servants, dinner parties, dances, and the theater. But in 1948, when her parents announced that they were getting a divorce, Joyce's world fell apart. Moving into a small apartment with her mother, she resigned herself to a simpler, quieter lifestyle.

Soon afterward Joyce met Bruce Todd, a handsome and soft-spoken young man several years her elder (Joyce had just passed her 19th birthday), with jet-black hair and sharp blue eyes. Although Joyce could have had her pick of almost any man in New Rochelle, she was attracted to Bruce, whose commanding six-foot-five presence dominated social gatherings. Bruce, too, was smitten—so much so that the day after the two had met he presented Joyce to his parents, introducing her as "the girl that I'm going to marry." Within a year they were indeed wed.

Two years later Bruce was presented with the opportunity to purchase a company in Michigan that sold light fixtures to schools and businesses. Jumping at the chance to be his own boss, he and Joyce, along with their young daughter Meb, packed their belongings in 1951 and headed for Detroit.

Bruce's company faced challenges, and the young couple struggled to make ends meet. While Joyce took care of the children—another daughter and a son had joined the family in quick succession—Bruce worked long hours to keep the company afloat.

One Sunday Joyce decided on a whim to visit a Baptist Church in the village of Rochester, Michigan. She listened closely as the minister read Jesus' words from Revelation 3:2: "Behold, I stand at the door and knock. If any man will open that door, I will come in and sup with him." Joyce, uninitiated in God's Word, felt as though a lightning bolt had hit her. She sat up straight, wondering how it was she could go about opening that door.

For most of her life Joyce had felt estranged from God. As a child her mother had taken her to a Christian Science church, but Joyce had felt more like a spectator than a member. After listening to the minister that morning in Rochester, she realized that she had never responded to the message of salvation. Bowing her head, she prayed then and there to receive Christ as her Savior. Joyce could hardly wait to tell Bruce all about it when she got home.

Desiring to become a member of the church, she announced to Bruce the following week her plans to be water baptized. Bruce, though happy to see his wife growing close to God, would have preferred that she not join a church. It wasn't that he objected to baptism, he just wasn't all that interested in religion. He explained to Joyce that his own relationship with God was private—and that he preferred she keep hers the same way.

Joyce took a sip of coffee as she continued to read Wilkerson's book.

". . . if these boys were going to change dramatically," the author recalled, "the transformation would have to come about in their hearts. I knew I could never bring this about: it would have to be the work of the Holy Spirit."[9]

Joyce read with interest what Wilkerson had to say next:

"There was one way to find out. . . . I would speak to these boys, trusting the Holy Spirit to reach them where I could not. . . . I chose John 3:16 as my text: 'For God so loved the world that He gave His only begotten Son that whosoever believeth in Him should not perish, but have everlasting life.' I told them that God loved them as they were, right then. . . . He knew their hatred and their anger. He knew that some of them had committed murder. But God also saw what they were going to be in the future, not only what they had been in the past."[10]

At that point in the narrative four of the gang leaders had asked Wilkerson a question: "What are we supposed to do?"

Wilkerson had responded boldly, "I want you to kneel down right here on the street and ask the Holy Spirit to come into your lives so that you will become new men. 'New creatures in Christ' is what the Bible says. This can happen to you, too."[11]

The gang leaders, Wilkerson remembered, had tossed aside their cigarettes, pulled off their hats, and dropped to their knees on a busy street corner, after which Wilkerson had led them in a prayer.

Joyce put the book down. *Could God's love be so strong,* she marveled, *that even gang members couldn't resist?* As she thought about the dramatic scene in New York City, a vision unfolded before her eyes: Joyce witnessed dozens of young people running up a hill and tumbling over a cliff to the rocks below. In the vision she sat, benumbed, for several moments watching this horror unfold. When the vision ended Joyce was so shaken she burst into tears. For the rest of the day she carried a weight in her heart.

That evening she related the incident to Bruce. "I could hardly sit still as I read the book," she shared. "It was so powerful, Bruce. And then, all of a sudden, I had a vision."

Bruce glanced up, skeptical, over the top of his reading glasses.

"I know it sounds crazy," she hurried on, "but I saw young people running up a hill and then falling over a cliff to their death."

Bruce set down his newspaper.

"They were like sheep without a shepherd," Joyce continued in a quavering voice. "Every one of them plunged to their death. That's when I knew I had to do something. I need to help them, Bruce. I don't know how, but somehow I have to help."

Bruce slipped off his glasses and drew a deep breath. "Pearshape," he reasoned, addressing her by his pet name, "we don't know anything about gangs. We don't know anything about drug addicts or prostitutes, either. What makes you think we could help?"

"Even if we don't know what we're doing," Joyce pleaded, "I still have to do something. I've got to help those kids."

Bruce had never seen her like this. Perhaps God had really spoken to Joyce, but he wasn't at all sure what this might mean.

The next evening Joyce placed a call to Bruce's sister Honey Lou, who lived in Florida. Honey Lou and her husband, Ray, were brand new Christians, so Joyce hoped they might be able to offer some advice. Honey Lou listened to Joyce's story and then handed the phone to Ray. "Listen, Joycey," Ray told her, "there's no doubt in my mind that God has something for you to do. I know a youth minister in Chicago by the name of Clair Hutchins. I'll give you his phone number so you can call him. Tell him about your vision. I'm sure he'll be interested."

Joyce waited till the next morning to make her call. Bruce was in the shower and the kids already at school. Her heart pounded as the phone rang at the other end.

Someone picked it up. "Hello, this is Brother Ed Maurer . . ."

"I'm looking for Clair Hutchins."

"He isn't here right now. Can I help you?"

"No, thank you. I just need to talk to Mr. Hutchins. I thought I could reach him at this number."

"Well, normally yes, you can, but there's no one here right now. I just happened to be walking by and heard the phone ringing. I'm a minister too—are you sure I can't be of some assistance?"

Joyce sighed. "It's these kids . . . ," she began. "All these teenagers on drugs are destroying their lives. I want to help, but I don't know how. I had this vision . . ." She paused for Brother Ed's reaction.

"Go on," he said.

"I saw dozens of kids falling off a cliff to their death. It was horrible. I just knew that if I didn't help them they'd keep right on falling. But I don't know what I'm supposed to do. I don't know what *God* wants me to do. I was hoping Clair Hutchins could help."

"Well, sister"—Ed's smile was conveyed right over the phone—"You came to the right place. I care about those kids too. I want to see every one of them saved."

Maybe this is who I was supposed to talk to, Joyce realized.

Ed told her he had just come up from Sarasota, Florida, to park his motor home behind Clair Hutchins's church prior to assisting his friend with a week of revival meetings. "Joyce," he put in thoughtfully, "I'd say this is a divine appointment. You and I both feel the same way about young people. How about if my wife and I swing by Michigan on our way home, and we can talk about it? How does that sound?"

Joyce was thrilled; she felt so certain God had brought her and Brother Ed together for this moment that she invited him to park his motor home in their driveway. After hanging up, though, Joyce's heart sank as she realized she had forgotten to ask Bruce.

Her husband was just finishing his shower, so Joyce called to him sweetly through the bathroom door. "Bruce, someone is coming to see us in a couple of days. He's from Chicago."

"Who is he?"

"His name is Ed Maurer," Joyce replied. "He's an evangelist who thinks he can help us with the kids. It's okay if he stays a few nights, isn't it? He's bringing his own motor home . . ."

The door flew open and Bruce appeared, wrapped in his robe with a shocked expression on his face. "Joyce," he thundered, "what have you done now?"

By the next morning Joyce was sorry she had ever placed a call to Chicago. As she stirred Bruce's eggs on the stove, she scolded herself for being so reckless. *What was I thinking? How could I have invited him here—a perfect stranger?*

Bruce sat at the kitchen table, silent and frowning over the *New York Times* in his hands. He hated the thought of houseguests, but it was too late to do anything about that now. Brother Ed was on his way. Bruce shook his head and turned to the business page. *A motor home in our driveway . . .*, he scoffed to himself. *What will she think of next?*

"I'll tell you what," he stated in a conciliatory tone as he folded the paper in half and laid it down. He sounded much calmer than he felt. "When the kids get home from school today, tell them to get on the phone and call everyone they know. Ask them all to come over tomorrow night. That'll give this man a few teenagers to talk to when he shows up." This was the best Bruce could come up with on such short notice. Joyce was ecstatic.

The kids were happy too. Having friends over on a weeknight was an occasion that didn't happen often. It sounded like fun. And Brother Ed sounded as though he'd be entertaining too. The phone lines were buzzing that evening as news of the gathering spread across town. Joyce assured Bruce that only a handful of teens would show up, but she would make an extra pitcher of lemonade just in case. None of them really knew quite what to expect.

"So in walks this short, wiry, gray-haired little man," Joyce was telling her friends over coffee the next day. "Sixty-five years old and full of fire."

The women chuckled appreciatively as Joyce described how Ed and his wife, Ethel, had appeared on their doorstep, toting two suitcases—and a poodle that immediately took a strong disliking to Bruce. All day long the scrappy little dog had nipped at Bruce's heels whenever he walked by. Later that night Bruce had gone so far as to threaten to "kick the little beast to kingdom come . . . along with Ed and Ethel, too."

"If there ever was a man on God's green earth who could drive Bruce up the wall," Joyce admitted to her friends, "it would be Brother Ed. He and Bruce are like oil and water."

While Brother Ed was brash, Bruce was soft-spoken. Ed was outgoing, Bruce reserved. Ed was a Spirit-filled Pentecostal, while Bruce's faith was intensely private. Bruce kept to his office in the basement for the rest of the day, while Ed shut himself off in a back room to pray. The only interaction between the two men took place at dinnertime—and Bruce preferred to keep it that way.

The next evening, as though on cue, teenagers began filing into the house. Brother Ed rubbed his hands together in delight, while Bruce retreated sullenly to the basement. Joyce sat on the couch, ready for whatever might happen next. In the meantime the kids kept pouring into the living room.

When everyone was settled, Brother Ed stood up to speak. Gazing around the room at his fresh-faced, expectant audience, he smiled. "I don't know what most of you expected when you came here tonight, but this is no ordinary gathering, is it?" His voice was high-pitched, and his Southern drawl caused some of the kids to snicker.

"But I've got a feeling," Brother Ed went on, "some of you might be interested in hearing about God tonight. Why else would you have come? There's plenty of other things to do on a Tuesday night. But you came here, and I believe God wanted you here, too."

"Amen, brother!" a boy called out with an edge of mockery in his tone. Everyone laughed.

Ed stayed the course: "Young people, I'm here to tell you God is interested in you. He knows where you live. He knows where you go to school. And He knows what you're thinking right now. You see, God isn't some impersonal being somewhere up there in the sky. He isn't a UFO. Amen?"

"Amen," a handful of kids responded politely, unsure of where this was headed.

"He's the loving, caring Father who created you. And not only does He know everything about you, He wants you to know about Him, too. Isn't that amazing? He knows you, He loves you, and He wants you to get to know Him. Think about that for a minute."

Ed paused long enough to glance, individually, into the face of each person in the room. The place grew quiet, with only the soft ticking of the mantle clock to punctuate the stillness. "So, how do we do that? I mean, how do we get to know this God? Well, young people, I've got some good news tonight. Jesus Christ came down to earth two thousand years ago with a message for us. Do you know what that message was?"

Ed started to pace. His breathing quickened, and beads of sweat began to appear on his brow. "This is the message: Repent! That's it! Repent, for the kingdom of God is at hand. But, you might be wondering"—Ed slowed down and lowered his voice here—"what does 'repent' mean?" He smiled into several of the blank faces. "Well, I'm gonna tell you now: It means change your direction. Go a different way. Be sorry for your sins and ask God to help you turn everything around. Did you catch what I just said? *Be sorry for your sins.* The Bible says, 'Believe on the Lord Jesus Christ and you shall be saved.' *Hallelujah!*

"So, now, what does this business of being 'saved' mean? Saved means you've been rescued. Rescued from sin and from hell. If you want to you can be saved right here and now—tonight—so you'll know you

213

won't have to spend the rest of eternity apart from God. Repent, young people, because you need to be saved. Short, tall, good, bad—*everyone* needs to be saved.

"This world is passing away, and when it does you don't want to have one foot in God's kingdom and one foot in the world. The Bible says '*Today* is the day of salvation.' There's no time to put this off. The time to decide is *now*."

Ed pointed to Joyce as she sat on the couch. "Do you know what happened to Sister Joyce a few days ago? She had a vision, a vision from God. He showed her a bunch of kids running up a hill. They ran up that hill and then fell right off the edge of a cliff to the rocks below. I want you to know that was a pretty scary sight for Sister Joyce. But the Holy Spirit spoke to her. He said, 'You need to help those kids. You have to keep them from falling over the cliff!' Well, she didn't know what to do about it. She isn't used to hearing from God that way. I don't think too many of us are. But when God gives you something to do, brother, you do it. So Sister Joyce prayed and asked God to show her what He wanted." Brother Ed smiled. "That's when she called me . . ."

Ed's voice grew quiet, and everyone's eyes were riveted on him. "She had no idea when she placed that call to Chicago that I'd be the one to answer. When she told me about her vision I said, 'Hallelujah, I'm going to Michigan!' Because you see, young people, God gave me a burden too. The same burden He gave to Sister Joyce, He gave to me. So I packed up my motor home and drove here to Rochester." Brother Ed let out an audible sigh and set down his Bible on the coffee table. "Young people, God cares so much about you he gave somebody a vision and somebody else orders to leave Chicago, just so you could hear this message tonight. The question is: what are *you* going to do about it?"

Joyce glanced at the rapt young audience. The kids, some open-mouthed, were hanging on to every word.

"You may ask," Brother Ed continued, "'What am I supposed to do? How do I get myself saved?' Well . . ."—he broke into one of his winning smiles—"I'm glad you asked. People have been asking that question for a long time. And here's the answer." He picked up his Bible and opened it to a bookmarked page. "In the second chapter of Acts—right here in the New Testament, chapter 2 verse 38—a group of people asked the apostle Peter that same question: 'What must we do to be saved?' Here was his answer:

"'Repent, and let each of you be baptized in the name
of Jesus Christ for the forgiveness of your sins; and you
shall receive the gift of the Holy Spirit.'

"*Three thousand* people received Jesus as their Savior that day. I'm
looking around this room right now and wondering how many we have
in here. Twenty? Maybe twenty-five. And a lot of you may be wondering
what to do next. Well, the answer is the same today as it was back then:
repent. Repent, be baptized, and you'll receive the Holy Spirit.

"The Lord is in this room right now, and He's tugging on a lot of
hearts. I'm going to ask each of you to bow your head so I can say a
prayer with you. If you want to meet the Lord Jesus tonight, repeat these
words after me: Dear Jesus . . ."

"Dear Jesus," the kids murmured in unison.

Brother Ed felt a lump rising in his throat. He swallowed and started
again, pausing at regular intervals to allow the kids to repeat the words.
"Dear Jesus, I come to you tonight knowing I'm a sinner. I ask you to
forgive me for my sin and wash me clean. Give me a new life, Lord. I believe you sent Jesus to die on the cross for me. I welcome you as my Lord
and Savior tonight. Thank you that I am now a child of God. Amen."

Ed looked over the sea of bowed heads. "Amen," he whispered as a
hush settled over the crowd. One by one the kids began to look up, tears
streaming down their faces. Joyce brushed away her own tears as well.
She had read in Wilkerson's book about the presence of tears:

> I think I could almost put it down as a rule that the
> touch of God is marked by tears. When finally we let the
> Holy Spirit into our innermost sanctuary, the reaction
> is to cry. I have seen it happen again and again. Deep
> soul-shaking tears, weeping rather than crying. It comes
> when that last barrier is down and you surrender your-
> self to health and to wholeness.[12]

"I'll never forget it as long as I live," Ed shared with Joyce the next
day. "Never seen anything like it before—all those kids crying at the
same time. Those were genuine conversions last night, Joyce. I've been
in this line of work a long time and seen a lot of revivals, but nothing like
that. I'm surprised the carpet wasn't drenched with their tears."

CHAPTER 32

No Turning Back

"**A**ll of a sudden they looked up at us with these happy, shining faces," Joyce told Bruce the next day. "They weren't the same kids who'd walked into our house an hour before. Something was different."

Bruce wondered whether this had been an isolated event or whether it would happen again. Brother Ed had invited the kids to come back the following evening, only this time he asked them to bring along their friends. Bruce looked out the living room window at the motor home blocking his driveway. He wondered how long it would be before he could once again park his car in the garage. Ed had no idea, he fumed, how irritating his presence, not to mention his personality, was. And Bruce had no idea how to get rid of him.

"As long as those kids keep coming," Ed announced to Joyce with enthusiasm, "I'll keep preaching."

The next night the living room was packed again as young people returned to the Todd house, this time in company with their friends. The crowd spilled over into the kitchen, and concerned neighbors wondered what could be happening on Charlesina Avenue, their peaceful, oak-lined street. For a second evening the road was congested, for more than a block, with noisy teens and beat-up cars. Ed's soon-to-be-infamous motor home was already becoming the talk of the town. Joyce, unflappable as usual, just smiled. None of her friends would believe her if she were to explain that a full-fledged revival was taking place at her house.

On the second night Ed taught the kids about the Holy Spirit. Most came from good homes, the children of parents who regularly attended church. They had a general knowledge of God, though few knew much about the Holy Spirit. Ed explained that the Spirit wants to take up residence in every believer's heart. At the end of the meeting he strolled around the room, placing his hands on each person's head and praying in a thunderous voice that rattled Joyce's china plates. "Speak it out!" he commanded. "Speak it out in tongues!" Suddenly the kids began praising God in the sounds and syllables Ed referred to as "tongues." "That's it!" he shouted. "That's it! You're doing it!" Some, thinking the cacophony sounded like gibberish, laughed off the spectacle, while others marveled at what was taking place in their hearts.

So the meetings went on, night after night, as teenagers continued to give their hearts to the Lord. Joyce suspected that some might be humoring Ed, but she was grateful for every young person who came.

When the weekend arrived Bruce assumed that Ed, Ethel, and their obnoxious poodle would depart. *They can't stay forever,* he reasoned. But when kids showed up yet again for a Saturday meeting, the motor home didn't budge, obliging Bruce to retreat yet again to the sanctuary of his basement. He was beginning to feel like a fish out of water. It was easy enough to perceive that God was up to something, but Bruce couldn't decide where he himself fit in.

While Brother Ed preached to a roomful of teens, Joyce tiptoed downstairs to speak to Bruce. She found her husband looking physically worn, almost ill. "Bruce," she asked in real concern, "What's going on? What are you doing down here?"

In a weary gesture Bruce closed the book he was reading and set it down hard on the desk. "I didn't think it was going to turn out like this, Joyce," he admitted.

Joyce's heart sank.

"One or two of these meetings was fine, but we're in it up to our elbows." He glanced in the direction of the living room above their heads. "And those kids don't want me around. Look at me—too big and too straight." He shifted in his seat and shook his head. "I'll just scare them off."

"No you won't, Bruce . . ."

"Still . . ." Leaning back, he returned the book to its place on a shelf. "This came into our home, didn't it? So maybe it *has* to involve me. Maybe even I can't miss this." With a resolute sigh Bruce rose, turned off the light, and started up the stairs with Joyce. Later that night, after everyone had gone home, he knelt down beside his bed. Folding his hands and bowing his head, Bruce asked the Holy Spirit to fill his heart as well.

The numbers continued to increase, and evenings settled into a routine: dinner with Ed and Ethel, followed by a horde of teens marching into the house. At 7:00 Bruce would station himself in his chair near the front door and greet each visitor with a nod. The kids soon began referring to him affectionately as "Big B," and Joyce, ever on fire for the Lord, became known as "Sister Furnace."

Joyce heard about other prayer gatherings as well, meetings just like theirs being held all over the Detroit area. Similar happenings were occurring in Ann Arbor, Livonia, St. Clair Shores, and Warren. Young people were meeting in homes, dorms, and church basements to pray and read the Bible. It had never occurred to Joyce that her group might be part of an ever-expanding movement of God. *Time* Magazine reported that the phenomenon was popping up all over the country:

> Jesus is alive and well and living in the radical, spiritual fervor of a growing number of young Americans who have proclaimed an extraordinary religious revolution in his name. Their message: the Bible is true, miracles happen, God really did so love the world that he gave it his only begotten son. . . . It is a startling development for a generation that has been constantly accused of tripping out or copping out with sex, drugs and violence.[13]

One Catholic leader was quoted as saying that "we are on the threshold of the greatest spiritual revival the U.S. has ever experienced."[14]

People began conducting Jesus rallies all across the country. They carried signs, sang, and marched down city streets. Denominational walls tumbled as churches began to hold ecumenical meetings intended solely to lift up the name of Jesus. The movement was spreading faster than the journalists could type. Prayer meetings began cropping up in Canada, Europe, and Latin America as well. It appeared that a worldwide revival was underway.

One night after the kids had departed, Joyce sat on the couch reading *Time* Magazine. She held it up to show Bruce an article about the Jesus Movement. "It's like we're on a stage," she commented with a chuckle, "and you and I are moving through the script like puppets on a string."

Bring Him to Me

CeG

April/1970

Bob pulled himself up from his prone position, then, sitting, sank back deep into the couch. Glancing around the room, he took in the scene: empty beer bottles everywhere, the stale stench of marijuana hanging in the air, an assortment of drug paraphernalia scattered across the coffee table, and two flies droning over a pile of wilted french fries from the night before. A young couple, fast asleep on the floor, still held each other in a passionate embrace. Bob ran his hand through his curly brown hair and reached instinctively for a pack of cigarettes. Empty. Crumpling the packaging, he rubbed his eyes hard and scratched his beard.

Steve was passed out in a chair. With one leg draped over the arm and an empty beer bottle in his lap, he looked wasted. All Steve had talked about the night before was killing himself. Bob knew it had been the acid talking, but he had still taken the threat seriously. Ever since returning from Vietnam Steve could talk of little else. Life had no meaning, he kept repeating, his eyes desolate. Death was the only way out—the only way to escape the nightmares that had followed him home from Saigon.

Like so many others returning from Vietnam, Steve had relied on heavy drug usage to keep the pain at bay. But the same pills that had helped him cope were now destroying his mind. Bob had stayed up most of the night trying to convince his friend of that fact. "There must be a reason you survived the war," he had pleaded. "Everybody is put on this earth for a purpose. You can't just throw away your one chance at life." Steve hadn't been moved. "Listen, man," Bob had tried one last time: "Just reach out to God, and he'll help you. Jesus is there to help."

It had all sounded so good the night before. Bob stood up to stretch his arms. Unfortunately, it had been a rehash of platitudes he wasn't sure he believed himself.

As the sun thrust its way into the room, it washed away some of the drabness. Bob reached for his sandals and glanced at a newspaper lying on the floor. "Jesus Freaks Hit the Beach" the headline read. Intrigued in spite of himself, Bob picked up the paper and started to read. A man quoted in the article sounded a lot like someone he had known years ago. "Sandy" described himself as a "born-again" Christian. Bob shook his head. This couldn't be the same person with whom he used to party. *But then,* he wondered, *how many guys have a name like Sandy?* The article mentioned Revival Tabernacle, a church in Sarasota that had been experiencing a religious revival. *That's not too far from here,* Bob recognized. Acting on an impulse, he grabbed a pile of discarded clothing and stuffed it into his backpack. *If I leave now,* he chuckled to himself, *I might even make it in time for church.*

In the early 1960s Gerald Derstine had pastored a Mennonite church in Minnesota. One night as he prayed God answered by filling him with the Holy Spirit. It was not long afterward that Derstine was offered a position at a small Pentecostal church in Florida. Revival Tabernacle thrived under Derstine's leadership, with young people in particular flocking to hear the fiery preacher. When it became clear that a spiritual awakening was taking place, Derstine began to hold prayer meetings every night of the week. Hundreds participated, with many committing their lives to Christ. The church multiplied in numbers, and long-time members rejoiced to see a revival in their day.

One Sunday Derstine's younger brother Willy took his usual morning stroll to church. The service wouldn't start for another hour, but Willy liked to arrive early. He'd let himself in the back door, open the windows to let the air circulate, and spend an hour in prayer. It was 8:00, too early for visitors, yet Willy spied a figure lying on the front porch of the building. It was a scraggly young man, bearded and shabby—the kind who showed up at their church on a regular basis these days. The man was fast asleep with his back against the door and his legs stretched out in front of him. On his feet were dusty sandals; he may well have walked for miles. Willy touched his shoulder lightly. "Can I help you with something, son?"

Bob lifted his head and shielded his eyes from the brilliant sunlight that formed a halo around Willy's head. "Sure, Preacher."

Willy helped him to his feet. "I'm not the preacher, son. That'd be my brother, Gerald Derstine. He's the pastor here. My name's Willy."

Bob shook his hand and smiled. "Bob Holt. Nice to meet you, Willy."

"Are you here for the service, Bob? It starts at 9:00, but people don't usually start coming for a while."

"No, I'm not here for church. I'm looking for an old friend of mine, a guy by the name of Sandy."

Willy smiled. "Everybody knows Sandy."

Bob stretched his arms into the air and yawned. "I read about him in the newspaper. They interviewed him about this place. I figured I'd look him up to see what's happening."

Willy unlocked the church door and held it open for Bob. "Why don't you come in and have a seat? Church will start in a little while."

Bob stepped inside and gazed around the sanctuary. A wooden cross hung at the front, and a large oak pulpit stood center stage. He sat down in a pew, wondering how the Sandy he had known could ever have ended up at a place like this. The back door swung open to emit a ray of sunshine.

"Praise the Lord," someone called out. A thin man in his sixties strode up to Bob, took his hand, and began priming it like a pump. "Brother Ed Maurer. Glad to have you here, son."

At first opportunity Bob thrust his hands back into his pockets, nodding his acknowledgment. "Thanks."

"We have a lot of young people attend our church," Brother Ed continued. "All hippies, every one of them." Ed glanced down at Bob's sandals. "Looks like you've come a long way, son."

Bob lifted his feet one at a time, inspecting each one. "Yeah, I put on a few miles today." He hoped Brother Ed wasn't planning to sit down.

"Wait right here," Ed told him, all the while moving away in his quick, fluid motion. "I've got something to show you." He left the room, returning only moments later with a photo album in his hands. Settling himself, uninvited, next to Bob, he opened the book. "I wanted you to see these; they're from our water baptism last week. That's me in the Gulf of Mexico. See all those kids standing in line? Every one of 'em baptized that day. Pretty amazing, isn't it? I never saw so many young people giving their lives to Christ. The Holy Spirit is pouring out His power, Bob. God is doing a mighty work."

Bob glanced back at the door to see whether anyone else might have arrived. He didn't care much about water baptisms, not to mention that he was still buzzing from three nights of drinking and dropping speed. *This guy has no idea how high I am right now*, he thought.

Brother Ed, undeterred, continued to turn the pages. "It's happening all over the country. Hippies are giving their lives to Jesus and getting baptized." He rested his hand on Bob's shoulder. "I hope we have the privilege of baptizing you one day, son."

Bob shifted in his seat and wondered what could be taking Sandy so long. The sanctuary began to fill, but there was still no sign of his friend. He watched as an assortment of hippies and bikers streamed into the pews. By 9:00 there was standing room only. Guitar music filled the air, and loud singing was accompanied by impromptu shouts of "Hallelujah!" and "Praise God!" Bob watched in amazement and, in spite of himself, clapped in time to the music. He finally noticed Sandy standing in a corner with his hands raised in the air. When Brother Ed wasn't looking, Bob slipped away to join his friend.

As Pastor Gerald Derstine began to speak, Bob felt uncomfortable. He was certain the preacher was talking directly to him. Sharp words cut into his heart like a dagger, and by the end of the service Bob found himself kneeling in the front of the sanctuary confessing his sin. He asked Jesus to forgive him, to become his Savior, and to fill his heart with peace. Someone laid a hand on his shoulder. It was Pastor Derstine, who stood over Bob and began to pray. Bob couldn't shake the feeling that his life was about to change.

A few days later he packed his belongings and moved to Sarasota. Toting his guitar to the church, he quickly learned how to play the worship songs at Revival. The music was nothing like the rock and roll he was used to strumming, but when Bob's deep baritone filled the church people stood still to listen. He would later write a ballad to describe the change that had taken place in his life:

> *Jesus, walked on water; Jesus calmed the angry sea.*
> *Jesus raised Lazarus from the dead,*
> *And he did the same thing for me.*
> *Now I know he's real. Now I know for sure.*
> *Now I know I'm gonna spend my life with him*
> *Both now and evermore.*[15]

"Bible camp?" Bob had never heard of such a place.

"It's up in Minnesota," Pastor Derstine explained. "I started the camp a few years ago. It's a great way to get close to God. I'm thinking it might be good for you. You could study the Bible and learn how to lead worship. Stay the whole summer, Bob. And don't worry about the cost— it's covered." Pastor Derstine laid his hand on Bob's shoulder. "It would mean time away from your old life, son, and give you a fresh start. What do you say?"

Only 20 years old, Bob had no family ties, no job, and no plans. He accepted Derstine's offer and on June 1 boarded a Greyhound for northern Minnesota. When the summer was over Bob returned to Revival Tabernacle as the new worship leader. Each day he grew stronger in his commitment, and as his faith grew he became increasingly prepared for anything God might ask him to do.

❧

In November 1970 Brother Ed and his wife, Ethel, finally packed up their motor home, left Michigan, and headed back south for the warm climate of Florida. That Sunday, as Ed stood before the congregation at Revival Tabernacle, he described what was taking place in Detroit. Bob listened quietly, his guitar on his lap.

"I'm looking for someone to go back to Detroit to help run those meetings," Ed informed the gathered crowd. "So if you're feeling a tug in your heart right now, it might be that God is calling you."

After the meeting Brother Ed sat down next to Bob. "It would just be for a couple of weeks, Bob. Just to lend a hand. You wouldn't believe how many kids gave their hearts to the Lord while I was there. They just need someone to teach them the Bible. Someone young like you."

"All right," Bob agreed with a shrug. "Maybe I'll go for a week or two. If that's what God wants, that's what I'll do."

Ed contacted Joyce and told her that a young hippie was on his way to Detroit. Joyce knew they needed someone to help lead the ongoing meetings and appreciated Bob's willingness to play that role.

Brother Ed had been the firebrand God had used to get things started, but someone else was needed to keep the momentum going. Bob could stay at their house for as long as he wanted, she assured Ed.

Two days later Bob strolled through Detroit Metro Airport with a guitar strapped to his back. He saw Meb, the Todd's oldest daughter, holding up a sign with his name on it. She was there to pick him up and drive him to the Todd home. Upon their arrival Bruce rose from his chair in greeting, and Joyce came in from the kitchen, wearing an apron. A pot of spaghetti sauce simmered on the stove, and the table was set for six. A yellow parakeet chirped brightly in its cage near the dining room window.

Bob stood for a moment to take in the idyllic scene: it was like something from "Leave It to Beaver." The Todd home was warm and inviting, each room tastefully decorated in antique collectables. Setting down his guitar, Bob grasped Bruce's hand, noting that his host wore a shirt and tie and held a copy of *The Wall Street Journal*. Joyce had a disarming smile, and her friendly chatter put him at ease. She showed Bob to his room and announced that dinner was almost ready. Bob was glad to hear it; he was starving.

The next evening young people began arriving at the Todd house, all anxious to meet the new young guy from Florida. By 7:00 more than 40 kids were settled in the kitchen and living room. It was cold outside, with snow falling steadily, but inside it was toasty. The kids, packed together like sardines, looked expectantly toward Bob as he perched himself in the front of them, guitar on his lap. He whispered a quiet prayer before beginning.

"How's everyone doing tonight?" he opened. "My name is Bob Holt, and I just came up from Florida to help run these meetings for a week or two. We're gonna start out with a couple songs I learned this past summer at Bible camp. After that I'll tell you a little about myself and how I came to know Jesus Christ." Bob strummed his guitar a few times. "And if you don't know Jesus, my prayer is that you won't leave this place tonight till you've met Him."

> *I found a new way of living; I found a new life divine.*
> *I have the fruit of the Spirit; I'm abiding, abiding in the vine.*
> *Abiding in the vine, abiding in the vine.*
> *Love, joy, health, peace, He has made them mine.*
> *I have prosperity, power and victory, abiding, abiding in*
>   *the vine.*

The kids stood up, swaying and clapping in time to the music. Once they knew the words the walls vibrated with their singing. They loved the melody and the message: it described their new life. Bob introduced a second song, and then a third. He strummed hard on the strings, and his voice rose high above the crowd. When he slowed the tempo, a hush fell over the room.

Everyone's eyes were closed. Hands were raised in the air as Bob continued to lead in a simple chorus:

Lord we love you . . . Lord we love you . . . Lord we love
you . . . Lord we love you.

He set down his guitar and asked everyone to be seated. Joyce sat in her usual spot on the couch as Bob began to describe how drugs and loose living had nearly destroyed his life. Some of the kids who had been experimenting with drugs nodded in agreement. Bob went on to explain how he had been filled with anger and bitterness for most of his life. Smoking pot, he said, had been just a cover-up for his pain.

He opened his Bible and started to read. "Isaiah the prophet wrote this: 'All of us like sheep have gone astray.' That means you and me. In one way or another we've all wandered far away from God. Everybody needs the Savior, man—His name is Jesus Christ. We need forgiveness and a brand new start. That can only come from Jesus."

When Bob started to pray the kids bowed their heads, and the Holy Spirit spoke to their hearts, leading them to sorrow, then repentance, and finally joy. Within moments the room was brimming once again with smiling faces. Bob shook his head in wonder. He had never before seen anything quite like this.

⌐⊖⌐

Two weeks later Bruce and Bob sat at the kitchen table while Joyce stood at the sink, her hands immersed in dishwater. Bob, setting down his coffee cup, leaned back in a stretch. "Well, folks," he announced, "it's been a great couple of weeks, but I'm about ready to head back to Florida."

Joyce turned around with a start. "You can't leave now!" she exclaimed in real consternation. She was sure God wanted Bob to stay in Michigan. After all, the meetings were exploding. There were so many kids they were running out of room. He *couldn't* leave now.

Joyce had just that week started making phone calls to local churches in quest of a more adequate facility for the meetings. Ted Mosies, the pastor at Leach Road Community Church, had shown some interest. "We're busting at the seams over here," she had told him. "Do you have any room at your church for a bunch of kids?"

Mosies's congregation had just completed an addition to the building, a large meeting space he referred to as Solomon's Porch. "It *would* vork perfectly for you," he assured Joyce in his thick Dutch accent. "You're more than velcome to bring the kids here. There's plenty of room."

Bob agreed to stay on until things were settled at Leach Road. The next week Mosies stood in the doorway of Solomon's Porch, admitting more than a hundred young people. The kids tossed their shoes into a corner before settling cross-legged on the floor. When the music began to play, the 60-year old pastor bent over the pile of shoes and began laying out the pairs in neat, straight rows so they would be easily accessible when the meeting adjourned.

Bruce found a chair near the back of the hall that afforded him a good view of the room. Bob was up front with his guitar, Joyce sat on the floor with the teens, and Mosies had posted himself near the door to welcome each new arrival. After a few worship songs Bob read from the Bible and preached the gospel before closing with a prayer. That was Bruce's cue to make his way to the front, where he seated himself strategically to pray with anyone who might come forward. Over the past several weeks, he had found, the more he had prayed with the kids the stronger his love for them grew. He had finally found his niche.

Many of the young people who found their way to Solomon's Porch walked in with broken hearts. Some were caught up in the drug scene, while others were angry over past hurts or struggling through the fall-out of their parents' divorce. They yearned for stability in their lives—precisely what the Todds, with the Spirit's help, were eager to provide. When the meeting ended a handful of teens always gathered around Bruce for some prayer and sound advice.

After the meetings had moved to Leach Road, Joyce was freed to resume the life she had for the past few months placed on hold. She gave the house a thorough cleaning and stocked up on groceries for the family, drove the kids to school, and began helping them again with their homework. Life was getting back to normal. But she never stopped thinking about her "Jesus Kids" and invariably looked forward to the next meeting at Leach Road. En route to the church Joyce would marvel at the radical changes in her life, despite the return to routine and schedule. She no longer took the time for coffee klatches with the ladies of Rochester; her circle of friends consisted primarily of the hippies and teenagers who packed into Solomon's Porch. Joyce's heart and priorities had changed drastically, and there would be no turning back.

CHAPTER 33

Brand New

T he elm trees at Balduck Park formed a canopy over East Warren Avenue in Detroit. Balduck was known for its beautiful trees and the steep toboggan hill that drew hundreds of kids to the park each winter. In the summer people played ball on the baseball diamond and enjoyed Sunday picnics under the trees.

By 1971, however, all but a few of the trees had died of Dutch elm disease. The park looked barren and had deteriorated into little more than a party hangout for teens. Every night dozens of youth gathered there to buy, sell, and use illegal drugs. It had all started with marijuana, quickly followed by LSD, mescaline, and even heroin. Any drug any night of the week. Wooden picnic tables once reserved for family outings were now covered in graffiti and littered with drug paraphernalia. Every dealer in the Detroit area knew about Balduck; it was the ideal place to make a sale.

Nervous neighbors peered out of living room windows every evening and called repeatedly for stepped-up police surveillance. By midnight several teenagers had usually been arrested, handcuffed, and hauled off to jail. The next morning the kids were released with a fine and ordered not to return to the park.

One hot evening in June Detroit police officers launched a surprise raid on Balduck. Two helicopters hovered over the park, directing their searchlights over the milling crowd of kids. An officer announced through a bullhorn that the park was now closed. On the ground policemen marched shoulder to shoulder, sweeping across the area and sending teens scurrying in every direction. Hundreds were arrested that night for drug possession. Afterward anyone in violation of the curfew was hauled away.

Jan had heard all about the raid. Several of her friends had been arrested—and held—on that fateful night, and she wondered when they would be released. She also wondered whether it would be safe to return to the park. It was June 30, her 17th birthday, and her friend Nancy had offered to spring for a hit of mescaline. Jan had never tried mescaline before and looked forward to the new experience. It was a warm night, and the girls headed to the park in worn cut-offs and tank tops. They first needed to find out whether any dealers had ventured back.

"There probably won't be much going on tonight," Nancy commented as they walked along East Warren. The park was guarded, as usual since the raid, by a row of officers who stood at attention on its outskirts. They were intimidating, but Jan squared her shoulders and stepped through the barricade. *These pigs can't make us leave*, she thought defiantly.

Dozens of teenagers were standing around with their hands in their pockets. Jan and Nancy joined the group and then paused to listen. Unexpectedly, the sound of guitar music wafted over the scene from some distance away. Jan nudged her friend, and the two headed across the park. Some people had set up a makeshift stage, and two musicians were strumming guitars.

"Oh, good," she called out in a jeering tone. "*Kumbaya*—my *favorite!*" The gathered kids laughed along. "Let's show those pigs we can outlast them," she challenged the others. Trying not to erupt into laughter, they all joined the singing, many in loud, mocking tones.

The musicians played with their eyes closed, and several people in the front row had raised their hands in worship. A crowd was forming as the music drew the curious from across the park. When the song ended a young man with a dark beard and black leather vest made his way to the front, a Bible in his hands.

"How's everybody doing tonight?" he asked. "You doing all right? Well, you're probably wondering what a bunch of Christians are doing out here at Balduck. How come we're singing all these songs and carrying Bibles? Well, my name is Frank, and I'm gonna tell you tonight about Jesus Christ and how He changed my life—how He took something really bad and turned it into something good. Okay with you if I talk for a few minutes?"

"I heard about this guy," Nancy whispered to Jan. "He used to sell dope; now he's a Jesus Freak."

Someone picked up a stone and hurled it at Frank. It hit him in the side before bouncing to the ground.

"Hey," Frank shouted. "Who just threw that rock at me?"

No one answered.

"I just want to know, man, because I want a souvenir of the first time I got stoned for Jesus Christ. That's what they used to do to people, man. They'd stone 'em just for believing in the Lord. And I'll tell you what, you greasers back there, you think you're so tough, but here's a chance for you to meet Jesus tonight. Are you up to *that?*" Frank went on to talk about his life: the drugs, the jail time, and the fights he'd started. Next he described the prayer meeting at Gesu's where he'd surrendered his life to the Lord.

Jan was starting to feel uncomfortable. A young woman moved through the crowd passing out fliers, repeating over and over again "God loves you." Jan took a flier, stuffed it into her back pocket, and tugged on Nancy's arm. "Let's get outta here."

"*That* was a wasted night," she muttered as they trekked home. The girls said goodnight in front of Jan's house as she turned up the driveway. The lights were out; her parents had gone to bed hours earlier. Making her way into the kitchen she saw a birthday cake sitting on the table, along with some gifts. *They must have given up on me,* she thought with a stab of guilt, dabbing her finger into the frosting. It tasted good, but she felt awful. No celebration this year. All she'd done was listen to a crazy, bearded Jesus Freak. Climbing the stairs to her attic bedroom, she dropped into bed in the hot room.

An hour later Jan was still awake. The moon was full, shining brightly through her window. Propping herself on an elbow, she pulled the flier from her pocket. It stated that Frank spoke every Friday night at a church over in Warren. *How could an ex-con know anything about God?* She doubted that anything he had said was true anyway. *He just made it all up,* she decided, tossing the flier to the floor.

As the night wore on, however, Jan found herself carrying on in her head both sides of an argument with Frank. Finally, disgusted, she turned onto her back and stared up at the ceiling. "Okay, God," she challenged aloud, "if you're real, like this guy says you are, then come into my heart and change my life."

Jan bolted up in the bed and put her hand to her throat. "Oh my *gosh!* He did it. He came into my heart." She looked somewhat frantically around the room. There was no one there, yet she could sense a palpable presence. She looked up at the ceiling. "God, did you just come into my heart?" *Maybe I'm hallucinating*, she thought. But she hadn't used any drugs for days and had never felt more alert.

The flier was still on the floor. Jan reached over and retrieved it, after which she tiptoed down the steps, slipped on her flipflops, and headed out into the night. For three hours she walked the neighborhood, repeating over and over again the same question: "*What* just happened to me? *What just happened?*"

It was only when the sun started to rise that she returned home. Her mother, unaware of her absence, was in the kitchen making breakfast, so Jan sat down at the table and took a deep breath. "Mom," she began, "you're probably not gonna believe this, but I think I've just been reborn." She wasn't exactly sure why she'd chosen that word.

Her mother turned around. "What are you *talking* about?"

"I'm sorry I wasn't here for my birthday, Mom, but I think I was meant to be somewhere else. I gave my life to Jesus last night, and now I'm brand new. I'm reborn!"

Jan rose from her chair and started to clear away dirty dishes from the night before. She washed, dried, and put them away while her mother watched in disbelief. Except under compulsion, Jan had never lifted a finger to help before. Next she pulled out the vacuum cleaner and began to run it through the downstairs.

The phone rang. It was her boyfriend, Ray. "Hey, I'm sorry I didn't call you yesterday to wish you a happy birthday," he opened.

"You know what, Ray? Something happened last night, and I need to tell you about it."

"What's up?"

"I gave my life to Jesus. I heard these guys talking over at Balduck . . ."

"You went to Balduck? Are you *nuts?*"

"It wasn't like the other night. There were these Jesus Freaks there, and this one guy was talking about God as if he really knew Him. When I got home I couldn't stop thinking about it. Then I prayed and I accepted Him into my heart. Now I'm brand new!"

Having no idea how to respond, Ray came up with a reason to get off the phone and hung up. Jan proceeded to call Nancy with the same news, asking whether her friend would accompany her to the prayer meeting on Friday night. Later that week the pair hitchhiked from Detroit to Warren.

Arriving at the meeting they found kids scattered everywhere: in chairs, on the floor, and leaning up against the wall, all killing time waiting for the meeting to start. Jan could sense the same presence at Saint Sylvester that she had felt in her room the night of her birthday. When the music began she stood to sing, but this time it was from her heart. She felt washed—clean all over.

When Frank came up to speak, Jan hung on to every word. And when he asked the attendees to close their eyes and bow their heads, she did so. Then, when Frank led the gathering in a prayer, she prayed along with him.

"If you prayed that prayer tonight," Frank invited, "I want you to raise your hand."

Jan shot her hand into the air. *Who wouldn't want this?* she wondered. *Who wouldn't want to know Jesus Christ?*

The girls returned on the following Friday night. This time Nancy gave her heart to the Lord, and the two friends began reading the Bible together. They never missed going to another meeting. The two Detroit city girls, hitch-hiking to Warren every Friday evening, brought along dozens of friends over a period of time. They sang, prayed, and observed as, one by one, each of their friends became new.

∞

"Hey, Cassady, can I get a lift?" Alex called. Mike was backing out his car from a parking space at Macomb Community College.

"Sure," Mike agreed. "Hop in."

Alex tossed his books into the back and slipped into the passenger seat. Rubbing his hands together, he blew on his stiffened fingers. "Cold out tonight, man."

"What happened to your wheels?"

"At the repair shop. Glad you came by, Cass. I appreciate the lift. God was looking out for me."

Like most of Mike's friends these days, Alex managed to inject God's name into nearly every conversation. Everyone who attended Frank's meetings seemed to talk like this.

"You know, Cass, it's looking more and more like we're in the last days," Alex reflected.

Mike winced. *Here it comes,* he thought.

"The Bible says there'll be some who will mislead many."

Mike turned the car onto Twelve Mile Road.

"Nation will rise against nation . . ."

"Uh-huh."

"Kingdom against kingdom, man. It says that in some places there'll be famines and earthquakes. And it's already happening, Cass."

The traffic was moving at an unusually slow pace this evening.

"You know," Alex continued, "when the Lord returns you want to be ready to meet Him."

"Yeah, for sure," Mike concurred in a noncommittal tone as he pulled into Alex's driveway. "Good seeing you, man." He left the motor running.

Alex reached for his books. "You wanna come in for some coffee, Cass?"

What could Mike say? It was only 8:00. "Okay. Sure." He turned off the car and followed Alex into the house.

Alex entered the living room carrying two mugs. Setting them down on the coffee table, he reached for his Bible. Opening up to Matthew 24, he pointed out prophecies describing the end of the world.

Mike set down his mug and rose to leave. "Listen," he told Alex, "I need to be shoving off."

"Before you go, can I pray with you?"

"That's cool." Feeling cornered, Mike shrugged and sat stiffly back down.

"You don't have to say anything, Cass. Just let me pray for you." Alex bowed his head. "Lord Jesus," he began, "help Mike to make the right choices for his life. Help him to know you, Lord, and to trust you as his Savior."

The prayer didn't take long. On the way home Mike couldn't stop thinking about what Alex had said. The whole tone of the encounter had made him feel uncomfortable, restless, and anxious about the future. He thought about his friends from Cousino. So many of them had become Christians. It was as though some alien "thing" had dropped from the sky and taken over their lives. *Alex is serious about all this,* Mike realized. *And so is Frank. And Randy too. Everybody's getting so serious about this stuff.*

At Frank's meeting last week Mike had watched more of his friends giving their hearts to Jesus. *They can't all be pretending,* he conceded. *Frank and Randy aren't faking, that's for sure. Who knows? Maybe this is for real.*

The next day Mike drove to Detroit to visit his friend John. John used to be one of the toughest kids at school, a scrapper like Frank. His conversion had been nearly as dramatic as Frank's, too. Now John spent all of his time at the House of Prayer. Walking into the storefront church, Mike was greeted by Pastor George Bogle.

Pastor Bogle was an imposing figure. He wasn't tall or particularly well dressed, but his handshake was firm and penetrating gaze disarming. Without warning Pastor Bogle placed his hands on Mike's head. "Father God," he began to pray aloud, "the time is right for this young man to receive your Holy Spirit."

It was a simple but powerful prayer. Waves of heat poured over Mike's head and trickled down like a stream of hot oil. Peace washed over him as well, and he felt lighter than air. His friend John, standing near the door, had witnessed the whole thing.

"What happened?" Mike asked, bewildered, as he and John stepped into the church.

"Pastor Bogle prayed for you, man. You just received the Holy Spirit."

"What are you talking about?

"We need to pray again, Mike. Pray that God will continue to fill you with His Spirit." John bowed his head, laid his hand on Mike's shoulder, and prayed. Immediately Mike began to speak in tongues. He had never done such a thing before, but as he prayed a new language emerged from his mouth. Later on Mike drove home overcome with joy and anxious to talk to Frank. Whatever had happened inside him, there could be no doubt it was from God.

CHAPTER 34

"This Must Be Frank"

Joyce pulled into the parking lot at Saint Sylvester. It was the summer of 1971, and warm weather had beckoned hundreds of teens out on a Friday night. By 7:00 the lot was full, so the overflow of motorcycles and junkers began to park along side streets.

Everywhere Joyce looked there were young people. Some lay on the grass reading a Bible, while other sat cross-legged on top of their cars. This was a rag-tag bunch of kids—many of them loud, obnoxious, and unruly. Joyce's heart sang as she walked into the social hall. *And they're all here to learn about Jesus,* she enthused.

"God bless you!" A girl hugged Joyce and held the door open for her.

"Praise the Lord!" A young man shook her hand.

Folding chairs were arranged in neat rows, but Joyce took a seat on the floor and leaned against the wall instead. From here she could see the podium, the musicians, and the steady stream of kids pouring into the room as though a spigot had been opened. Teens made up a majority of the crowd, but there were also businessmen in tailored suits and nuns in flowing habits. Everywhere Joyce looked people were laughing and hugging. The air was electric, and she was beginning to get excited too.

A side door opened, and several musicians filed out, followed by a train of young girls carrying tambourines at their sides. Each girl's hair reached to her waist, and all wore colorful granny skirts that swished across the floor.

Joyce, watching the procession, wondered about the bearded young man as he strode to the microphone.

"How's everybody doin' tonight?" His voice boomed, sending

feedback squealing through the speakers. The room fell quiet as all eyes turned to the podium.

Joyce smiled to herself. *This must be Frank.*

"How 'bout we all stand up?" Frank pointed to a young man seated near Joyce. "You too, Charlie. It's Friday night, man. The week might be over, but God's just gettin' started in here. *Amen?*"

"Amen!" roared the crowd as all rose to their feet.

"Now you all had a chance to groove for a while and say hi to your friends," Frank continued, "but now it's time to praise the Lord, okay? My buddy Dale here is gonna lead us in a few songs. Let's do it, man. Don't hold back. We're here to worship Jesus Christ with everything we've got." Frank raised his Bible in the air. "'Cause He's the King of kings and the Lord of lords!"

"*Amen!*" The crowd was fired up.

A tall young man in a T-shirt, faded jeans, and cowboy boots stepped up to the microphone.

"All right, Caveman," Frank told him, "do your thing."

Dale, a 22-year-old convert, sported a thick red beard reaching down to his chest, and his strawberry blond hair hung to his shoulders. He strummed his guitar a few times and began to sing in a clear tenor that permeated the room:

> *Jesus, Jesus.*
> *Jesus in the morning, Jesus in the noontime.*
> *Jesus, Jesus,*
> *Jesus when the sun goes down.*

The place exploded in song. Joyce looked around. *What a sight!* she thought, relishing the moment. *I've never seen anything like it.*

Dale moved quickly from one song into the next.

> *I shall not be—I shall not be moved.*
> *I shall not be—I shall not be moved.*
> *Just like a tree that's planted by the water,*
> *I shall not be moved.*

Hands were raised and eyes closed as the worship rose to a crescendo. The crowd became increasingly energized with every song.

Joyce, who could feel her heart pounding in her chest with each beat of the drum, exhaled deeply when Dale finally slowed the tempo.

> *Holy, holy, holy is our Lord God Almighty.*
> *Who was and who is, and who is to come.*

A hush fell over the room, and the atmosphere was transformed into one of quiet reverence. One by one voices broke out in spontaneous praise. "Bless your name, Lord," someone next to Joyce sang out. "Praise you, Jesus. We worship your holy name." To Joyce the praise sounded like a choir of angels, as more and more people joined in. Voices blended in beautiful harmony as the singing continued spontaneously, without verse or chorus, and the volume continued to escalate once again until the room felt ready to burst its seams. Someone started to clap, and the room thundered with applause. Finally, as though on cue, the crowd grew quiet once again, and everyone waited in silence. Joyce glanced up at the song leader. Dale was nodding to the musicians, who began to play.

> *We are one in the Spirit, we are one in the Lord.*
> *We are one in the Spirit, we are one in the Lord.*

All over the room people reached for the outstretched hands of neighbors. A nun grasped the hand of a biker and a hippie that of a businessman. Charlie took Joyce's, and they swayed as one to the music as their singing filled the air with a wistful melody.

> *And we pray that all unity will one day be restored.*
> *And they'll know we are Christians by our love, by our love,*
> *Yes they'll know we are Christians by our love.*

Now Joyce understood how Frank was able to draw together so many people every Friday night. It was by the power of the Holy Spirit. When the song ended everyone sat down. An empty Kentucky Fried Chicken container was passed around for the offering, and people began to toss cash into the bucket. Joyce handed it to Charlie, after which he shook her outstretched hand. "I'm Charlie," he volunteered. "Nice to meet you. We're not too formal around here, in case you haven't noticed. Is this your first time?"

"Yes," Joyce replied. "I came from another meeting. It's a lot like this one."

"Well, when you hear Frank preach, you'll know there's no place like this anywhere."

Joyce watched Frank as he greeted people in the front row, pointed at a tall man leaning against the wall. *"Tarzan!"* Frank called out. "Where you been, man? Good to see you. Stick around after the meeting, okay? We need to talk." As he made his way back to the podium the crowd quieted yet again. "All right," he began. "How many of you are here for the first time? Let me see your hands."

Several hands went up.

"Okay," Frank acknowledged. "I want those of you who brought someone here to start praying right now that the Holy Spirit will speak to everyone's heart tonight. Can you do that? This isn't about me, man. It's about Jesus Christ. He's the one who's gonna get the glory for what happens tonight, okay? Amen.

"You know what? I saw a sign on the road this mornin' out on Van Dyke; it was a donut shop or something. And it said, 'Coming Soon' on it. That was all. So what I want to know is: how many of you believe that Jesus Christ is coming soon?"

Applause broke out, and people in the front row started to cheer. Frank motioned with his hands for everyone to quiet down. "You know, the world will tell you 'He's not comin'.' The world don't really care if He's comin' or not. But He *is* comin'.

"Way back in Noah's day they laughed at him too. Noah was out there trying to tell 'em all. And do you know what the world was like back then? It was full of violence, crime, drinking, partying . . . the whole nine yards. Our world is the same way today, isn't it?

"How many of you have ever seen the movie 'On the Waterfront'? You know, the one with Marlon Brando. All you ladies know who Marlon Brando is, right? Heh, heh. So what was Marlon Brando's famous line? 'I coulda been a contender.' What was he trying to say? What he meant was, I coulda *been* somebody. I coulda had class . . . but no, instead I'm a bum, and I'll always be a bum.

"Well, that's pretty much the way I felt for most of my life. I was always going to be a bum. I was raised on the other side of the tracks, so to speak. The Christian world was alien to me; it was foreign. I didn't know nothin' about it. I was brought up in a church, in a particular denomination, but still I didn't know what was going on. It came in one ear and flew out the other just as fast as I heard it. And where I lived, I didn't see any real Christianity, man. I didn't even know that Christ died for me. It makes a difference if you know that because that's where it happened, on Calvary, where Jesus Christ shed His blood for every one of us in here."

Joyce was mesmerized. Frank's speech was coarse and his style unpolished, but every word he spoke had the ring of truth.

"I'll tell ya what," Frank continued, "back when I didn't know Jesus I had a big mouth. I had the biggest mouth in De-troit City, and I thought I was the baddest and the coolest dude. I knew it all. You know the type? There's a million of 'em around. They're a dime a dozen, and that was me. I bad-mouthed people so much I got shot in the head one time. And I got what I deserved. I started bad-mouthing a guy that didn't want to fight, and so he shot me! And then the Lord looked down and said, 'Hey, I'm gonna get this cat; he's got a big mouth!'"

Frank laughed—and the crowd with him.

"You know what I'm saying? Praise God! The Lord got a hold of me. You know, the first time I heard about Jesus Christ was from my best friend. I was a super-doper back then, man. My head was so spaced out it was unreal. I was like a vegetable. I took so much LSD my mind was *full* of LSD. I snorted till my nostrils caved in. My head was gone, man. I thought dope was my answer. I thought dope was everything. I thought perverted sex was my happiness. I thought everything out there in the world would bring me pleasure.

"The world says, 'This is where happiness is, man. C'mon. It's in Boone's Farm Apple Wine. It's in hash, opium, booze. C'mon! This is where it's at!' But it's a lie, and you're being deceived by the devil! And I fell all the way into that trap.

"I hated my mom and dad. They weren't my real parents—I was adopted. I was fostered out about three times in my life and got thrown back three times, 'cause I was a strange, unusual kid. People didn't want me, man. And I'll tell you what, when you get the feeling nobody wants you, it's pretty heavy. What happens is you grow up hating people, and all my life the only thing I knew was hate. I was hateful each and every day I lived.

"My mom and dad adopted me from Canada. I was born there in Canada, man—Nova Scotia. I was adopted from there and taken across the border. And then I grew up in jails and juvenile homes till I tasted all life had for me. And that's the way it was for a kid that nobody wanted.

"At 14 years old I almost killed my mother. I hated her so much I turned against her and tried to strangle her, till finally my brother pulled me off. I was a rebellious kid, but God looked down and saw my rebellion. Then He breathed His Spirit upon me and melted me just like a stick of butter. Heh-Heh.

"I'll tell you guys, this morning I saw two greasers hookin' it. And it brought back memories of how many times I used to hook it. 'Cause that's where I thought happiness was, proving that I was 'bad' and that I was on the top. 'Ain't nobody gonna beat Frank Majewski . . . if you think you can, brother, you better prove it now.'

"Back then a lot of guys would look at me 'cause I'm so little, you know, and they'd say 'that little shrimp?' Well, you know the old saying, 'dynamite comes in small packages.' Ha-ha.

"Anyhow, when I was a greaser I was out there fightin' everybody, man. I learned how to fight in the joint—the juvenile home. And they sent me to this one place, a work farm, for 17 months. I had my own personal head shrink working with me, trying to get into my head. He couldn't do it, man. He didn't have no answers for me. You know, all they can tell you is 'you got hit with a swing when you were a kid and so now you're nuts.' And then they put you away and that's that!

"Anyhow, I learned how to fight in the joint, and after I got out I took my fighting to the streets. That's when I started fighting with anyone who messed with me. Man, I was juicing it real heavy.

"And then, like I said, I bad-mouthed the wrong guy one night, and he shot me at point-blank range in the head. The bullet went up my nose, curved under my eye, and then stuck in my temple, right here. I had blood coming out of every opening in my head: my ears, my nose, my mouth . . . and I can tell you at that split second I didn't think about God. I didn't think about eternity. As a matter of fact, at the time I didn't even believe in heaven or hell. But if there *was* a heaven or a hell, I knew where I was going. Straight to hell. You didn't need to tell *me*—I already knew it in my heart.

"I broke into so many places, I stole so many things and busted up so many buildings—I was just a terror, man. And I'm telling ya, when Jesus got a hold of me He did society a favor. He blessed 'em. He said 'I'm gonna take this problem right out of your hands!' And that's exactly what He did, because man's system failed with me. They couldn't do *nothin'* for me.

"They locked me up, and I got to see their jails, their holes, their everything. Nothing could change me though; I only got worse."

During Frank's speech not a soul rose to leave. Not a sound was heard while he was preaching.

"So that's exactly what happens behind a jail cell wall," Frank went on. "People don't get any better. All they do is get worse. And I'll tell you, man, when you go to jail you learn how to do freakier things than you did before you got in there. It's true! You know I never pulled a B & E till I went to jail and the guy next to me said 'When we get out, Frank, we're gonna pull us a job! We'll get the biggest job and then we're gonna be rich!'

"And I said 'I can dig it!' So when I got out I started pulling all these jobs until I got caught. So what then? You get locked up after you're caught. So back to jail I go.

"But getting back to the time I got shot. At first I didn't think about nothin'; it was just like 'Oh, wow!' I hit the ground. When I got up my head felt like somebody had hit me with a sledgehammer. My ears felt like somebody had put a big firecracker in them and blew them off. They were still ringing from the sound of the gun. And then my head swelled up to about three or four times its size; it just blew up. When I woke up lying in the street, I said 'What happened?' I had two friends of mine that got shot along with me. Right after me, the guy shot my two friends. *Boom! Boom!* He shot my buddy in the stomach and my other friend in the groin. Everybody was just lying on the ground bleeding. I woke up and I said, 'What happened? What *happened*?'

"And my buddy MoJo says, 'You been shot!'

"And I says, '*Ahhhhhhh!*'

"I freaked! I dragged myself down the street and put my fist through a door. I was scared, man. Next thing you know I'm in a hospital bed, dying. Just barely breathing. A priest is there, saying goodbye to me. He had come to give me last rites.

"*Whoa!* What's gonna happen NOW, Frank baby? You're checking out, man. The doctor looked at me and says 'How many bullets has this guy got in him?' My mother looked at me later and started crying. I was a bloody mess, I'll tell ya. And all I could think about at that time was eternity. Now it had caught up with me and I said 'Oh-oh.'

"You know, I'd heard a whole lot about Jesus, and I heard about Satan and all about hell. I got bribed with heaven and blackmailed with hell. I had heard all about it, man, but now I started to get this eerie feeling that I'm about to find out if it's real or not. You know, in the Scriptures it says 'First comes death, and after that the judgment.' And there I was. 'First comes death.' And then, after I died, the judgment. And if I would have faced the judgment seat of God on that day, I just couldn't go near Him! I was so freaked out. And I knew exactly where I'd be for all eternity. Not so much the burning in fire, but being without God—being without Jesus and knowing that I blew it.

"Heaven and hell. You can hardly comprehend what they mean. Our natural minds can't comprehend infinity up there. All you would know, man, is eternal separation from God. There you'll be, just knowing you blew it! For all eternity, that's gonna be hell in itself, just knowing you blew it, you know what I mean? And I blew it by my own free will! I blew it! And I knew there were no more chances.

"You know, I'm not trying to scare you, but this is reality. This is what I faced at that time in my life. And this was when I was a big bad greaser—had it all together. But all of a sudden I was scared. I wasn't big and bad then. I was like most typical human beings that cop out at the last minute. So I said to God, 'God, I'm sorry. Let me slide for everything I did. If there's a heaven, I want to go there, 'cause what I heard about the other direction is pretty bad.'

"Then the next thing you know, I didn't die. They put me on the operating table but couldn't get the bullet out for another 10 days. After I got out of the hospital the doctor told me I was one out of a billion that ever made it. The way that bullet was traveling—straight up—there was nothing to make it curve. But it did curve. If it had continued straight it would have been all over for me. I believe God had his hand on my life even then. And I believe everything works out for the glory of God. All my life God had his hand on me. He was just drawing me to himself, though I didn't know it at the time.

"After I got out of the hospital, I quit fighting. I said, 'Well, this greaser trip better end for me, man. I can't fight no more.'

"So then I became a hippie and got into drugs. After a few years of that, Jesus called me through my best friend who was now turned on to Christ. Did you ever have your best friend turn on to Jesus, come back, and shine the light on you till it just blows your mind? It took about four months of him rapping to me, telling me that Jesus loves me and that He cares about me, before I finally accepted Christ into my heart. I was born again, man. And that's what the Lord wants for everyone in this room.

"My conversion was somewhat like Paul the apostle's. I got thrown right out of my chair. It's a Ripley's Believe It Or Not, brothers and sisters. It didn't happen to you, so you don't have to believe it. It happened to me. *I'm* the one that's gotta believe it.

"You know, I tell people and they say, 'You mean you actually fell right out of your chair? Man, you really *are* nuts!'

"But Jesus breathed His life into me and changed me into a new creature. It's been over a year now that I've been following after Him. I've been baptized in the Holy Spirit, and I want more of everything Jesus has got. If He's got it, I want it, man! Give me all of it, Jesus!

"So anyway, brothers and sisters, all I can tell you tonight is that I'm a new creature in Christ. It's a miracle that God ever got a hold of me. He said that in the last days He's gonna perform signs and wonders, and believe me, *I'm* one of them wonders. Heh, heh.

"My mom couldn't believe it. After I got saved I went up and I hugged my mother and told her I loved her. After she watched me live this new life for about eight months she knelt down on the floor and asked Christ into her own life. She said, 'I *know* this kid has changed! What you gave to him, Jesus, give to me.'

"Since then God has called me to be a witness. That's all—just telling people the truth. I'm not some great preacher up here—you know what I mean? I'm just a simple dude, that's all! I've been called to witness about who Jesus Christ is. We're all supposed to do that: tell people what He's done in your life—be a witness. I'm just trying to build up *His* kingdom, not my own.

"The other night I went to a park with a lot of brothers and sisters from Detroit. It was a park like any other park—a place where people go to freak out. They get high and they groove, you know, on pleasure trips. So we went out there and put up a little stage where we could stand right in the middle of all these freaked out people. And nobody was saying 'Amen' after everything we said, you know what I mean? In here we got a whole lot of Christians saying 'Right on, brother! Amen! Hallelujah!' but that wasn't the kind of audience we had this time. They were booing and hating us in their heart, man. We were telling them about the answer, but they hated us.

"Anyways, there were some motorcycle guys there. Greasers, real greasers, sitting on their choppers. I used to own a chopper myself. I had a big old Harley Davison, extended frame, you know, the whole shot.

"So anyhow, I saw these guys sitting there, and one guy picks up a rock and throws it at me, hits me right in the side. I said, 'Hey, man, who threw that rock? You know, I want that rock, man, as a souvenir of my first time getting stoned for the cause of Jesus Christ.' That blew his mind, ha-ha. Then I challenged him and told him about Christ.

"You know, in meetings like this we always have a few that sit back and kinda laugh. Inside their heart they're just scoffing. The Bible says in the last days scoffers will come. They'll be scoffing at the return of Jesus Christ. And I believe He's on His way back.

"So anyway, tonight I'm gonna leave you right here, right now with the same choice I gave those greasers the other night. Inside your heart if you think God is not real, I ask you right now to stand up! I give you the *same* thing Jesus offers to everyone that if any man knocks, the door shall be opened.

"You know, I can get up here and preach my guts out, but some people just won't take that step. Right now I'm gonna ask everybody, man, to bow your head and close your eyes. I'm gonna ask you to pray along with me. I don't want nobody leaving right now, all right? The greasers are at the back door, and you ain't getting out! Heh, heh.

"Seriously, I'm gonna ask you to pray along with me that Jesus Christ will become real to you right now. Let the Holy Spirit just work and give you that little extra shove you need to make a stand for Jesus. Let Him speak to your heart and show you He's alive today. Now while our brother Dale is playing, I want you to listen to the words of this song. Think about where you're at tonight. Do you need to ask God for forgiveness? He's here tonight, and He's speaking to you. Go ahead, Dale."

Frank stepped away from the microphone as Dale started to sing:

> We're all gathered here, because we all believe.
> If there's a doubter in the crowd, we ask you not to leave.
> Give a listen to our story. Hear the message that we bring.
> Feel the faith well up inside you. Lift your voice with us and sing.
> Accept Him with your whole heart and use your own
>   two hands.
> With one reach out to Jesus —and with the other . . . bring
>   a friend.[16]

Joyce looked across the room and felt a lump in her throat. It was a familiar feeling, reminding her of her own living room. She brushed away a tear and listened again to the words:

> *Many know him well, others just by name.*
> *If you don't know for what he stands, you've really much to gain.*
> *With faith you can move mountains. These are common*
>   *words, but true.*
> *Well I'm not quite a mountain, but he's moved me here to you.*
> *Accept Him with your whole heart and use your own two hands.*
> *With one reach out to Jesus—And with the other . . . bring*
>   *a friend."*

When the song ended Frank stepped up to the microphone. "That song pretty much says it all, don't it?" he asked. "Everybody keep your heads bowed for another second. This is your moment. The only reason you came here tonight is because the Lord drew you here. And tonight is your chance to accept Him into your heart. Now, while every eye is closed, I want you to repeat this prayer after me: Lord Jesus . . ."

A low murmur rippled across the room as people repeated the prayer.

"I'm sorry for all of my sins. Come into my heart and make me clean. Wash me in your precious blood and make me a new person. I want to be born again. Amen.

"Now, while our heads are still bowed, if you prayed that prayer with me let me see your hand—slip it up, right now. All over . . . c'mon, don't punk out! This is your night, man. All right, for those of you that raised your hands, I want you to stand for a minute. Just stand up, all over the room. C'mon. Praise you, Jesus. Hallelujah. There's more of you, too. C'mon. Thank you, Jesus.

"Now we want to pray with you and give you a Bible. Thank you, brother. Hallelujah. C'mon, the rest of you that raised your hand, stand up. God's tugging on your heart, man. You're not going to be embarrassed; just stand up right where you are. Thank you, brother.

"Okay, for those of you who are standing, we're not gonna ask you to join a church or anything. Do you know what Jesus said to do next? He said, 'Go and sin no more.'

"That's what he tells everybody, okay? So we wanna give you some

help in that department. Everybody who stood, I want you to go with
my buddy Greg over there by the door. Raise your hand up, Greg. See
that guy waving a Bible? Just follow him to the next room, and there'll
be some counselors there to pray with you and talk with you. They'll get
you started on your new walk with the Lord, okay? Now don't sit back
down! Just go over by Greg, man. Praise the Lord. Hallelujah."

More than 30 people filed out of the room as those who remained
behind started to clap.

"Praise God," Frank exclaimed. "That's what it's all about, man—the
power of Jesus Christ. Anybody know what the word 'gospel' means?"

"Good news," someone shouted.

"That's right. It means good news. And today I think we could all
use some good news, couldn't we?"

Everyone clapped again.

"Hallelujah. Let's all stand up and sing one more tune before we get
kicked out of here. Dale, another song, man."

Once again, the room broke out in jubilation:

> I've got that joy, joy, joy, joy down in my heart.
> Down in my heart, down in my heart.
> I've got that joy, joy, joy, joy down in my heart.
> Down in my heart to stay.
> 'Cause I'm so happy, so very happy. I've got the love of Jesus
>   in my heart.
> Yes I'm so happy, so very happy. I've got the love of Jesus
>   in my heart!

As Joyce walked out to her car, Frank's sermon resounded in her
head. His words had burned like a prairie fire, consuming everything in
its path. Frank's message had fallen like a hammer, breaking up the hard
places in everyone's heart. *How strange,* Joyce thought as she reached for
her keys. *At the same time God began to use Frank, He was starting a prayer
meeting at our house. That couldn't all be a coincidence.*

"Hey, Joyce!" Charlie called from across the parking lot. "I want to
see you here next week!"

Joyce waved back. "Don't worry," she assured him. "I'll be back."

CHAPTER 35

"Wipe the Dust Off Your Feet"

Randy spotted Frank from across the room. He stood near a window in the social hall at Saint Sylvester, surrounded as usual by a group of kids. The ever exuberant Frank was waving his arms in the air as he described for his appreciative audience his fall from the chair at Gesu's. Randy made his way over to the group and waited for Frank to finish. Several others wanted to speak with him too. It was like this every Friday night.

When the crowd finally cleared Randy reached out to shake Frank's hand and introduce himself. "Listen," he offered, "if there's ever anything I can do to help around here, just say the word. I can set up chairs, run a book table, or give the announcements. Whatever you need, just let me know."

Frank studied him for a moment. Randy was tall, more than six feet in height, with a curly blond Afro that made him appear even taller. Frank liked his Fu Manchu mustache and admired his signature cowboy boots and brown-fringed jacket as well. "Hey man," he remarked, "I dig them boots and that hippie coat, but how are you at speaking in front of people?"

"Pretty good," Randy replied. "I can handle it."

"Okay, cool, bro. Next week you do the announcements."

On the following Friday evening Randy arrived at the meeting earlier than usual. Setting a bagful of books next to a table in the back of the room, he made his way to the stage. A small stack of papers sat on the podium—several announcements that needed to be made. There would be water baptisms, Bible studies, prayer meetings, and a street rally in

Detroit—all scheduled for different evenings the following week. Randy made a mental note of the street rally set for the following Saturday; he didn't want to miss that.

As the crowd began to arrive Randy emptied his book bag onto the table. He laid out an assortment of reading material, some of which he had purchased from Howard Christian Bookstore; the other items were donations. In the front he placed popular books by Billy Graham, Hal Lyndsey, and Watchmen Nee, also prominently displaying a couple of King James Bibles, a commentary, and several worship cassette tapes. The donated items he would give away for free. The rest he would sell, allowing him to return to the store to purchase more goods for the following Friday.

A group of teenagers stopped at the table and perused the material. "Thanks for setting all this up, man," one of the boys acknowledged.

"Just doing the Lord's work," Randy replied with a smile.

By 1971 the Jesus Movement was in full swing. Christian coffee-houses, prayer meetings, and communes were popping up everywhere. From Los Angeles to New York underground newspapers were spreading the message that Jesus is the only way. Randy laid out several copies of *The Hollywood Free Paper* and *The Fish*, all of which were snatched up almost immediately.

There were albums for sale too. Artists like Larry Norman, Honey-tree, Randy Stonehill, and Phil Keaggy soon offered a variety of genres— from gospel to folk to rock and roll—all with a Christian message. These musicians had together launched a new genre, still today known as Contemporary Christian Music. Churches had begun to hold Jesus Festivals—open-air gatherings that were replacing Woodstock music with praise and worship.

Paul Clark and Phil Keaggy had been invited to perform at Frank's meeting the next time they were in town. Like many other artists they had left the professional music scene to devote their talent solely to the Lord. One Friday evening more than a thousand kids packed into Saint Sylvester, unaware that they were about to enjoy a gratis concert. Keaggy sat up front, facing the crowd, on a metal folding chair. A Les Paul guitar rested on his lap as he leaned in to the microphone. "There's no doubt in my mind," he told the crowd, "that God is reaching out to a lost generation. So if you don't know Jesus tonight, I pray that these songs will introduce you to Him." Keaggy began to play his guitar with the consummate skill of a master musician—a performance unlike anything those present had ever witnessed. The lyrics touched cords deep within many hearts.

Frank stood off to the side, smiling. As he watched the crowd he mentally rehearsed the sermon he was about to give. When the band had finished playing Frank waited for the applause to die down before stepping up to microphone. When the meeting was over, many had once again given their hearts to the Lord.

As time passed Frank became aware that the Friday night meeting was in need of some structure. He assigned leadership roles to people he trusted: Dale became the worship leader, Randy took charge of the announcements, Greg led the salvation room, and Alex helped set up chairs.

Mike Cassady organized a "God Squad"—a group of bouncers who kept an eye on the parking lot. "Don't come inside here with that beer!" Mike warned a teen who was stumbling forward between two rows of cars. "Beat it, man," he told someone else who smelled like pot. "No blowing joints around here." Occasionally, if someone in the crowd got out of hand, Frank would verbally call on the God Squad for help. Mike's team wouldn't hesitate to grab someone by the collar and escort him from the room.

One night Police Chief Groesbeck's son Eugene hid with some friends behind a hedgerow in the parking lot. The kids were there to get high, drink a few beers, and smoke a little pot. Eugene pulled a joint from his pocket and was passing it to his friends while reaching into another pocket for a book of matches.

The bush parted with a rustling sound, and a dark, bearded face appeared ominously between the branches. "*Busted!*" Frank yelled, and the kids, utterly spooked, scattered. But Frank grabbed Eugene by the collar and pulled him toward the building. "Why are you out here *smoking weed*, man? You could be inside getting high on *Jesus* instead."

Eugene struggled until he had worked himself free. "I'm not going in there, man!" he muttered, scowling and shaking his head as he backed away. "You guys are too freaky." At that he too turned tail and ran.

"I'll be watching for you to show up here next week, bro," Frank called after him, laughing. But it would be two years before Eugene returned to the meeting. When he did, he would surrender his life to Christ.

Every head turned as two rough-looking men made their way into Leach Road Community Church. Frank and Jim strolled up the aisle before sitting down together in the first pew. Ted Mosies and his wife, Myrna, hurried over to welcome them before the service began. Mosies had heard all about Frank and was glad to finally meet him.

Frank sported a black leather vest over a pair of frayed bell-bottom jeans. His arms were covered in tattoos, and a gold hoop earring hung from one ear. His beard had grown thick and long, reaching down to his chest. Frank's expressive eyes flashed as he took the pastor's hand and shook it firmly. Although Frank didn't fit the mold of most preachers, Mosies had long since learned that God doesn't care much about molds.

"I'm so glad you came by today," Myrna affirmed warmly to Frank when the service was over. "There's some people I want you to meet."

She led Frank over to Bruce and Joyce and introduced the two. Bruce, in his typically understated manner, greeted him with a nod, but Joyce was thrilled to finally meet Frank in person. "How did you ever hear about Leach Road?" she bubbled. "It's a long ways from Saint Sylvester."

"JJ told me about it." Frank turned with a nod toward Jim.

"I came to one of your Friday night meetings a few weeks ago," Joyce enthused. "It was wonderful. So many young kids. And everyone was hanging on your words. I'd love to hear the rest of your story sometime."

Frank's eyes shone as he glanced at Bruce. "How about if I come over to your house this week and give you my testimony. How would you like that?"

Joyce beamed. "That would be *great!* Come for dinner."

Frank took Bruce's hand and began to pump it. "Sounds like we'll be seeing each other soon," he commented before turning to leave. Not many people could disarm Frank, but Bruce had managed, unintention-ally, to do just that. His imposing stature and solemn stare were intimi-dating, but Frank, characteristically, liked him all the same.

On Wednesday evening he arrived as promised and sat down at the kitchen table before dinner to flesh out his story for Joyce. Frank started at the beginning, talking about the orphanage, the youth home, and the prayer meetings at Gesu's, while Bruce listened from the living room. The truth was that the two had infinitely more in common than Frank might ever have realized: both were absolutely committed to Jesus Christ.

That Friday evening Bruce drove himself down to the prayer meeting to listen to Frank. He found a seat in the back of the room and watched intently as hundreds of teenagers filed into the hall. By the time Frank was finished preaching, more than 30 converts had given their hearts to Christ. Bruce returned the following week, and the week after that. He made certain, in fact, from that point on never to miss a meeting.

The two men began to spend their Friday afternoons together. They would fast and pray during the day, following up with dinner at a Detroit restaurant prior to the meeting. Some days Bruce would drive Frank to Belle Isle Park to walk, talk, and pray with him; this helped to clear Frank's head and to prepare him, mentally and spiritually, for the evening's ministry. Bruce understood that preaching every Friday evening could eventually take its toll on Frank and hoped the lower key Friday afternoons would be restorative for the intense young man. People remarked that the unlikely pair looked a little like Mutt and Jeff as they strolled through the park, but Frank didn't care—he was grateful to have found such a wise and fatherly friend.

oⲐo

"Moj, I'm going on a 40-day fast." Frank had made up his mind. He wanted to show God he was serious about following Him.

"You gotta be kidding." MoJo was used to Frank's crazy ideas, but this was the craziest.

"Nope. I'm serious. Forty days, bro. The Lord told me, and I'm gonna do it."

"You'll starve to death, Frank."

"No, man. God'll take care of me. I'll just fill some water jugs and head into the wilderness like John the Baptist. "

"Where you gonna stay?"

"I don't know. Up north somewhere. Some place where nobody can find me. I gotta get alone with God. And after the 40 days are up you can come get me."

"What about the prayer meeting?"

"It's covered, bro. Matt's gonna take it while I'm gone."

There was no point in arguing. MoJo helped Frank fill the jugs with water and then drove to a parcel of state land in northern Michigan.

"I'll see you later, man." Frank waved his friend away. Toting the jugs into the woods, he found a spot to set up camp.

This won't last, MoJo reflected in concern as he headed back to Detroit. Not only was Frank without food, he had no shelter, no bathroom—not even a bed to sleep on. He couldn't even call anyone on the phone. *This definitely won't last,* MoJo repeated, aloud this time, hoping he was right.

Frank didn't know anything about fasting, but he did know God had told him to set aside 40 days to pray, and he firmly believed the future of the prayer meeting depended on his obedience. The first few days in the woods he felt hungry, lonely, and cold. But by day five his hunger pangs had abated, and he became keenly aware of God's presence.

On day six a state trooper pulled off the highway and gazed into the woods. Something was moving, and it wasn't a deer. Stepping gingerly from his patrol car, he rested his hand on his gun as he made his way, squinting, into the dark woods. There in the distance sat a bearded young man, surrounded by several jugs of water.

"What are you doing out here?" the officer demanded. "Are you some kind of hermit?"

"No, man," Frank replied. He felt weak, and his head was spinning. "I'm on a 40-day fast, Officer. Did I break the law or something?"

"Camping on state land without a permit? Yeah, I'd say you broke the law. There are campgrounds for things like this. I want you to pack up your stuff and get out of here. I won't arrest you if you clear out now."

"How am I gonna do that?" Frank rubbed his forehead. "I don't have a car."

The officer sighed. "Let's go," he directed, picking up a few jugs. "I'll drive you back to the station, and you can call whoever it was that dropped you off. Tell him to come get you."

"Frank, you're such a nut," MoJo sighed on the drive home. "Look at you. You're all skinny and starving to death. When we get back I'm cooking a turkey dinner, and you're gonna eat every bit of it."

"No I'm not, Moj. Don't cook me no doggone turkey, man, 'cause I won't eat it. The Lord told me to fast, and I ain't quittin'."

MoJo ignored him. He roasted a turkey and laid the platter in front of Frank. "Eat it," he ordered, pointing to the meat.

"Moj, I appreciate what you're trying to do." Frank stood up to leave. "But I said I'm not eating turkey, and I'm not. You're gonna have to eat this one all by yourself, bro. I'm outta here."

⊂⊃⊂⊃⊂⊃

In Bible times God often performed miracles through ordinary men and women. Sometimes diseases were healed, or the Israelites were able to defeat a powerful foe. In other instances the miracle was a changed heart. But whenever such a wonder took place opposition always arose from the enemy. Jesus encountered the devil many times during his life on earth. And he warned his disciples to be wary of his schemes—to be "wise as serpents but gentle as doves."

Frank noticed the same phenomenon occurring in his own ministry. Whenever he preached people responded and gave their hearts to Christ. But afterward darkness would seem to descend on him in unexpected ways. It might be a drug addict calling at three in the morning, or a gang member waiting for him out in the parking lot. Frank understood himself to be on the front lines of a spiritual battle—and he knew he needed the Holy Spirit's help.

Halfway through his 40-day fast he paid a visit to Sister Angela, who gasped when Frank appeared at the convent's front door. Frank's face was thin and drawn, and dark rings had formed under his sunken eyes, accentuating his ashen face. He couldn't have weighed more than 140 pounds.

"Frank, are you sure God wants you to do this?" she asked in alarm.

"Yeah, Sister," Frank confirmed with obvious resignation. "I gotta finish it. The Lord is breaking me. He's cleaning me out, getting rid of the garbage inside. I'll be okay, Sister. I just wanted you to know I'm still around."

Plucking a crucifix from her desk and hanging it on a chain around Frank's neck, she gave him a hug and promised to pray for him. "Come see me when you're done with all this."

Frank fingered the crucifix with a wan smile. "You know I'm not big on this kind of thing, Sister, but since it's a gift from you I'll wear it."

A few doors down from Frank lived a woman by the name of Dorothy, who had started a commune at her house more than a year earlier. Some believed her to be a woman of great spiritual insight, while others were of the opinion that she ran a cult. Frank decided to move in with Dorothy while he completed his fast. The two had long sessions together, sometimes lasting till two in the morning.

One night Dorothy, pacing the living room floor, began to point out Frank's weaknesses and sins. "You've got lust in your life," she accused him. "The Lord says you've got to shave your hair off."

255

"Why do I have to do that?" Frank asked a little petulantly.

"Because you've got pride in that hair," she told him. "And you've got to shave that beard off too, all of it."

Frank complied. Enervated as he was from a lack of food and restorative sleep, he was like putty in Dorothy's hands. He had forgotten the sound wisdom Bruce had worked so hard to instill in him.

Dorothy pointed to a relative stranger seated next to Frank. "From now on this man is going to be your partner. I want you to listen to him."

Something didn't feel right. Frank glanced at the individual to whom Dorothy was referring. It was no secret the man loathed Catholics—he had shared his feelings on the subject many times. Despite his lethargy Frank rose to his feet and put his hands on his hips. "How can this guy be my partner," he asked brusquely, "when I work with so many Catholics? He ain't gonna be my partner, Dorothy."

"Yes, he is!" she roared.

"No, he ain't!" Frank could yell as loudly as she. "No way is this guy gonna work with me!" Frank glanced around the room at the others seated there. "And you know what? All of you people are *nuts*, man." He pointed at Dorothy. "And what you're doing is *wrong*."

Someone was pounding on the front door. Dorothy froze, but after another thunderous round of banging she opened the door a crack. "Who's there?" she asked, her tone slightly tremulous now.

"Brother Bogle."

"*Who?*"

"Pastor George Bogle from the House of Prayer. Open up this door *right now!*"

Dorothy's hands shook as she pulled the door open a crack. "B-b-brother Bogle . . ."

George Bogle pushed hard enough against the door to force entry. Glancing quickly around the room, he glared at Dorothy before addressing her in a thunderous voice: "I rebuke you, you spirit of a high priestess!" Dorothy dropped into a chair as Bogle strode over to Frank. "And you! Get your things together—*you're* coming with me."

"Where we going?" Frank asked, shaken and bewildered.

"To the House of Prayer, where you'll be safe."

Frank began to follow, but Bogle paused, holding up his hand. "Stop!" he ordered in an authoritarian tone, pointing to Frank's shoes. "Wipe the dust off of your feet." This was the command Jesus had given his disciples whenever they were about to depart an ungodly place.

Frank brushed off his shoes before docilely climbing into the car with George Bogle. For the next five days he stayed at the House of Prayer while completing his fast. When Brother Bogle prayed with him Frank finally received the message from God for which he had been waiting: the meetings would forever be known as a place of love.

The next week Frank resumed his preaching at Saint Sylvester. Relying on the Holy Spirit as never before, he faithfully conveyed the message of God's love to the gathered assembly. The fast had taught him two important lessons: (1) that demonic forces depart whenever someone preaches the gospel and (2) the indomitable power of God's love. After the fast, agonizing as it had been, Frank was more prepared than ever before to break up hard ground and knock down trees.

CHAPTER 36

The Jesus March

"**H**ow many of you know this message by heart, 'cause you've been comin' to this meeting for a few months?" Looking over the crowd at Saint Sylvester, Frank watched dozens of hands shoot into the air. "Okay. All of you that raised your hands, follow my buddy Cassady over there." Frank pointed to Mike. "He's gonna tell you all about the baptism of the Holy Spirit."

A large group followed Mike into a classroom. After handing out some Bibles he sat down on the edge of a desk. "Everybody here has made a commitment to the Lord, right? So now you need the Holy Spirit to fill you so you have the power to be a witness. We're going to look at a couple of verses in the Bible and then ask God to fill you with His Spirit. Open up your Bible to the second chapter of Acts, verses 2–4:

"'Suddenly there came from heaven a noise like a violent, rushing wind, and it filled the whole house where they were sitting. And there appeared to them tongues as of fire distributing themselves, and they rested on each one of them. And they were all filled with the Holy Spirit and began to speak with other tongues as the Spirit was giving them utterance.'"

Mike closed his Bible and looked around the room, making eye contact with several of the rapt young faces. "That same Holy Spirit that filled the apostles wants to fill your heart too. God doesn't change, man. He offers the same gift to His people today. How else can we be His witnesses in the world? We're going to pray right now for each one of you to be empowered with God's Holy Spirit."

Every head was bowed as Mike prayed. Soon he looked around the room in amazement as people began speaking in tongues. Thirty minutes later they walked out of the room with Bibles in their hands and hearts suffused with joy.

One of the girls, a student from Rochester High School, approached Frank and tapped his shoulder. "Hey, Frank," she announced, "I just got a great idea."

"Lay it on me," Frank replied.

"What if you came to my sociology class to talk about the Lord? You could tell everyone about the Jesus Movement, and how it's not just another religion. I think my teacher would be cool with it."

"Tell you what," Frank responded. "Talk to your teacher, and see if he's into it. Then you set everything up and I'll come."

The very next week Frank was on his way to the high school. He had asked Bob Holt to accompany him, bringing his guitar. Bob and Frank had met at Leach Road and had become instant friends. By the time the two men arrived the room was packed with students. Bob played a few songs and then turned over the meeting to Frank.

Frank stood up and opened his Bible. "There's a passage here in the book of John I want to read to you. Jesus said, 'Unless a man is born again, he cannot see the kingdom of God.' So listen up. I'm here to tell you that according to Jesus it don't matter who you are or what you've done. Everybody needs to be born again. It don't matter how old you are, either. You can be seven, seventeen, or seventy. It's the same deal for everybody. You must be born again. I don't know how much you've been following the news, but this Jesus Movement has been happening all over the place. In California where the freaks hang out, and in New York City, people are calling on the name of the Lord. It's God, man. He's reaching down to you because He wants a close relationship with you. He loves you. And you're not gonna hear too much about that in sociology class. Not unless a biker like me comes to tell you about it."

By the time Frank offered an invitation for people to receive Christ, every hand was in the air. He prayed and told the kids about the Friday night meeting. Afterward the teacher pulled open a partition and invited more students to join the group. "Can you stay longer and speak some more?" he asked Frank.

"Sure, Teach. I can do whatever you want."

More than a hundred teenagers squeezed into the two rooms. Some sat in chairs, while others made themselves comfortable on the floor.

Latecomers drifted in and headed for the back of the room to lean against the wall.

Four hours later Frank was still going strong. "I was one of those people that was born to be wild," he told the captivated young audience. "I didn't care *nothin'* about God. I went to church all my life, but it just went in one ear and flew out the other."

Bob heard a *pssst* from the corridor and turned to see the principal beckoning him. Slipping from the desk on which he had been sitting, he withdrew into the hallway. "Hi Mr. Drew," Bob greeted him. What's up?"

"You need to stop him, Bob." Mr. Drew's face was red and his eyes bulging. "You need to stop this meeting *right* now."

"Hey, man," Bob laughed good-naturedly. "*You* stop him. *I'm* not gonna stop him."

"I'm serious, Bob," Mr. Drew repeated, livid. "I want you to call this off. It's too much. Things are getting out of hand."

"All right, all right." Bob raised his hands in resignation before stepping back into the classroom to speak with Frank. "Hey, Frank—."

"*What?*" Frank, his momentum disrupted, sounded petulant; he didn't like to be interrupted, especially when he was preaching.

"The principal is out in the hall, and he wants to talk to you."

Frank turned toward the kids and raised his finger. "Hold that thought," he told them. "I'll be right back."

Mr. Drew's temper had cooled by the time Frank arrived. "Now, young man," he addressed him, taking a step backward, "I know you mean well, and you're excited about your faith, but really, this is too much. You're *scaring* those kids."

"Mr. Drew," Frank replied, "I heard you were a Christian."

"Well, yes, that's true."

"Then how about if you put your head on the choppin' block along with the rest of us, man?"

"No, listen, you don't understand. I think you're *scaring* everybody."

"Hey, man," Frank responded in as reasonable a tone as he could muster, "I don't think we're scaring the *kids*—I think we're scaring *you*. I'll tell you what, Mr. Drew, why don't you let them decide? If they say we're scaring 'em, we'll leave right now."

As the two walked into the classroom, the expectant crowd fell silent.

"This assembly is a little unusual," Mr. Drew addressed his audience. "These young men have come, and they've probably said enough. It's time for everyone to leave. I want all of you to go back to your classes."

A boy stood up near the back of the room. "*No, man,*" he countered loudly. "We should have heard about this a long time ago."

With one accord the kids rose to their feet to give Frank and Bob a standing ovation. The applause didn't end until an exasperated Mr. Drew had thrown his hands into the air and exited the room. Frank motioned for everyone to take a seat before picking up his Bible. "Now," he continued with a grin, "where was I?"

The following week Frank took Randy with him as they drove to Macomb Community College, where the two had been asked to speak to a psychology class. Randy spoke first. He talked about his childhood, about how growing up without God had made him feel alone and empty. He described his work as a medic in Vietnam and the unspeakable suffering he had witnessed there. Finally he told the students about falling to his knees in a church and crying out to God.

Randy poured out his heart, yet there was a noticeable chill in the air. No one was responding. The teacher sat stonily in the back of the room, arms folded across his chest in a dismissive stance and a scowl on his face. Occasionally he would roll his eyes and shake his head.

Frank stepped forward. "Hold on a minute there, bro," he said to Randy before turning to the class. "Listen," he told the class seriously. "Your teacher back there isn't getting into this." Everyone turned around to look at the professor, whose posture hadn't changed.

Oh man, Randy thought, instinctively ready to bolt for the door. *It's about to get real uncomfortable in here.*

"I'm guessing your teacher doesn't believe you guys wanna hear what we're saying," Frank went on. "So I'll tell you what. We're ready to leave right now if you want us to. Are you sick of what we're telling ya? Do you want us to go? What do you say?"

"No!" they shouted in unison, before beginning to chant "No, no, no!"

"All right, all right." Frank motioned for everyone to quiet down. "We've been spilling our guts out to you guys, trying to tell you how Christ changed our lives. I want you to be honest now and spill your guts for us." Frank took the time to look each person in the eye. "I wanna know how many of you in this class—you're in a psychology class here, right?—I wanna know how many of you have ever thought of taking your own life? Be honest now! Raise your hands. I wanna see."

All over the room hands went up. Frank shook his head in amazement before turning to the professor. "Now, Teach," he addressed the man, "did you know you had all that right under your nose?"

The professor shook his head slowly.

"So do we have your permission to continue?"

"Yes," the professor replied, mollified. "You may continue."

Frank's ministry soon expanded beyond the Detroit area. Schools, colleges, churches, and county festivals began booking him for appearances. School administrators thought Frank was blunt and crude but recognized that he was just the person their students needed to hear. All alike appreciated his street-level approach and asked him to return time and again. Whenever Frank spoke something resonated in his listeners' hearts, and they responded by surrendering their lives to Christ. Frank adamantly declined to take credit for what was happening—like great evangelists before him he wanted the spotlight to shine solely on Jesus Christ. Whether the gathering attracted 50 or 500, he challenged everyone to make a decision. "Was Jesus the Son of God or not?" Frank would ask. "Was He an imposter or the real deal? It's up to you to decide."

For the next few years thousands of kids were introduced to Christ through Frank's meetings. Bible studies were launched in church basements and prayer meetings held on campuses. Like a stream surging unchecked down a mountainside, the Friday night meetings were sprouting new gatherings all over the state.

⊷⊖⊶

"Got it." Jim strode into the barbershop, decisively waving a permit in his hand.

"All set?" Mike asked.

"Yep. Everyone's on board: the police, city hall, and Saint Sylvester. We even got an advertisement on the radio. This is gonna be *huge!*"

"Cool, man." Rising from the barber chair, Mike headed for the door. "I'll see about making some signs."

Michigan's first "Jesus March" was about to be held in Warren. Mike had heard about similar marches taking place all over the country. Hundreds of young people were prepared to carry signs, sing, and march for the Lord down major streets. Some would even tote a huge wooden cross behind them as they walked. Newspapers loved to cover the marches, which provided a breath of fresh air in contrast to the violent anti-war protests of the day. People who marched for Jesus were invariably joyful—and well behaved.

The march was to take place on Saturday, September 19, 1971. In preparation, more than a hundred people parked behind Saint Sylvester Church and gathered around Frank. The plan was to march along Twelve Mile Road until they reached Macomb Community College, after which the crowd would sit on the lawn to listen to Frank preach.

A large wooden cross was placed on wheels, and people carried signs stating that "Jesus Is the Answer," and "God Loves You." When the media arrived cameramen filmed longhaired hippies as they strummed guitars and practiced worship songs. Alex directed the participants to form a line behind the cross, with Frank and Randy at the front. As the march was about to begin a large blue Buick pulled in to the parking lot. Bruce uncurled his great frame from the car and raised a forefinger in the air, signaling "Jesus: One Way." Stepping from the passenger side, Joyce moved quickly through the crowd, smiling and hugging each person she met.

Frank hefted one end of the cross and began pulling it down the street. The cameras continued to roll, with no one paying much attention to the media: the focus was solely on Christ, Frank, and the enormous cross. Everyone, including many of the onlookers lining the street, broke into song.

As the marchers wended their way down Twelve Mile Road, drivers honked and neighbors waved from their porches. By the time they reached Macomb College the crowd was several hundred strong.

"Praise God, everybody!" Frank called out into a microphone. The crowd settled expectantly on the grass under a brilliant sun. "You know, I came here to Macomb a while ago to speak to about 300 people, all of them in the hippie scene. They had it all together, too, man. They looked at me and said, 'This guy ain't blowing grass anymore, so he ain't hip.'"

Everyone chuckled.

"Then these people started laughing at me," he went on. "I mean ALL of them! Even the teacher that brought me! I didn't say but two words, and they all laughed. Wow. Did you ever get up in front of people and they just laugh at you? It's a heavy trip, man."

Frank's words quieted the crowd. He had touched a personal cord with many, and every ear was tuned in.

"So, anyhow," he continued, "I looked at 'em all, and I said 'Well, I'm sorry, man. I didn't mean to bum you out or anything.' I told them, 'I'm here to tell you about Jesus Christ.' And they laughed some more. Then when I started telling them about how God moved in my life —that's when the anointing of the Holy Spirit came. Things aren't the same after the anointing comes, believe me. Not by the words of Frank Majewski but by the power of the Holy Ghost.

"So, then, in the middle of my talk they bust out in another laugh. I said, 'All right, man, this is it. You people that don't believe God is alive, I challenge you *right now* to come forward.' I thought the teacher's glasses were going to fall off. I hardly knew what I was saying, man. You know what I mean? My buddy MoJo was sitting back there saying, 'Aw, there goes Majewski again. What's he doin' *now?*' It had never happened to me like that before. You coulda heard a pin drop in that room. And then all these people came forward and got saved. It was heavy, man. And it all happened right here at Macomb College."

Frank wiped his brow. After toting the cross for three miles he had worked up a sweat. "So now I'm gonna give all of *you* people a chance to answer a simple question—even you guys with the big cameras. Do you, or do you not know Jesus Christ? Is He your Lord and Savior? If your answer is yes, then you're in the right place, man, with other believers marching for Christ. But if your answer is no, then you're *still* in the right place, 'cause I'm here to tell you that Jesus is real."

Frank took the microphone off the stand and started to pace. "The Bible says 'How can anybody hear if there's no preacher?' Well, that's what I'm doing today, man—preaching. And I'm here to tell you God loves you. He loves you so much he gave His only begotten Son, and whoever believes in Him will not perish but have eternal life. Now, we didn't just march down Twelve Mile for the fun of it, man. We did it because we love Jesus Christ and want everyone to know that He's the King of kings and Lord of lords. He's coming back one day, brother, so you might wanna get your life together!"

The crowd had grown extremely quiet.

"Let me tell ya, if you don't know Jesus Christ, then this is your chance to meet Him right now. Everybody just bow your head for a minute, okay?

For those of you that have never met Jesus and want to meet Him today, just stand up right where you are and repeat this prayer after me."

Several people rose to their feet.

"Lord Jesus, I come to you and ask you to forgive me for my sins. I came here today, Lord, and I'm not sure why. I saw a crowd, and I just joined it. But now I know that something is missing in my life—and Jesus, it's you. I ask you to come into my heart and make me a new person. I want to be born again, Lord. I give you my life today, and I don't ever want it back. Amen."

Randy and Alex made their way through the crowd, passing out Bibles and praying with each new convert. The musicians started to play, and Frank stood back to take it all in. A young girl sat cross-legged on the grass with tears streaming down her face, a friend who had accompanied her to the march kneeling next to her in prayer. All over the lawn people stood to give their hearts to the Lord.

"Praise God," Frank intoned quietly. "Thank you, Jesus."

As the crowd started to disperse Alex, Randy, and Mike began gathering the signs and laying them in a pile, while several others started pulling the cross back toward Saint Sylvester. Bruce waited for Frank, and together the unlikely pair trekked slowly back to the church. This was a day neither man would forget.

Epilogue . . .

The book of Genesis begins with a story—the account of creation: "And God's Spirit moved over the surface of the deep." Then God spoke, and for the first time light appeared.

God's Spirit has been moving over the earth ever since. He shines His light into dark places by pouring forth His Holy Spirit. And He brought new birth to thousands of people during the turbulent 60s and 70s. Nor was this just in America: revival was taking place all over the globe. Wherever people were hungry for God—in Canada, Europe, Asia, Latin America, and South Africa—souls were touched and hearts revived. God summoned back into His fold many of His prodigal children, and new believers were being welcomed daily into the Body of Christ. They came in droves as thousands of young people either joined churches or established new congregations.

We read in the Gospel of Mark, Chapter 9, that no one was able to heal a demon-possessed youth until Jesus came along. He told his disciples "Bring him to me"—and changed the boy's life forever. In Detroit God reached out to gang members, delinquents, and drug addicts, all in need of a new start. It was Christ, and Christ alone, who could heal them.

No one could reach Frank, either. But through the prayers of Father Melczek, Jim and Judith Johnston, and Sister Angela, Frank found healing in Jesus Christ, and his new life began. Christ offers the same new life to anyone who asks. Everyone can be born again.

After several years Frank's meetings evolved into a church. Randy suggested the name Fisherman's Net, and it became a sort of spiritual hospital—a healing place for broken lives. Alex became the pastor, with Bruce his associate, while Frank continued to preach for several more years. Countless thousands were introduced to Christ through the Friday night meetings. And for years the church enjoyed weddings, baptisms, Bible studies, and park outreaches. In 1985, after 10 years of leasing school auditoriums for Sunday Services, Fisherman's Net purchased a building in Utica, Michigan, and for the first time put down roots.

Missionaries were sent out from The Net to places as far away as Mexico, Colombia, Turkey, Afghanistan, Thailand, and the Philippines.

One missionary, Dave Keller, describes the mighty work of the Holy Spirit during the 1970s:

> When I think of those Friday night meetings, it really was part of a revival that swept all over America. I often use it as a measure of what revival really is, because having lived through it, I know that I witnessed something very special. Even though it can never come back the same way it was before, it's important for each generation to experience a visitation from the Lord. It's so easy to fall back into a routine, where even good things that come from a revival become techniques and traditions. Finally they lose their power. Thinking back on those days, I long to see a new visitation among our young people, and pray that we older ones who experienced it don't lose what it means to give ourselves fully to the Lord. Not that we look back and try to repeat it, but we look forward and say "Oh Lord, do it again."

Where are they now?

Father Dale Melczek served as co-pastor at Saint Sylvester Catholic Church until 1972, after which he was appointed pastor of St. Christine Catholic Church in Detroit, Michigan. Later he was appointed Auxiliary Bishop of Detroit and then Bishop of Gary, Indiana, until his retirement in 2014. He continues as Bishop Emeritus of Gary and also pastor of St. Mary of the Lake parish in Gary. He still remembers Frank's Friday night meeting with fondness.

Sister Angela Hibbard, I.H.M., still serves at Gesu Parish in Detroit as the congregation's Pastoral Associate. She also teaches a class titled "An Introduction to Christian Worship" at the Ecumenical Theological Seminary in Detroit. Her vibrant faith and love for the Lord continue to inspire others. She describes Frank's fall from the chair as a moment she'll never forget.

Larry (MoJo) Wolf graduated from barber school in 1972 and has been cutting hair for 44 years. He and his wife, Denise, have two children and four grandchildren and are serving the Lord at a worship center in Romeo, Michigan.

Chuck Majewski attended Frank's meeting and gave his heart to Christ in 1975. He passed away unexpectedly in 1979 at the age of 31.

Mike Cassady became a schoolteacher and, after teaching for 36 years, worked as a school administrator. He and his wife, Mary, have two children and seven grandchildren and continue to attend Fisherman's Net Church.

Bob Holt helped to lead worship throughout the early days of the Friday night meetings and then became the pastor at Christ the King Church in Oxford, Michigan. He and his wife, Ruth, have four children and ten grandchildren. Bob still smiles at the thought that he never made it back to Florida.

Randy graduated from Oakland University, pastored a church, co-owned a landscaping company, and now co-owns a landscape design firm with one of his sons. He has been actively involved in pro-life work and attends Shrine of the Little Flower Catholic Church in Royal Oak, Michigan. Randy is regularly asked to share his testimony and has launched a speaking ministry to American veterans. He and his wife, June, have six children and eight grandchildren.

Joyce and her husband Bruce raised three children and had 6 grandchildren. Joyce taught a ladies' Bible study for many years at Fisherman's Net. She loved and encouraged her "Jesus Kids" until she went home to be with the Lord at the age of 80.

Bruce became Alex's associate and worked alongside him until his passing in 1994. A father figure to countless young people, "Big B's" love and wisdom helped guide the course of the Fisherman's Net.

Jim and Judith Johnston moved to Tennessee and served with Retrouvaille, a Catholic ministry geared toward helping marriages in need of restoration. The Johnstons returned to Michigan in 2014 and on February 22, 2017, Jim went home to be with the Lord.

Alex and his wife, Sue, raised three sons and have three grandchildren. In 1975 he became the pastor of Fisherman's Net Church and has served the congregation in Utica, Michigan, for the past 40 years. In the pulpit or in his community he is always looking for an opportunity to tell others about Jesus Christ. Sue went home to be with the Lord in 2004.

Frank was married to Becka and had two grown children and three grandchildren. He continued to cut hair and share the gospel for many years at church gatherings and outreaches. On February 24, 2018, God called him home to glory.

The mark that Frank left on the Detroit area and beyond cannot be measured. The ripples of his ministry will be felt for generations to come. That's how God keeps His Kingdom moving forward: one spark at a time. Frank lit a fire in many hearts that will burn forever. He will be greatly missed . . . but never forgotten.

Acknowledgments

After more than 30 hours of recorded interviews, I'd like to thank the wonderful people who allowed me to pepper them with personal questions as they shared their story: Larry (MoJo) Wolf, Bob Holt, Meb McFaddon, Jan Verschaeve, Sam Spano, Caroline Murphy, Chuck Cardamone, Dave Keller, Dennis Majewski, Former City of Warren Police Commissioner Charles Groesbeck, Eugene Groesbeck, John and Jan Sauter, Emil and Marge Cardamone, Marcia Teed, Stephen Teed, Ray Rafferzedar, Shirley Cusatis, Phil Keaggy, Mike Cassady, Randy Marcial, Jim and Judith Johnston, the late Joyce Todd, the late Pastor Jim Beall, Pastor Dick Bieber, Pastor Alex Silva, Sr. Angela Hibbard, Bishop Dale Melczek, and Frank Majewski.

Thank you to Jan Schwartz for taking time out of her schedule to help with proofreading.

A very special thank you to Donna Huisjen, my encouraging and skillful editor. And what a privilege to work with my brilliant and Christ-centered publisher, Tim Beals, president of Credo House Publishers and Credo Communications. You truly were God's gift to me!

Also to Sr. Florence Kennedy, Archivist, from the Sisters of St. Martha Archives in Antigonish, Nova Scotia, Canada: Thank you for digging back in history to rediscover Little Flower Institute. When describing the orphanage became challenging, you kindly filled in the blanks.

And grateful, heartfelt thanks to . . .

Dick Bieber—Your encouragement has meant the world to me. Your writing is an inspiration and your love for Jesus contagious.

Emil and Marge Cardamone – you opened up your home to a scruffy bunch of teenagers, thereby allowing Frank's meetings to continue. Thank you for the love and support both then and now.

Jan Verschaeve—Thank you for sharing the story of that life-changing moment at Balduck Park. The fruit of that night—lives you have touched, people you have led to Christ—displays the power of God's love.

Mike—What a great source of information you are! You helped Frank's story come alive in the retelling. Many thanks for letting me scrounge through your bins of old photos: when it comes to picture taking, you are king!

Randy—You shared your personal story with me in such a moving way. How can I ever thank you enough for preaching on that memorable night when I first met Jesus Christ? It changed my life.

Jim and Judith—You are the anchors for this account. Without your unquenchable love for Christ and commitment to the gospel there never would have been a Friday Night Meeting. Thank you for taking young Frank into your hearts and giving him a chance.

Joyce—I will always remember you sitting curled up on the couch with a cup of coffee as you related the stories of your Jesus Kids. Your laughter filled the room, and I was transported in time. Till we meet in glory, Mrs. T . . .

Alex—I'll always treasure our trip down memory lane in the old neighborhoods of Detroit. Thank you for sharing your life and your heart . . . and for teaching me that "it's a gift to be simple."

Sister Angela Hibbard (aka, the Psychedelic Nun)—You were available when the Holy Spirit knocked, and we are grateful to you for leading Frank in prayer on that memorable night. It changed his life, and later ours.

Bishop Dale Melczek—Thank you for praying with Frank in the hospital. It opened the door for God to begin working in his heart. And thank you for allowing hundreds of lost and lonely youth to gather at Saint Sylvester's to hear the gospel. You will always hold a special place in our hearts.

Frank—From the moment you gave your heart to Christ your life became an open book. Thank you for obeying God's call to preach night after night, week after week, year after year. Your ministry continues to produce more fruit than any of us could ever have imagined. One day you will hear the Lord saying "Well done!" and a cheer will arise from the sidelines: it'll be thousands of Jesus People shouting "Amen!"

Denise and Marianne—my "Aaron and Hur"—you held me up when my arms grew tired. Your prayers, love, and support helped me keep my eye on the prize. Thanks for loaning me to the world of writing . . . now how about lunch?

Jason, Jonathan, Paul, and Alex—you encouraged; critiqued; bounced ideas around; and, most importantly, loved and supported your mom on her crazy adventure. You mean more to me than words can say—this book is really for you.

Callie, Corinne, and Little Baby Z—If Grandma could leave you with one gift from her heart it would be this story—the story of God's love. I pray you will always know that it's true.

Tommy Z—What a ride it's been! From my first interview with Joyce to our final moment of completion you have been my rock, my cheerleader, my coach, my chief advisor, and my dearest friend. Guess that's why they call you "Tuffy." There would be no *Bring Him to Me* without you, my love, and I feel the Lord smiling down on us today.

Lord Jesus—You are the "why" of this book. Thank you for coming into my life and making my heart "the pen of a ready writer." In 1974 you saw a young girl sitting on the carpet at Frank's prayer meeting and knew that one day she would write this story.

> ". . . the wind is at my back, and I can't wait to see you,
> Jesus, face to face!" [17]

SHARE YOUR THOUGHTS

If Frank's story has touched your heart in some way,
we'd love to hear from you.
To contact the author, please visit www.SallyAnnZito.com

Endnotes

1 "76 Evacuated In Orphanage Blaze." *The Post Record* [(Bras D'Or, Nova Scotia) 5 March 1953.

2 Wasser, Julian, et al. "The New Rebel Cry: Jesus Is Coming!" *Time* 21 June 1973: 56–63.

3 Ibid.

4 The Jimi Hendrix Experience. "Purple Haze." Single. Track (no. 604 001), 1967.

5 *Macomb Daily* (Warren, MI) 20 June 1970.

6 The Four Seasons. "Sherry," Sherry and 11 Others. LP. Vee-Jay Records, 1962

7 The Shirelles. "Mama Said." *The Shirelles Sing to Trumpets and Strings*. Scepter, 1961.

8 Sly and the Family Stone. "Thank You Falettinme Be Mice Elf Agin." Single. Epic. 1969.

9 Wilkerson, David. *The Cross and the Switchblade*. (Pyramid Publications, Inc., 1963), 56.

10 Ibid., 56, 59.

11 Ibid., 61.

12 Ibid., 68.

13 Wasser, Julian, et al. "The New Rebel Cry: Jesus Is Coming!" *Time* 21 June 1973: 56–63.

14 Ibid.

15 Bob Holt. "Now I Know." Waiting On the Sunlight. Utica Music Company, 1978.

16 Love Song. "Two Hands." LP. Dunamis Music, 1972.

17 Phil Keaggy. "Let Everything Else Go." Town to Town, Sparrow Records, 1981.

Made in the USA
Middletown, DE
15 April 2023

28708655R00170